PRIESTLEY AT KISSING TREE HOUSE

Rosalie Batten

GREAT NORTHERN

Great Northern Books
PO Box 1380, Bradford, West Yorkshire, BD5 5FB
www.greatnorthernbooks.co.uk

ISBN:
Paperback edition: 978-1-912101-94-8
Hardback edition: 978-1-912101-93-1

Design by David Burrill

CIP Data
A catalogue for this book is available from the British Library

For more information about the J. B. Priestley Society
and for contact details go to *www.jbpriestley-society.com*

Rosalie Batten

Rosalie Batten (née Lowrey) was a woman with a lively enthusiasm for life, a keenly observant eye and a rigorous attention to detail which she doubtless gained from her father, an engine designer.

She was born in 1931 in London of Geordie parents. After training as a nurse and then attending Secretarial College she married an RAF pilot, Ronald Mortimer Batten, son of the Naturalist, H M Batten. They had two children before leaving the Forces and moving to Warwickshire. Here she was an active member of various charitable and business organisations, holding Chairs for a local Altrusa International Club and also the Women's Institute for a number of years.

As a talented artist, gardener, unpublished author and lover of life she had much in common with Priestley. They were introduced by a mutual friend and formed a close working relationship from 1968 until his death in 1984.

After Priestley's death Rosalie continued as PA to his widow, Jacquetta Hawkes and retired in 1996.

She died shortly after her husband in 2015.

J. B. Priestley

J. B. Priestley was born in Bradford in 1894. He was educated locally and later worked as a junior clerk in a wool office. After serving in the army throughout the First World War he went to Trinity Hall, Cambridge before setting up in London as a critic and renowned essayist. He won great acclaim and success with his novel *The Good Companions*, 1929. This and his next novel *Angel Pavement*, 1930, earned him an international reputation. Other notable novels include *Bright Day*, *Lost Empires* and *The Image Men*.

In 1932 he began a new career as a dramatist with *Dangerous Corner*, and went on to write many other well-known plays such as *Time and the Conways, Johnson Over Jordan, Laburnum Grove, An Inspector Calls, When We Are Married, Eden End, The Linden Tree* and *A Severed Head* which he wrote with Iris Murdoch. His plays have been translated and performed all over the world and many have been filmed.

In the 1930s Priestley became increasingly concerned about social justice. *English Journey*, published in 1934, was a seminal account of his travels through England. During the Second World War his regular Sunday night radio *Postscripts* attracted audiences of up to 14 million. Priestley shored up confidence and presented a vision of a better world to come.

In 1958 he became a founder member of The Campaign for Nuclear Disarmament and later in life represented the UK at two UNESCO conferences.

Among his other important books are *Literature and Western Man*, a survey of Western literature over the past 500 years, his memoir *Margin Released*, and *Journey Down a Rainbow* which he wrote with his third wife, the archaeologist Jacquetta Hawkes. J. B. Priestley refused both a knighthood and a peerage but accepted the Order of Merit in 1977. He died in 1984. His ashes were buried near Hubberholme Church in the Yorkshire Dales.

Contents

A Note from the Editor   7

A First Word *Tom Priestley*   9

Foreword *Nicolas Hawkes*   10

On JBP *Susan Cooper*   11

PRIESTLEY AT KISSING TREE HOUSE   15

Notes   241

'He who must be obeyed' – Recollections of Priestley   247
Sophie Fyson, Rosalie's Daughter

A Note from the Editor

Rosalie Batten wrote this book in 1986, some two years after J. B. Priestley's death. Samples were sent to publishers but nothing happened. At regular intervals, the family suggested that she contact other publishers or find an agent. She declined to do this, feeling that if her book wasn't snapped up straight away by the best publisher available then it wasn't good enough. Later, the family suggested self-publishing, but Rosalie didn't approve of such an approach and wouldn't agree to it. I am told she wasn't the sort of person to follow other people's advice.

When she died in 2015 her daughter, Sophie Fyson, decided that she wanted to do something with the manuscript. Correspondence with Priestley's stepson, Nicolas Hawkes, led to the manuscript being brought to the attention of the J. B. Priestley Society and together they collaborated to seek a publisher. The result of their effort is this book.

For myself, it has been an honour and a delight to have had a hand in bringing Rosalie's words out into the open. I am only sorry that Rosalie never saw it in book form in her lifetime. I like to think she would have been pleased.

The book offers a very unique insight into the personal and the working life of one of the twentieth century's great literary figures. Rosalie knew her subject well and her portrait of Priestley is an honest, unflinching, and sensitive testimony of the time she spent with him. More than that, I believe it is a testimony of the love and admiration she felt for him. We can really only love those we know well and I believe Rosalie Batten knew Priestley not only well, but in ways many others did not. How she knew him is this book and what she writes is worthy of publication.

The notes in the book are not meant to be exhaustive and are there to provide clarification as well as additional information I felt would be of interest to the reader. They also provide biographical details of some of the personalities who visited or wrote to Priestley at Kissing Tree House. Every effort has been made to ensure all details are correct.

Acknowledgements

Books are invariably a result of the efforts of more than one person and there are a number of people I would like to thank. Firstly, Sophie Fyson for her work typing and re-typing the manuscript, for her patience with all my questions and for allowing access to family photographs. A big thank you to Nicolas Hawkes for his assistance proofreading the text and for checking my notes and biographical details. Thanks to Tom Priestley for supporting the project and for permission to use photographs held in the J. B. Priestley Archive at the University of Bradford; it was important to all concerned that publication received backing from the Priestley family. I would like to thank Susan Cooper for finding the time to read the manuscript and for her kindness in offering to write an introduction to the book; Priestley had enormous admiration for her and her involvement makes publication even more special.

Thank you to Alison Cullingford, Special Collections Librarian at The University of Bradford for sending digital copies of photographs from the J. B. Priestley Archive and providing copyright information. Thanks also to Sheri Bankes for permission to use photographs from her collection; further details can be found at www.sheribankes.co.uk.

Every effort has been made to contact copyright holders. Any copyright holders we have been unable to reach or to whom inaccurate acknowledgement has been made are encouraged to contact the publisher.

Lee Hanson, Yorkshire, 2018.

Lee Hanson is the series editor of the Rediscovering Priestley Series for Great Northern Books. He is also Head of English at Bradford Grammar School, a writer and Chairman of The J.B. Priestley Society.

A First Word
Tom Priestley

It is impossible to say how many times I met Mrs Batten, as we knew her. Yet oddly enough I don't suppose it could have been that many times. The decade 1970/80 was a busy one for me, working and travelling, so I would only have visited Kissing Tree for the occasional weekend when normally Rosalie Batten would have been off duty. However, I clearly remember her as a very pleasant, friendly person, and we got on well enough together to develop a secret code. She told me she enjoyed visiting Greece and was learning the language. Well of course I had spent thirteen months in Greece after leaving Cambridge. I was in Athens teaching English at an evening school. I learnt Greek. So Rosalie and I used to salute each other in Greek whenever we spoke on the phone, no need to ask who was there. But I did invade her territory when we were preparing to shoot our film *Time and the Priestleys*. Her office shared space with the billiard table where we laid out a mass of books to demonstrate my father's great output. How lucky he was to have found such a helpful and understanding assistant. In another life I would hope to have a secretary, a cook housekeeper and a house maid to deal with all the small irritations of everyday life, travel arrangements, laundry, meetings, interviews and food. And if fate allowed, a secretary as helpful, intelligent and understanding as Rosalie Batten.

© Tom Priestley, 2018

Tom Priestley is one of Britain's most highly acclaimed film editors. He won a BAFTA in 1967 for his work on the now cult classic Morgan: A Suitable Case for Treatment and was Oscar nominated in 1972 for Deliverance directed by John Boorman. He has worked on numerous prize-winning films with many talented film-makers including Karel Reisz, Lindsay Anderson, Bryan Forbes, Michael Radford, Jack Clayton, Blake Edwards and Roman Polanski. He now spends his time more in the world, lecturing on film editing and promoting his father's life and work. He is President of The J. B. Priestley Society.

Foreword
Nicolas Hawkes

As J. B. Priestley's stepson through his marriage to my mother Jacquetta Hawkes (nee Hopkins) I knew Rosalie Batten well from 1968 to Jacquetta's death in 1995, especially in the later years when she carried the whole burden of support. She was therefore a great strength to me, my mother's only son, yet living in Edinburgh at the time. This situation revealed to the full the qualities of intelligence, observation, attention to detail and a wonderfully positive attitude to her life. I think JBP perceived these qualities in her - he was ever a shrewd judge - and was aware of how lucky they were to have Rosalie as the manager of their affairs. The portrait she provides here is an unusual and highly interesting blend of the public and the private, in that it sheds light directly into their daily working life together, not hesitating to share it with the reader. Though the Priestley working arrangements were of a kind that must have all but died out by now, it is tempting to see the relationship as in part unique to Priestley and in part revealing of a 'late 20th century successful writer' who was determined - despite taxes - to remain living and working in his own country, which he loved despite his many grumbles.

Rosalie throws light on many aspects of JBP's character of a kind not usually shown in public, but her very careful observation and description confers great integrity on the process; it was close but never too close. To be sure of the detail she must have kept a regular diary and drawn on it throughout the writing up. Priestley was a giant of the literary and national world in his time, who achieved prodigious productivity both in his writing and in his numerous public commitments. He - and we who benefit - were fortunate that Rosalie's professional support was there to make sure that nothing slipped through the net.

This book is a fascinating portrayal of a personal working relationship, made all the more so by the fact that Rosalie writes beautifully. This makes it not only accessible but enjoyable to readers with no previous encounters with author or subject.

© Nicolas Hawkes, 2018

On JBP
Susan Cooper

I must have first seen Kissing Tree after I became friends with the Priestleys in 1962; it seemed a beautiful, spacious country-house equivalent of their flat in Albany: peaceful, book-filled, eminently civilised. A year or two later I married an American and moved to the USA, to the horror of my family and my editor at *The Sunday Times*, and Priestley wrote me a letter ending with the kindness tinged with gentlemanly flirtation that Mrs Batten describes often in her book: "At 70 and with a beautiful wife to adore, I can have favourite girls, and you happen to be one of them - and I might be useful about work - so let us keep in touch." So we did, through letters and weekend visits, for the next 20 years.

I say "Mrs Batten" because that was always how she was known, in that mildly Upstairs, Downstairs household. The invaluable Gertrude had her first name because she was technically the maid; Mrs Batten and the wonderful Miss Pudduck, secretary and housekeeper, were elevated to surnames. Similarly, though Priestley's friends of his own age called him Jack, those under about 35 - like Bob Robinson* and me - were instructed to call him JB.

The secretary situation was a matter of importance; it turns up later in my box of Priestley letters. "Our only trouble," wrote Jacquetta in the summer of 1968, "has been deciding to part with our secretary after she has been with us for about nine years. We've just taken on another girl, but it's meant a fearful lot of letter writing, interviewing, telephoning."

By September that year the new secretary was in place. "She is in the sharpest contrast to Miss Smith," wrote JB, "being in her 20s, mini-skirted, a bit sultry and moody and probably with a private life straight out of an offbeat novel or film."

But for whatever reason, the miniskirted one didn't last, and Mrs Batten took over, for good. In my box there's a friendly note from her written in 1970, telling me that my current letter to JB would await his return from Ceylon. This was a good thing, since a day or two later a handwritten letter arrived from Ceylon, complaining that Colombo was an unattractive city and that it never stopped raining. "I don't really like the tropics," Priestley wrote, "the mosquito netting, the fuss about water, the monotony of the food - even the fruit. Send me a note to greet me at Kissing Tree." The envelope was under stamped by 35 cents; clearly he needed his secretary.

By then I had written a book about him, after many long talks on visits to Kissing Tree. I hadn't really intended to write one. But when I moved to the USA Priestley had introduced me not only to his oldest friend Edward Davison, now a New Yorker, but to Ted's children - and one of them, Peter, was not only a poet like his father but also a publisher. Around 1966, Peter asked me if I would edit a collection of Priestley's essays. So I did; the book was eventually called *J. B. Priestley: Essays of Five Decades*.

He'd written an enormous number of essays; reading them was great fun, but took me forever. I wrote to him facetiously, "I know so much about you now, I could almost write a book about you."

And a telegram arrived. It said, "Heinemann offer five hundred pounds advance."

So I wrote *J. B. Priestley, Portrait of an Author.* I also wrote a cover story about him for the *Sunday Times Magazine*, with pictures by Lord Snowdon, to celebrate his 80th birthday. In 1978 John Braine wrote a Priestley biography, but its subject, undeterred, was clearly encouraging Mrs Batten to write a book about him as well. And now we find that she did, with great affection, after he died. So did a number of others; he'd have been pleased.

Well, he was vain - but he was also a lovely man: funny, warm-hearted, loyal and prodigiously talented. During my first homesick years in America his letters were a lifeline: "Remember," he wrote, "you will find you write better about a place when you are away from it." In his last couple of years, the letters and talk began to fade, and Jacquetta and I grew closer and remained so after his death, until she too began to fade. What an astonishing couple they were.

And as talismans, perhaps, there are two pictures on a wall of the study where I write my own books. One is a gouache landscape, painted by Priestley. The other is the black-and-white photograph taken by Alfred Bernheim that was on the jacket of *Essays of Five Decades*: the round face, contemplative, pipe in mouth.

"For Susan," says the inscription, "from her friend, J.B."

Susan Cooper is the author of the classic five-book sequence The Dark is Rising, which won a Newbery Medal, a Newbery Honor Award, and two Carnegie Honour Awards. Born in England, she was a reporter and feature writer for the Sunday Times before moving to the United States. Her writing includes books for children and adults, a Broadway play, films, and Emmy-nominated screenplays. Her most recent books for children are King of Shadows and Victory, and for adults a portrait of Revels founder Jack Langstaff called The Magic Maker. In 2012, Susan was given the Margaret A. Edwards Award and in 2013 she received the World Fantasy Award for life achievement. Her children's novel Ghost Hawk was published in 2013. Susan lives and writes in Marshfield, Massachusetts.

*Robert Robinson (1927-2011) was a journalist, author and well-known broadcaster. He is perhaps best remembered as the presenter of *Brain of Britain* for Radio 4 and the host of *Call My Bluff* for BBC television.

PRIESTLEY AT
KISSING TREE HOUSE

Rosalie Batten

26th June, 1979

One day I very much hope that Mrs. Batten will write a book about me because, as I have pointed out to her, she knows me better than anyone else who might want to write such a book. If she does, then I give her my full permission to quote from any of my correspondence or my work that she feels is necessary.

B. Priestley

The letter given by J. B. Priestley to the author.

CONTENTS

November 1984   21

First Meeting   25

Making a Start   29

Christmas at Kissing Tree House   35

Talk by Firelight   40

The Edwardians   45

An Active Year   62

Interlude for a Small Dog   81

Ceylon   84

Birthdays   91

Theatre   103

Other Occupations   113

Expedition for Paper and Paint   122

April 1985   126

Differences   130

More than Ireland   132

The Good Companions   148

Bradford   158

Echoes of War   170

The Freeman   180

Four Score   187

A Few Asides   195

Award for Merit   198

At Kissing Tree   203

A Final Volume   212

The End of a Decade   218

Into the Eighties   222

Preparing for Ninety   229

The End and Onwards   234

November 1984

The whole house misses him, and yet it does not miss him at all because he is there in all his old places. In the study his seat on the sofa seems to have settled about him and when winter dark draws in, the sidelights are lit to cast their comforting glow, as if they had to throw their illumination over his shoulder for he is still there, reading. In the corner his desk and his typewriter remain untouched and waiting. The big glass ashtray is there on the coffee table with the books and pamphlets that he was browsing through until those last few days. Sometimes he would sit there for hours with the page unturned, thinking, remembering, his memory fighting with age's attempts to slow the mechanism, and if you entered he would turn and smile. Age fought hard but it did not defeat him.

It is as if he were only along the hall, but it is a long hall and so you must wait for him a long time. There is a sense of feet shuffling, slippers scuffing the floor, for his legs and his back have been troubling him lately and he travels with effort. Possibly there is a pause while he sits and recovers in the chair that stands half way between cloakroom and study. He sits there and rests his hands on his walking stick, but if you approach him he will turn and smile. It is the smile of an infant and imp, a bright smile, a wicked smile, a 'there is a secret between us and the world' smile.

Most men grow old in their seventies, but not him. He has been too busy to find the time. It was only at the end of his eighties that age managed to take hold of him. He grumbled about it, resented its limitations, but he did not give in to them. The long slow effort from end to end of the hall continued, his routine continued as far as possible, although it had altered by slow degrees to accommodate the changes as they came to him. A big wing-backed chair was placed by the coffee table in the place where the Victorian button-back had stood. It was a high chair and a firm one, but now it seems out of place there; it is only the shadowy memory of an old man sitting half sideways to ease his back. The sofa is his proper place and it is as if he has returned there and is waiting to let spill from his mind all the ideas that are surging in it. He could not sleep for them sometimes for they could not be switched off at will, but continued to shape themselves during the night hours as if they could not wait for him to take his place at the typewriter and release them onto the paper for us to share.

How strange to think that I was once afraid of him and stumbled here, nervously dropping things. A few years ago he said, "Don't knock when you come into the room. This is your home as much as mine and you have as much right here as I have."

Upstairs in his bedroom the curtains remain unopened. His bed is tidily made and the shelves of thrillers are there to occupy those sleepless hours. All is settled and waiting for him here, as if he might ascend at the appointed hour and make himself comfortable between the warmed sheets, turning his mind to murder, mystery and small squares of bitter chocolate. He pretended that they were for his wife, but it was his face that would fill with dismay if the chocolate ran out.

"You had better go into town and get me some chocolate," he would say, his voice as full of consequence as if we were cabinet ministers dealing with important matters of state.

"You'll get fat!"

"It is for Mrs Priestley. She likes me to give her a square at bedtime."

I would regard him with incredulous eyes and say, "Oh yes," in quite a meek tone.

"Besides I'm already fat."

"You'll get fatter and have to go on a diet of fruit juice and lettuce leaves."

There would be a little grunt and a moment's silence before I was instructed, in meticulous detail, to get the precise kind that was currently favourite. Its wrapper, brand and size would be described, its price conjectured, with the opportunity taken to complain of continuing inflation and the impossibility of ever knowing what a thing would cost. It would invariably have gone up since it was last purchased. "See that you get the right kind or I will growl until you quiver with fear!"

I would smile at him then. Did he really suppose that I could ever be afraid of him? He had taught me better than that.

Just as when he was alive the house is filled with him. One day I heard the tap of his pipe against the glass ashtray, felt the comfort of his presence, before remembering that he was no longer there. Crossing the short stretch of hall between our doors I looked in for him, sniffing the air for the scent of tobacco, but there was no sight of him. He was the heart of the house and we all felt it as we feel it now.

"You should write a book about me one day," he would sometimes say. "After all, you know me better than anyone else does."

I would smile at him, lowering my eyes to study my feet, for I did not want to write such a book, in fact I was determined not to. It was not the kind of writing that appealed to me; many people had already written about him and more would do so in the future. Besides, I had my own reasons. My silence never daunted him and he would bring it up again, "One day I hope you will write a book about me." Sometimes towards the end I would look at him from behind and send out strong thought waves that I would never write a book about him. If he felt the bombardment his back remained as it was, unmoving, solid; he might even look up and smile at me.

Outside the garden is kept as he knew it with gravel paths tidy and lawns mown smooth. He would walk round and round on those paths, would cross the grass to where the daffodils stretched in their thousands at the side of the paddock and would marvel at them. He would stand at the iron fence to watch the cattle, amused when they gathered to stare back at him. When the magnolia tree blossomed he would go to wonder at its blooms, would remain there motionless and then resume his round, deep in thought but yet aware of things. He used to stride through the garden when I first came, but over the years he grew slower. In that last hot summer of 1984 he walked there only occasionally, leaning on his stick and his wife's arm. Sometimes though I would hear him leave the study to descend the stone steps from the door and sit in the sun outside my window. Worried at the effects of heat I would go and fuss him, bringing his hat, fearful of dizziness.

"You're not too hot here?"

"No. I'm not too hot."

His replies were patient, good-natured, and if he resented my fussing he gave no sign of it, accepting it as well intended. I would be out there again and again to check that all was well with him. He sat on the bench, leaned against its white iron pattern of nasturtium leaves, his hands clasping his stick, his eyes distant, bearing my intrusions with courtesy.

"Do you want to come in now?"

"No, I don't, thank you."

"That sun is terribly hot!"

"Now that you've brought me my hat I'm all right. Thank you for thinking of it."

In recent times he had had the odd fall and we dreaded him hitting his head on the steps or breaking a limb. When he fell he lay like a stranded whale, patient, recovering, before he followed his own style of rising. He liked to do it his way, without help, if he could manage it, and if he had hurt himself he did not complain of it, except perhaps to say, "I've a bit of tenderness here." It was only about small things that he grumbled. If he was really ill he became a stoic, and falling when you are old is not a small thing, so that it was scarcely mentioned.

The garden is busy with life. The squirrels are there, and a great variety of birds. He used to call me to watch a hare leaping, or the gleaming green head of the woodpecker caught by a ray of the sun, or a cat crouched flat by the shrubbery watching with tiger eyes for something to pounce on.

"I had a cat once," he would say. "Big as any dog it was."

He would laugh at the memory and make a face at me to illustrate the cat's fierceness, his hands making stalking movements towards me. "Terrify any dog."

It is not the garden that keeps such a strong sense of him though, it is the house.[1]

FIRST MEETING

The room warmed to his presence. He was a round barrel of a man, but his entry was feather soft and later he told me how light he was as a dancer, which I could well believe.

"Mrs Batten?" He held out his hand.

"How do you do, Mr Priestley."

There was no shyness or stiffness now, only a sense of delight. It was like greeting an old friend whose thoughts, opinions and humour were known and very much valued.

"So you want to work for me, do you?"

His hand was soft, his smile was encouraging and I too smiled. Ever since at the age of fifteen I had read and relished *The Good Companions,* I had known this man. I had followed him through *Angel Pavement, Bright Day, Jenny Villiers* and whatever else I could lay my hands on. Happily there seemed no end to the supply. Fortunately I did not mention *The Good Companions* now. I was soon to learn that he did not like it being brought up first, as though it were the only book worth remembering. Later work, he felt, was of greater merit and he would prefer to be thought of for *Bright Day* or *The Image Men.* When, as it so often was, *The Good Companions* was mentioned, he would sometimes emit a low growl, or a grunt, or a sigh and his lower lip would pout.

There was no growl now; there was only the glow of him as he stood in a thin shaft of November sunlight smiling benignly, a roly-poly Pickwickian figure of good nature. He looked at me as though he liked and approved of me.

"I'm an easy man," he said. "You won't find me difficult to get along with. My previous secretary was here for eight years. No awkward reason for her leaving. We both felt the time had come for a change – that's all. We parted with good feeling on both sides." He did not mention the two unsuccessful beginnings that came between us. Lowering his head, his eyes gleaming, as if we might be about to enter into a conspiracy, "Just the two of us," he said, "The work will be interesting."

His approach was very different from what his wife's had been. I had seen her first and the encounter made me uneasy, an unease instantly dispelled by the warmth of him.

It was a big palace of a house and I had approached it nervously, not at all sure that I wanted to be there. I had not even asked to come, I had been invited. A mutual friend, hearing that the Priestleys needed a secretary and were having difficulty finding one, suggested that I might be interested in part-time work. As I was unable to drive then, a friend brought me, driving past the gardener's lodge, the big black wrought iron gates that were never closed, the greenhouses and the pergola where the wisteria grew. It was winter now and the wisteria bore no bloom, the stems of the roses were dark traceries on the white house walls, the conifers a line of deep green sentinels. We arrived at the foot of the steps where I left the car. It was a daunting prospect. Six steps led up to the mahogany door which was dark and solid in the chill light. Feeling small and timid I mounted them and rang the bell.

It echoed distantly and then there was the patter of feet against hard surface. They took a long time to reach the door, but at last it opened to reveal endless hall and an ocean of cream marble floor on which my footsteps clattered. Gertrude, the parlour maid[2], showed me into the drawing room which, I was relieved to discover, was at the near end of the house.

Mrs Priestley was there, Jacquetta Hawkes, writer and archaeologist in her own right. She seemed not to want to see me. This surprised me, for having been urged to come I had anticipated hope, perhaps even pleasure at the sight of me. That these feelings might abate on further acquaintance I knew was possible, but it was daunting to find no sign of them before I had even appeared. I had taken pains, wore my best navy dress, tied my hair tidily with a chiffon bow. Mr Priestley grew fond of those bows and used to admire them, was dismayed when I eventually had my hair cut. Mrs Priestley, however, was clearly not an admirer of chiffon bows. I moved my lips, tense with terror, into what I hoped was a smile, and greeted her politely.

After that there followed a short, rather stiff conversation about the job. Perhaps the two false starts had put her off secretaries, or maybe she hated interviews as much as I did. When I outlined the hours I had in mind Mrs Priestley looked immensely disapproving.

"We want someone full-time."

This surprised me even more, as I had been definite about the part-time bit when asked to come, had clearly emphasised it. Doing my best to sound easy, I replied that for me full-time was impossible.

She said, "Mr Priestley is used to having someone here when he needs them."

The dismissive tone did it. Somewhere, from the depths of nervousness, a spark was roused in me, grew into determination. I would not be dismissed. Family and home dwindled, stubbornness rose.

"Perhaps I could manage a little more."

This was considered for a while and I was asked what sort of salary I had in mind. Being out of practice as a secretary I named a figure so low that at last something was approved of, seized so eagerly that I did not like to explain that I meant for the first few weeks or so until I was worthy of more and had proved myself. Anyway, I only wanted enough to cover my son's school fees, and he was a day boy then so the figure would do this. There was further discussion then and I found myself agreeing to work every day from 9.30 until 4.30 with two weeks' holiday a year. It seemed to be that or nothing, although at that point I still doubted that I was being considered in any case. However, now that, like a jellyfish, I had agreed to such totally different terms from any I had originally intended, I had obviously passed the first test. Mrs Priestley rose and announced she would send her husband down to meet me. I sat and brooded on what I had agreed to and wondered whether to withdraw from it. With home, family and a largish garden to look after, it sounded to me like slave labour. Mr Priestley, however, settled it.

He said, his tone implying a wealth of wonderful things ahead of us, "There'll be interesting contacts for you. Theatre, television, the press, plenty of good books."

He, at least, seemed eager that I should join them. By now he was sitting close to me in an adjoining chair. He waved an emphatic forefinger.

"It will be far better than industry, an office, that sort of thing. You don't want that. What have you been doing recently? Anything?"

"I've been acting as conference secretary, but it was only for the odd week-end. It means going to conferences in different places, taking down what is said and typing it back at home so that the delegates get a copy of it."

"I can offer you better than that."

It was obvious that he had a low opinion of the business world.

"How about it then? Will you come to me?" He peered at me kindly from beneath bushy eyebrows.

"I'd love to work for you."

A rosy future stretched ahead of me. It would be good to work for this man. I would see that he had no troublesome things to bother him, no one would be allowed to interrupt him if I was there. I would protect him, make sure that his affairs ran smoothly. It was 1968 and he was seventy-four now; an age that deserved respect; an age of wisdom and experience. Perhaps his energy might be less than it had been. If so I would help him not to waste it. Obviously Mrs Priestley could not have disliked me as much as I had imagined or I would not still be here. I would keep her affairs running too and we could discuss archaeology. That was an interest of mine and I went to classes in it. We could discuss digs and things and I would learn from her.

He said, "How will you get here? Is there a suitable bus?"

When I produced a timetable we discovered that nothing would get me there in time. Living in a village on the opposite side of Stratford meant two buses were necessary and none of them linked before mid-morning. He announced then that he would send a car to collect me at his own expense until I could pass the driving test, and that I could leave at four instead of half past so that the homeward buses would link. My heart swelled at such kindness and my devotion firmed. With me to look after things he could write more books like *The Good Companions*.

He shook my hand again and again, I noticed how soft his was. One day he would roll up his sleeves for me to see the smooth, soft, wrinkle free skin of his arms, which he was rather proud of, and then he would roll up his trousers so that I could admire the smoothness of his legs. Now I was only aware of what small feet he had for such a large man, and how he moved, light as thistledown, from the room.

MAKING A START

He sat, brooding over the morning mail, chin in hand. It was a slightly stubbly chin as he had not yet shaved, and he wore leather slippers and a camel coloured dressing gown. It was a scene that I was to come to know well, for he was a man of habit. Breakfast was sharp at nine o'clock and by half-past he was in his study and his secretary had to be in his study too or else his face would darken. Sometimes it darkened anyway because the mail lacked interest, or a reply he was expecting had not come yet, there was a demand for income tax, or that magic something that he awaited always in the post was still eluding him. All this I was yet to learn, for now it was my first session with Mr Priestley and the mail and I felt small and timid as a frightened mouse as I knocked on his door, which was open anyway so that I could see that cogitating figure at the near end of the sofa.

He turned and smiled. "Come in," he said, his voice deep, smooth, rich and reassuring. Ever ready to take fright I used often to be tense at the thought of joining him, but as soon as I had done so all was well again, that voice calming alarm, that smile most often welcoming.

"Sit here beside me."

Trying to look alert and competent I advanced, tripped on the edge of the carpet, managed to regain my balance and continued to the blue velvet Victorian button-backed chair that was to be my place. It stood at right angles to the end of the sofa, fairly close to him, and there was a long coffee table in front of it on which he piled letters, newspapers and whatever books were at the time of interest to him. "I like punctuality," he said.

"I was here on time." I pointed this out with the utmost anxiety, in a nervous bleat.

"I'm aware of that," he said. "I am merely letting you know that it's important to me."

After that there was a long silence. The letter he was holding seemed to require much thought. Very quietly I sat and waited, my eyes absorbing the room which, like most in the house, was large and high ceilinged. There were three big windows, one at the far end facing the door, two on the left of the room as you entered it. In front of these was a desk, but it was not the one at which he worked. That stood in the far corner, facing the wall, for he said that views were distracting to a writer and he needed to keep his mind on things. A Mary Potter portrait of his wife hung over it, which seemed to me to have caught the essence of her. The walls were entirely lined by shelves of books and below the shelves there were cupboards containing typescripts of his books, published and unpublished plays, old magazines, some with articles by or about him, a box of letters to his parents from the First World War. The shelves and cupboards were all of mahogany and there were matching library steps. A similar chair to my own was opposite, the seating grouped round the marble fireplace, the coffee table stretching in front of it. The desk in the window, a big one, had drawers to both the front and the back of it. These, I discovered, housed Mr Priestley's tobacco, odd pieces of writing, important letters, old programmes, a pack of playing cards and a jumble of things that had at some time been of interest to him. At the far end of the room, in the corner opposite his working desk, was a grand piano, behind it an L shaped arrangement of yet more bookshelves, these of a simpler kind than the built-in mahogany and painted white. They contained mainly paperbacks, while the grander shelves were filled with hardback, some of them in matching sets. The carpet, which covered most of the floor, was red and an oriental rug was spread in front of the fireplace.

At last he began to dictate, "Dear Mr Smith," and I found myself straight in at the deep end of his private affairs. Mr Smith was his London solicitor and the letter was of a kind that in all my years with him was never to be repeated. Someone had taken exception to a harmless remark he had made on television and was having a 'try-on' about it. After that he wrote to Basil Dean.

"He produced a great many plays of mine," he said to me. "Did a very good job with them too. Once, when I was a much younger man, I acted in one of them myself. The actor who was playing the part was involved in a road accident so I took his place for three nights until a suitable substitute was found."[3]

I looked at him awed. "What was the part?"

"Ormonroyd. The drunken photographer in *When We Are Married*. Do you know the play?"

I shook my head. It seems astonishing now that I was then unfamiliar with it. It has many revivals and is in constant demand for amateurs.

Memory of the play obviously amused him. He chuckled merrily as he outlined the story of three Yorkshire couples sharing their silver wedding celebrations. "Ormonroyd turns up to photograph them. He is rather drunk and talkative."

As he spoke his voice slurred slightly, his eyes glazed and he made such exaggerated movements with his hands that Ormonroyd took shape in front of me, a loquacious, bibulous northerner who I felt must have dominated the stage. Clearly if Mr Priestley had not elected to write he would have made a marvellous actor.

He said, "I think I was all right in it," and smiled complacently. Modesty was not a dominant virtue with him. "Do *you* think I would be all right?"

With tremendous enthusiasm I assured him he would, then he went on to dictate a letter to his daughter Mary. Afterwards I went upstairs to Mrs Priestley's study, a small room which lay beyond her bedroom and bathroom. Here she worked each morning until it was time for their pre-luncheon drink. That day she wrote to Dimitrios Harissiadis in Athens, the photographer whose work had illustrated her recent book, *Dawn of the Gods*, and then to Sir Mortimer Wheeler, dashing bringer to life of the ancient past whose charm had beguiled me on television. Both letters stirred my imagination, for there was talk of Crete, Knossos and Minoan artefacts, of classicists and non-classicists; also Mrs Priestley accepted an invitation to dine with Mr Harissiadis and his wife in Athens. She was going there on an archaeological cruise as a guest lecturer with Swan Hellenic. It seemed as if I hovered on the edge of a fascinating world and longed to see it, but if that was impossible at least I could enjoy it vicariously.

After that there was a fresh ordeal ahead, for I had to master an electric typewriter. It proved to be quite different from a manual model and I had only to pass my hands near the keys for them to act on their own volition, producing letters haphazardly. Js and Ks in particular lived a life of their own and turned up everywhere. It took two weeks to gain control of it.

While this was going on Mr Priestley, as he always did, had gone upstairs to dress and shave, had come down again to settle in front of his typewriter, his ears stuffed with cotton wool against disturbance, and was writing. That is to say he was typing rapidly with two fingers and seldom a pause, the sharp tapping sounding professional. Although he insisted it was two fingers it always appeared to me to be four, but they went so fast that I could not be sure. There were never torn up sheets of false starts in his wastepaper basket; he got it right first time. Preparations were in his mind, for he did not use notes and said it was important to brood. When he handed me the work to be copied there was scarcely a flaw on the page, only the occasional overtype, the odd word crossed out. If, very rarely indeed, there was something to add he would type it on another sheet and attach it to the page with a paper clip, giving detailed instructions on where it should be inserted. He had firm notions about how he wanted things set out, but later, when we had learnt each other's ways, he would say that he would leave it to me. Until then he directed the setting out very carefully, particularly of plays, because as he said, there was a proper way to do these.

Sometimes he worked in a cloud of smoke, at others with an empty pipe gripped in his mouth, and the tapping of keys was broken occasionally by the tapping of pipe against his big glass ashtray. The pipe might be laid on his desk, but it was always to hand and there was a pot of them in the corner if he should want a change. He was working on a book about Chekhov.

In the afternoon he entered my room, observed me with interest so that my hands felt all thumbs, spoke for a moment or two and then signed his letters. These were laid out on the billiard table which filled a good part of the room. Full sized, it was covered with an oriental rug. Apart from letters, cheques, contracts and anything else to be signed, which I spread round the edges on manilla folders, I discovered it was the repository for whatever came into the hands of either Mr or Mrs Priestley. It did not matter how often I tidied it there was always more and I would find piles of books, postcards, advertisement pamphlets, pictures and miscellaneous objects scattered all over it, so that Mrs Priestley remarked accusingly that it was time it was tidied. Mr Priestley, signing the letters for the first time, was encouraging, praising the layout and typing of them.

After that he used to come in often in the afternoons and presently began to spend quite a lot of time talking to me, walking about the room or hovering over me, watching with an interest that continued to be disconcerting. His room was directly opposite mine, at the back of the house which had originally been the front of it, so that there were virtually two front doors, the one at our end known as the garden door. From it stone steps led to a paved area and then there was lawn, flowerbeds, and further on shrubs. The meadow lay beyond, rented out to a local farmer who grazed cattle there. Immediately opposite the garden door an ornamental pond had a fountain of metal hoops to keep herons off. Unfortunately it could not prevent hedgehogs from falling in and drowning, an event which caused Mr Priestley much upset. He would call me sometimes to come and watch a hedgehog crossing the lawn, taking as much pleasure in it as a small boy might take in a toy train, but with more tenderness, for this was life.

All that first week he was patient with me, as in my nervousness I constantly tripped and dropped things. The corners of rugs never failed to catch my feet; files, letters and pens slipped from my fingers; Js and Ks leaped from the typewriter; and the more these things happened the more nervous I became. JBP appeared not to notice, stood tranquil and still, a rock of a man against whom adversity dashed and retreated. I picked the things up and recovered myself. For the first time with me he dictated a letter to his sister, Winnie, which I heard as Willie. I did not know then, of course, that he was a she and his sister. Nothing was said, he simply signed the letter and corrected the mistake in ink. Soon I knew more about those who were close to him as he named all five of his children, telling me something about each one of them, told me of his half-sister, Winnie, said with much satisfaction that he got on well with all of them.

I wished he would not stand and watch when I had to use the telephone. It was difficult then to speak naturally and my fingers fumbled the dial under his scrutiny. He entered my room.

"We'll need a car for Monday."

They were going to London for a few days and it would be the first time I had made the arrangements for them. I looked up expectantly, waiting for more. Duly he gave the details. I was to ring International Car Hire who would meet them at Paddington, as they always did. I must stress that "it should be a small car or they might send a big one, which would cost a lot more." Expense, I was already aware, was to be avoided whenever possible. In spite of his close attention I managed to organise this and then he asked me to get his agent, A. D. Peters[4]. Like a toastmaster at a Guildhall banquet I announced Mr J. B. Priestley. He seemed to approve of this and after his call stayed for a while, watching me typing.

"You're not as quick as Mary Smith," he remarked eventually. This stung for she had not been confronted with an electric machine which was purchased for the secretary who came between us. Besides, I had warned him it would take time to adjust to it.

"I can do more than 60 words a minute on an ordinary typewriter," I replied, a shade sharp about it.

"Can you indeed!"

If there was exaggeration in the admiring tone he used, I was not aware of it, but I realise now that the number of words one could type would convey little to him. He had never asked me for speeds or qualifications.

It was years before my nervousness left me and yet from the start, at the peak of my fumbling and stumbling, there was a sense of reassurance that eventually reached me and strengthened me. The world was a tough place, but with him there I began to feel more and more that there was someone at the helm, ready to take my side, to defend me. He had that effect on people. The house seemed to gather about him, to take heart from him. It is understandable that in so much of his work there is a figurehead, the man who sees and comprehends all, for there was undoubtedly something of that in him. Although occasionally he did not understand as well as he thought he did and there were times when he seemed out of touch with ordinary modern life, there was a solid core of true compassion and sensibility. He was above all a strong man with not a whimper in him. His strength steadied the house. I found myself going to work each day with a feeling of purpose and fruitfulness, for in his company the world was a more secure place and I had a part in it.

CHRISTMAS AT KISSING TREE HOUSE

Christmas was not a season to be greeted with pleasure. It disturbed his routine and involved giving presents, which he did with less enthusiasm each year, complaining about being expected to pour out money like water as if he were some kind of endless, bottomless lake of it. The Priestleys never sent Christmas cards, but they did write to thank people who sent cards to them, and the season generally involved him getting in touch with old friends, often happily.

This year the interruption was to the Chekhov book, which he was eager to finish. He was finding it a difficult book to work on and grumbled about it, saying that it required too much reading and that he preferred to get on with the writing. I did not know then that there was generally a stage when he announced that a book was difficult and that he was always increasingly eager to finish towards the end. A further frustration this time was that he was limited in what he could say by the volume being a small one. It was part of a series called *International Profiles* which, as the title suggests, were profiles of well-known writers. The first seven titles had been published on November 8th and his friend Ivor Brown had contributed *William Shakespeare* and sent him a copy of it. Looking at this he was gloomier than ever about the restriction of the length and said to me,

"It's always very difficult to do this sort of thing. There's a great deal to say about a man like Chekhov and I'm having to compress it into a fraction of what there should be."

From my place on the Victorian button-back chair I looked at him anxiously.

"Do you read Chekhov?" he asked.

"I've seen his plays – or at least some of them."

"Like them?"

"Yes."

It was a short reply, but I was extremely nervous in case he expected me to know all about Chekhov when in fact I knew very little. The prospect of having to speak intelligently on the subject was a daunting one, and although it was possible my ignorance might make him feel his work the more worthwhile I considered that silence was the best approach.

Mr Priestley sat back, considering me carefully. "He was a fine writer."

I waited for more.

"When they approached me to do something for the series I told them that Chekhov was the only one I wanted to do." He tapped his pipe against the ashtray, carefully placed some tobacco in it, lit up, looked at it reflectively then equally reflectively looked ahead and puffed for a moment. "What do you know of the man?"

"Not a great deal."

"He was a doctor of medicine. Did you know that?"

I shook my head.

"A caring man. A sensitive man. He knew a great deal about human nature." He broke off for a few more puffs. "Men who are artists, and by that I mean writers, actors and musicians as well as painters, artists in the full sense of the word, have a great deal of the feminine in them. Did you know that?"

"I suppose so," I said. "They have more sensitivity than most men."

The reply evidently satisfied him as he smiled approvingly, asked if I had read Jung and, hearing the negative, told me that I should do so, that Jung had tremendous insight into the creative spirit. He then resumed dictating his letters, writing to his accountant to complain about a tax demand and to Norman Collins to thank him for an appreciation of *The Image Men*. It was here that I began to learn something of the preferences he had among his own books. The letter opened:

"How very kind of you to write so promptly about *The Image Men*! You have very good taste in fiction because of course you are right about *Bright Day*, which has long been my favourite book, and equally right to give a very high place, as many people do not simply because it is funny, to *The Image Men*. The idea, which I'm afraid was mine, to publish it in two volumes with the better part of a year in between, has not really worked out very well, but Heinemann's are to do it in one volume next year in time, I hope, for my 75th birthday. Of all the characters I have created I think I had the greatest affection for Professor Saltana and Dr Tuby and left them finally with great regret."

In a letter he wrote to Mr Priestley in 1946 Jung had told him he was impressed by the two aspects of his personality, with one face turned so much to the world that it was a surprise again and again to meet another face turned "to the great abyss of all things". He then went on to read *Bright Day* and afterwards wrote again admiring the way JB made his characters real and the atmosphere he gave to places and situations.

Mr Priestley having completed the letter to Norman Collins, we both sat silent. I made a point of never moving until he announced that our session was at an end. Sometimes it was a long wait so that I began to wonder if I should get up quietly and go, but at other times he told me at once there was no need to stay, or that he was going to get dressed. Quite often I was informed that he was "going to the lav" now, that either I should wait until his return when we would continue, or that I had better go to my room and he would let me know if he had further need of me. I think that sitting and waiting was the right thing. It could be ruminating time that brought forth another letter, a request for a telephone call to be made, or for something to be noted. On the other hand it could produce nothing, or at least nothing that appeared on the surface. It was difficult to know from his expression whether deep thoughts were being pondered on or whether he was just having a rest. I felt that he liked me to be there so long as I kept still and silent, and of course his work required long broodings to develop in. After several years, when I had grown easy in his company, I might venture to break the silence. He would turn then and give me his attention, but if the interruption was inopportune the attention would be on the surface, with a smile that was over polite and words equally so. Having observed this exact attitude when he was with people with whom he did not feel sympathy, I would again fall still. Often enough, he was content to be spoken to, responding with teasing or questioning.

On this morning, as on so many others, he said, "Turn off the telephone before you go," as if this were something unusual.

The switching on and off of the telephone was quite an obsession with him, perhaps because it was important he should not be disturbed unnecessarily when he was working. Switched on the telephone rang in both our rooms, off only in mine so that I could vet the calls and put through only those that needed urgent reply from him or that I knew he would not wish to miss. He liked to remark on it, ask if the switch had been made, emphasised that when I left for home I was to enter his study no matter who might be visiting him there, nor what he was doing, and turn the instrument on again. He said that a great many important calls often came the instant I disappeared. Even if he was giving a television interview, so long as I could not actually hear him speaking, I was to open the door and go about my business. Although he knew perfectly well what it was I did, he liked to comment on it. "Putting the telephone on, are you?" or "That's right!" with an approving nod. When he had some noted visitor I would scuttle in shyly and hurry out again, but eventually he was able to catch me long enough to introduce me.

Having dutifully turned the switch to 'off' I was about to leave his study, but he stopped me as I reached the door.

"Do you like Christmas?" he asked, rather as if he might be inquiring whether I enjoyed illness.

I replied happily in the affirmative, at which he looked at me as if I had strange ways, shaking his head in despair and bafflement. I returned to my room and left him to his contemplation of the trials of Christmastime, and Chekhov. In the afternoon he came to join me, stood at the far end of the billiard table, smiling at me as a conjurer smiles when about to produce a rabbit.

"Do you like music?" he asked.

On hearing that I did and that I had a record player but not too many records he nodded contentedly, disappeared and returned bearing, with an air of triumph, a record.

"I'm going to lend you this!"

My expressions of pleasure were hardly formed before there followed earnest warnings to take care of it, not to scratch or damage it. This worried me so much that I took the record home, removed it from its sleeve and hastily replaced it, returning it intact to him the next morning. When he asked if I had enjoyed it I could only make embarrassed mumble, but he was used to awkward responses from me and probably did not notice. Later that day he brought me Elgar's *Enigma Variations* to borrow, spoke about Elgar, for whom he had much affection, of the Malvern Hills, of music and Englishness and Englishmen. This time I actually played the record and kept it, as instructed to, for several days. When I brought it back to him he said that in his music Elgar takes you on brisk walks from Edwardian country houses and suddenly points at the lost shining land of Avalon. After that from time to time he would produce some piece he had selected for me and would tell me firmly how much I would enjoy it. He liked to anticipate the pleasure he would give to others, whether with his writing or with some gesture or treat, and although I did enjoy the music I would not have dared to say that I had not. His resolution that you would enjoy a thing was so firm there could be no gainsaying it.

The week of Christmas arrived, setting the pattern for future Christmases. It made me a shade melancholy not to be at home giving the proper amount of time to preparations, but such thoughts did not trouble JBP. He expressed regret at the approaching two days' holiday, grumbled about it.

"Christmas is a busy time. There'll be more letters to deal with than ever and we'll need you here."

I said nothing. Surely he did not expect me to volunteer for Christmas Day!

He said, "There's far too much free time nowadays. People don't need it."

Much on the defensive I replied that there was no post on Christmas Day nor Boxing Day.

"There used to be when I was a boy."

I looked at him and then down at my feet. He sighed.

Despite his reluctance the spirit of the season must have got the better of him as on the day before the two day break he entered my room with the air of Father Christmas, his face shining with goodwill, and handed me two of his books which he had signed for me. They were *The Thirty First of June* and *Sir Michael and Sir George* in one volume and his book of essays, *Delight*. There was also a bottle of whisky. These gifts were so wholly unexpected that, momentarily, I quite forgave him the shortness of time I was allowed with my family and was filled with gratitude. Some of his own family were coming to stay with him and a Christmas tree had taken its place in the drawing room. There were cards spread on top of the grand piano and along the chimneypiece in his study, while in the hall there were sprays of holly, so that Christmas was felt in the house, spreading its warmth through the rooms as if the sun had entered it. He saw me off for my two days of leisure, smiling benevolently, well pleased with his own benevolence.

TALK BY FIRELIGHT

He was laughing to himself as I entered the room. Perhaps it was the heat of the fire that warmed his humour for it was not every day that one was lit in the study, but it was cold and he had asked for it and now he sat basking in its light, chuckling happily.

"I was thinking of a joke," he said. "Come and sit down."

I sat and waited for his next move.

"Have you ever heard about the elephant in the jungle who met another elephant and said to it, 'I keep thinking it's Thursday!'"

The telling of this brought on another burst of laughter so that he shook with it.

"No," I replied, doing my best to laugh with him, for I was not as amused as he was.

"I love that joke," he said. "The elephant kept thinking that it was Thursday!"

I smiled, looking into the fire which was blazing merrily. Cascades of sparks glittered and danced on the black of the chimney and there was an agreeable scent of wood smoke.

"Do you ever get that feeling – that you know perfectly well it's Tuesday but you keep thinking it's Wednesday?"

"Occasionally."

"That's what I've been doing today."

He leant to the fire so that its rosy glow fell on his face, which looked well contented.

"An elephant!" A final chuckle rumbled inside him, there was a pause, and then, "Did you see my play last night on television?"[5]

"Unfortunately I was out," I said.

"You should have stayed in! Remind me in the morning to write to Irene Worth. I want to tell her how much I enjoyed her performance, which was really magnificent. That's more than I can say for the way the BBC handled the play. They didn't follow my directions – and they often don't. Then the thing was ruined by the *Radio Times* having given away the surprise secret of the whole thing. When my directions called for a tremendous crash they altered the dramatic effect by having a lot of flames bursting out around Irene Worth as if she had suddenly turned into a Christmas pudding."

"It must be very annoying for you to have your work altered," I said.

Satisfied at having a sympathetic audience he replied, "It is very annoying indeed. After all I don't put in stage directions simply to fill a gap on the page. They're there because they're important to the whole."

"Of course," I said, indignant that anyone should fail to appreciate this fact.

Now he took up the role of sage giving instruction to an eager pupil, explaining earnestly, "My plays are very well constructed, and that's why they've endured. They're played all over the world, as you'll have seen from the royalty statements."

I assured him I had noticed this.

"It's a weakness with a lot of modern dramatists that they don't pay enough attention to the construction of a play, which must be tight. There is too much reliance on shock tactics in the Theatre these days. To shock is easy, but to write a solidly constructed play that widens and deepens our sympathies requires hard work."

Puffing away at his pipe he looked comfortably into the fire again for a time lost in thought. Outside, in the cold dark of winter, a branch of the climbing rose scratched at the window. Inside it was warm in the room and cosy. The fire crackled and chattered at us, sent shadows flickering; a log stirred and settled.

"I love to sit by a fire," he said.

"So do I."

"It's like a person," he said.

"Or a trip to the theatre – so much happening in it."

"Another world."

"Warmer than ours," I replied.

We explored the depths of the fire silently and then,

"The thing about logs is that you get creatures in them," he said.

"You have to rescue them with a poker like Beverley Nichols does."

"Do you know him?"

"No, but he says he does in his books."

"You read him, do you?"

"Yes – it was him who set me off gardening with *Down the Garden Path*."

I do not know what Mr Priestley thought of Beverley Nichols, but to me he was 'Consider the Lilies', which grew for him in a great bed so that he picked armfuls of them. He was statues and Evensong, woodland and the snow defying iris reticulata that you knelt to get close to.

Mr Priestley turned away from the flames, leant confidingly across the space between my chair and the sofa.

"When I was a lad I used to be a very keen footballer. Are you good at games?"

I shook my head.

"I was good at football." He laughed, half to himself half to me. "You may not think so, but I was pretty nippy on my feet. I could dribble the ball away from anybody."

There flashed before me the image of the stocky young Priestley, feet adroitly flicking between the feet of the other lads, seizing the ball.

"We used to play in the streets then," he said. "Many a game we had on the way home from school. It was a good life that. Simple and straight and you knew where you were. There was a lot of poverty but none of the discontent you get now. People didn't expect so much and weren't so greedy. Wages were low, but they seemed to buy more and people were grateful for what they had. The government hadn't taxed us out of existence then and you could get a bottle of whisky for three shillings and sixpence. There was a lot of hospitality. People could afford it at that price. A man might not earn much but he knew where he was with what he had. Ten shillings next year would be the same as ten shillings this year. Inflation is a bad thing."

He shook his head at the badness of it and I nodded with feeling. Suddenly he returned to the games.

"What did you do at school when they played them?"

I described to him the horror of having to hit hockey balls and catch netballs thrown hard at you, which I would have minded less had it not been so deadly serious, caused such an outcry if you failed to hit or catch the appropriate object. I told him how sometimes in the lunch hour when they were practising netball my friend and I took refuge in the chapel, hiding with books behind the organ.

"It's that chin." He put his finger gently into the cleft. "I told you you could never trust a woman with a dimple in her chin."

I said, "The letters are all laid out ready on the billiard table if you would like to sign them now."

We went through to my room which was as book lined as his. It had a chesterfield against the window at the side and at the far end, where my desk stood in the bay made by three large windows, French windows led down steps into the garden, immediately opposite the rose bed. Having signed his letters he stood regarding me. "I hope," he said presently, "that you are going to stay with me." His eyebrows bushed at me and beneath them his blue eyes watched almost with a look of anxiety in them, but he might just have been playing a game with me.

Shocked at the very notion of leaving him I replied, "I'll stay." I must have looked like a devoted spaniel.

"Good," he said. "I enjoy having you around. Finding the work suits you? Liking it here?"

"Yes," I said, nervous as ever.

"Lots of interesting contacts."

It was a statement, not a question. I had not really had any contacts at all, but he had. On one of his visits to London he had made a recording with Robert Robinson about Raymond Chandler. He had seen Stan Barstow who had visited him at Albany[6], he had had tea with the Prime Minister's wife, Mary Wilson. I had stayed at Kissing Tree House typing and answering the telephone. But at least he wanted me to stay, so that my tripping and dropping things, blushing and twittering had not entirely put him off and that was relief enough. I smiled at him happily.

Soon after that my husband and I were invited to dinner at Kissing Tree along with two mutual friends. Mrs Priestley's daughter-in-law, Rosalind, was staying then. It seemed strange to be there in the evening, following Gertrude down that endless hall, feet clattering as much as ever. Mr Priestley was waiting in the study to welcome his guests, the fire blazing behind him with a warmth as cordial as his greeting was, and behind my timidity I had almost a sense of home-coming. We ate roast duck and Miss Pudduck's renowned 'Floating Island' pudding. Seated on his left I set about, with the utmost diligence, an attempt at the intelligent, cultured conversation of the kind I imagined he was used to. My friend had told me beforehand to bring up Yeats if I could as JBP was very keen on him. Realising at once that I had nothing whatever to say about him, I leafed through my poetry books, remained uninspired. All the same, I managed to bring him up somehow, and art and music, for Mr Priestley was sure to want to talk of these things. He listened gravely, caught on quite quickly that I spoke of Millais, not Millet, expressed much interest in my words, turning towards me as though he had never heard such wisdom, laughing if there was anything faintly amusing to discern. Astonishingly my intelligence and culture could not have been too much for him as three weeks later, through the open door of his study, I heard the Priestleys discussing another dinner party and he actually suggested that I should be invited again! Mrs Priestley's opinion was, however, that as we met every day there would be nothing new to talk about. Indignant that my conversational powers should be underrated, for I can be relied on to utter something regardless of nerves, I was nevertheless relieved to be spared further study of Yeats.

However, we had talk enough in the afternoons. The mornings were devoted to work but every day after his lunch, sometimes before sometimes after his walk, he would come and join me, would stand close talking. Occasionally though he would ask me to come to the study to take a letter or two, and then he would keep me for a while in conversation. It was not all one sided for there never was such a listener as he was, his whole attention devoted to it, absorbing your point of view or experience, watching attentively. He spoke of earlier days, his opinions, his current book and ideas associated with it and very often I discovered that what we had been discussing appeared in his immediate writing, either before or after our talk. I do not know whether he was trying it out or whether these topics were so much on his mind that he wanted to speak of them, but I would take what he handed me to type and see almost a record of our conversation.

It was nicest of all on those rare occasions when the fire was lit for him, for the warmth of it was conducive to easy talk, and relaxing. So much alone in his work he had a need for company when he was resting from it, and on the few times when we were alone in the house he might invite me to bring my coffee in and join him or take tea with him. Now I have only to see a fire burning there to sense his presence, to turn to the sofa expectantly, but there is only the memory of that solid form with the pipe resting on the lower lip, the eyes gleaming and watchful – when they were not gazing into boundless spaces of that inner world.

THE EDWARDIANS

The new work was to be about the Edwardian period and would cover the years 1901 to 1914. It was to be one of those large, lavishly illustrated books in the style of *The Prince of Pleasure*, which he had produced the previous year. Mr Priestley had already told me that *The Image Men* was the last novel he would ever write, and so it proved. For the future it was to be these illustrated books, essays, a final volume of autobiography and some of his unpublished writing reworked. Although I had come in at the end of the Chekhov book, the Edwardian volume was the first that I was to follow through its entire course and I was interested to watch its progress from the very start. First it was arranged that John Hadfield[7] would come to Kissing Tree on 12th February to discuss the necessary research, illustrations and the general outline. He would bring some books about the period with him which JB might find of help.

In the meantime, at the end of January, I went down with an unpleasant form of flu, discovering in the process that I had joined an entirely different world. Staff were not expected to be ill, and if they were they must recover quickly. Daily reports were considered to be necessary, together with an estimate of the anticipated day of return. Oppressed by all this I was foolish enough to go back to work the following Monday.

Mr Priestley regarded me suspiciously. "I don't think you want to work for us. That's why you got flu."

"I do want to work for you."

"Then why get ill so soon after joining us?"

"Everybody gets ill sometimes."

His eyes remained accusing as he said, "It's in your subconscious. You don't really want to work for us."

Being still so limp I only managed to laugh weakly, not very pleased at his lack of sympathy. He in turn was not very pleased at the thought that I did not wish to stay with them and it took some time to change his mind about it.

John Hadfield duly arrived and after lunch there was a long discussion in the study about the planned book. It was decided then that Mary Anne Norbury should do the picture research as she had for *The Prince of Pleasure*, for Mr Priestley liked both her work and her personality. The book was to carry representations of the paintings of Augustus John, Sargent, Spencer Gore, Harold Gilman, Sickert, Sir William Nicholson and James Pryde. Yeats was to be included with the poets! Now, his appetite for the project thoroughly aroused, JB began to think about it in earnest and to plan the outline of his approach to it.

On his return to London, John Hadfield wrote about a current exhibition at the Royal Academy, pointing out that many of the pictures would be appropriate to illustrate the book and ought to be photographed before the exhibition ended in a fortnight's time. Some of the subjects which particularly appealed to him fell outside the strict limits of the Edwardian era and he wondered how far Mr Priestley was prepared to stretch the limits of the book. He felt, for instance, that a painting of Boulter's Lock by E. J. Gregory was a superb evocation of the social background of the period as well as being attractive, but it was painted and exhibited in 1897. JB's reply was that he considered it would be quite wrong to put in anything outside the chosen period, the years 1901 to 1914 providing a sufficiently wide choice of pictures.

His preliminary thoughts were that he would divide the book into three parts, roughly 1901 to 1906, 1906 to 1911 and 1911 to 1914. The various subjects would be dealt with inside each period and in each there would be reference to what was happening in New York, Paris and Berlin. As with the Regency book he would employ a researcher to go through memoirs, press material and other relevant papers. He thought that his treatment of the subject should be less historical than with the Regency and more psychological and personal. With the idea rooting he was eager to make a start and on 14th February he wrote to John Hadfield suggesting that the contract should be settled or that there should perhaps be a temporary and flexible kind of contract which would enable him to begin. Until he had some sort of agreement he did not wish to look for a researcher or spend time which might be wasted.

Fate, however, had another kind of hold-up in store for us. On 17th February the flu struck again with a vengeance. I had never quite thrown it off and it returned in full vigour, sending me to my bed and then the entire Priestley household. When I returned to work on the 24th I found Mr Priestley in bed and everybody else struggling. He must have been fairly unwell as he hardly mentioned the flu but sat up against his pillows dictating short letters. They were longer the following day and he began to speak, though not too earnestly, about his illness. He expressed some doubt about the Edwardian book, but then said that he felt doubtful about everything at that moment. A letter from Neville Cardus cheered him considerably and in reply he wrote:

There are some writers I read to make myself fall in love with writing again; Hazlitt and Stevenson when I was much younger, then H. M. Tomlinson – and you!

By the beginning of March he was about again and the flu was becoming a major topic. Correspondents were told that the whole house was decimated by it, that he had not known a worse flu since the epidemic of 1918, that he was dressed but not properly dressed, work was impossible and he could not go out of the house yet, nor could Jacquetta who was now in bed.

Although, like me, he continued to feel far from well, he had soon resumed his normal correspondence, writing a long and detailed letter to John Hadfield about the illustrations for a piece he had written for *The Saturday Book* of which Mr Hadfield was editor, having first given him a description of the flu of course. On 4th March he told his daughter Mary that "the flu situation here has gone from bad to worse," and announced that he and Mrs Priestley were hoping to go to the South of France on the following Monday where they might find sun in which to recuperate. Arrangements were speedily made and I was instructed to take care of things while they were gone.

"See to the mail, let people know when we expect to return and get in touch with me if there's anything urgent."

"I will."

My reply raised immediate apprehension. "I don't want to be bothered with things though. Don't contact me at all unless you have to and don't let anyone have our address unless it is for something very important."

"No," I agreed.

"I'll leave you some signed cheques so that you can settle the bills."

Alarmed in case these should get into the wrong hands I said, "What if there are burglars?"

"Hide the cheques where they will not find them."

Duly I concealed them in a place of the utmost safety but they were found by Gertrude and Miss Pudduck in the thoroughness of their spring cleaning and handed to me solemnly!

There was much to do before departure, a fuss of preparing, Gertrude sponging his suits, clucking her tongue at marks on them, washing and ironing his shirts. His time was taken up by the choosing of paints and paper, for he was an eager holiday artist of no small merit. There was much consulting with me about the choice as I myself went to art classes and was therefore looked to for opinion, although I had no experience at all of his chosen medium, gouache, and was no expert on suitable paper. He had a large black bag to carry his painting things and a folding easel[8]; the weight of them caused me to sag!

They had gone when I arrived on Monday, but he was taking no chances with arrangements and had left a note for me.

"MRS BATTEN

As I have already told Miss Pudduck, unless you hear from us to the contrary, we hope to return on Monday 24th on BEA 105 due at Heathrow at 3.55 in the afternoon. Arrange for International to meet us there.

Please note we shall be staying in London until Wednesday at the earliest. As there might be something I can attend to while in London, you had better get Miss Pudduck or Gertrude to bring up the more important letters.

Unless it is something really very urgent indeed, do not try to get in touch with us, and if you should have to, then send us a wire. People like Heinemanns, Peters and Peggy Ramsay have not got our address in Vence but if they have something really urgent, give it to them so they can wire us. We may move, perhaps to Nice, after about 10 days. It depends how we like Vence and the hotel there.

The signed cheques are for comparatively small payments, if there should be a big one (e.g. tax demand), leave it until I come back.

I don't want people to write to me in France as it is such a nuisance having to reply from there.

I hope all goes well with you – health, car test and all.

J.B.P."

Alas, paralysed by terror at the taking of it, I failed the driving test and for many months longer he was obliged to hire cars for me.

There was a great homecoming, the house filled with excited anticipation, flowers in the rooms, electric blankets warming the beds, everything sparkling from the spring clean, the mail sorted and ready with the letters most likely to please at the top of the pile. Sounds came from the front door, voices, footsteps, the shift of luggage on the hall floor. Not having seen him for a while I was ready to be nervous and strange again but the door of my room opened and he was there, with his most benevolent smile.

"Have you got letters for me?"

He quivered his chins at me. He did this sometimes, lowering his head and shaking it so that the chins rippled, laughing with his eyes at the delight that this action aroused in me.

I indicated the heap of mail but he merely gave it a glance before asking, making it sound like father bear being friendly to Goldilocks,

"What have you been doing while we've been away?"

"We've all been busy here," I said, anxious to show devotion to duty. "Was your holiday good?"

"Very good. The hotel, which was very expensive indeed, was excellent and we enjoyed the food." His voice in the aside about the cost was momentarily mournful, but it revived at the memory of the food.

"We had a separate little villa arrangement with a big balcony that gave us a tremendous view. Do you know Vence?"

"We've stayed there in our tent. We had a month on the Côte d'Azur once."

"So! My secretary goes off to the Riviera for a month at a time, does she! We could only have a fortnight there. What do you think of that?" He wobbled his chins again.

"You didn't stay in a tent."

"I've been in plenty of tents in my time, let me tell you. You wouldn't have cared for some of the tents that I've stayed in."

"Ours is comfortable," I said rather smugly. "We used to buy big bunches of lilies in the Market at Cannes and put them on our table. Roses too."

"You had a table in your tent, did you?"

"A folding one, and chairs and a cooker and shelves to keep our food on."

"Sounds very grand, this camping of yours."

"We used to get baskets of raspberries, strawberries, lovely fresh vegetables and fish, delicious new potatoes with butter on them."

"Your whole face lights up when you talk about food," he said. "Never seen such enthusiasm for anything else. I wish you were as keen on my affairs as you are about eating."

Slightly offended I asked him how his painting had gone and was told that although the weather had been variable with a good deal of rain he had enjoyed being up in the hills and had done quite a lot of painting, in spite of finding it difficult country. After that he looked at the mail, shuffled it about, tutted at it and said, "Nothing much here." I thought that there was a great deal, affectionate letters from his family, details of productions of his plays, some nice fat cheques, requests for him to speak at universities, colleges, clubs and a local school, invitations to dinners, letters asking if he would read other people's work, letters of admiration. Besides these there was the solid stuff concerning his work, television and radio interviews to be arranged, a French publisher wanting to do an edition of *The Magicians*. He was waiting though for that special, spectacular letter that would change his life, some psyche calling to his psyche, some revelation that would lead to a better and more brilliant world full of the kind of wonders that he knew existed somewhere so that he was always reaching for them, waiting for them. I wish I had seen him at the moment of his death for I have heard that sometimes there is a look of joy then, of recognition and fulfilment. As it was he resigned himself to reality and dealt with it efficiently without wasting unnecessary words in reply to it, keeping the substance of his energy for resumption of work on *The Edwardians*.

On 31st March Mrs Priestley went to London to attend a luncheon at the Mansion House and then Sir Julian and Lady Huxley's Golden Wedding party in the Fellows' Restaurant at the Zoo. He, in spite of the holiday, still felt the lingering effects of flu and decided not to go, instead settling to his work and producing a Prefatory Statement. A copy was sent to Charles Pick[9] at Heinemann and to John Hadfield at Rainbird Books, to whom he wrote:

"This "Prefatory Statement" will not be the actual Preface to the book, even though some of the thoughts here will appear there. But it does give you some idea of the way in which I see the book and will tackle the job of writing it. Do not hesitate to let me have any comments.

The question of the title is a difficult one and I shall be glad to consider any suggestion."

It was unusual for him not to have the title at the start of a book, which was when he liked to have it as it gave him a sense of direction. *The Edwardians* was not settled until towards the autumn and there were several alternatives which never felt really right to him. Writing to John Hadfield on 3rd April he said:

"After several days beating my brains out, I have at last come up with what seems to me a very good title. It is:
Edwardian Caravan
'a Very Personal Study of the Years 1901 to 1914'
Then, on the title page, I shall put this from Fitzgerald's "Omar":
'The Stars are setting and the Caravan
Starts with the Dawn of Nothing'"

John Hadfield was unenthusiastic, feeling that the word Caravan was not wholly appropriate to the spirit of the age, that it lacked impact without the quotation and that in any case the quotation was not a familiar one. It was he who suggested the eventual title, JBP who now expressed doubts, offering this time *The Edwardian Years*. When *The Edwardians* was finally agreed there was some consideration given to Vita Sackville-West's book with the same title which, although published in 1930, was still in print and widely read. The style of the books was different, their publication so far apart that there seemed no chance of confusion, and so it was settled, for it was a short crisp title that described what the book was about.

Mrs Priestley returned from London well pleased with her visit. Mr Priestley wrote to Lady Huxley to regret his absence with:

"I was very sorry indeed to miss your party last night and it was not laziness that kept me here. As Jacquetta probably told you, we went to Vence to recuperate after a rather bad go of flu, and although I improved out there I did not feel quite right, with a cough hanging on when we got back, so I felt I must keep out of London for a week or two."

He was still writing about the flu in May so it obviously made an enduring impression on him. Morosely I hoped he remembered that I had begun it all.

Not feeling quite right was not allowed to intrude on his working plans and he began to immerse himself in the period, writing on 15th April to inform his researcher that he had been doing some work on the first section and giving a long list of books that he had already gone through. She was asked to call on him at Albany on the 21st. Observing the pace he was going at I wondered if there would be anything left for her to read for him.

"I'm a lazy man," he would say. "Wouldn't do a thing if I wasn't obliged to." But he was obliged to, impelled by the writer's urge to hurry along, always with a sense of urgency, of time being short, of ideas and more ideas to be seized and put down on paper. Besides, he was now writing about his own period, the formative never-to-be seen again time before his world was smashed by the war and dissolved before him.

By the end of the month he was writing again to the researcher to thank her for some notes and tell her that the bones were there but he wanted more meat. Later he wrote again saying that her notes were all right as far as they went, but they did not go far enough. Eventually he decided that he would prefer to do his own research as he said his time was being wasted waiting for the notes he required. It was always a challenge to keep up with him, and if anybody lagged behind he soon lost patience. Indeed, I noticed with gloom the number of people who were seen no more if they failed his pace or if he fell out of sympathy with them.

April was not unbroken work. Iris Murdoch[10] came to dinner with her husband John Bayley. His friend Susan Cooper, over from America, came to stay a few days. She was writing a book about him and his work and I had later to send her vast parcels of his novels and plays if she had not already got them. There were a good many calls on him and he dealt with them all in time, travelling away from home if he had to, answering letters, supplying endless information, giving interviews patiently. These things had their properly appointed times and were kept to them, then he would settle into his corner at his typewriter, cotton wool wedged firmly into his ears, and type steadily. Whenever I opened my door I could hear the sharp, steady tapping. There might be an occasional short pause, but mostly it was like the high heels of a woman who has a train to catch rapping against the pavement of a silent street.

Often he liked to talk about the book, so that one afternoon when I took a book he had asked for to the study where he was reading on the sofa, he patted the blue velvet chair companionably, as he did sometimes, and I obediently sat in it.

"How are you today? All going well with your affairs? I hope so."

"Yes," I replied, thanking him.

"That's good. I'm very glad to hear it." He always gave to such remarks the utmost sincerity, as if he really cared. "All's going well with my affairs too. I'm enjoying this Edwardian stuff." He adjusted his pipe and took a few puffs at it. "You could say I'm an Edwardian myself. It was, after all, the period I grew up in."

I made a faint murmur to cover all eventualities.

"It was a very good period. Although there was a lot of poverty and hardship about, there were a lot of good things too. It was a better time than any time since in my opinion."

We sat in quite a long silence, he gently smoking his pipe, his eyes thoughtful, I very still as was my habit with him. Sometimes I peered sideways at him, sometimes at the shelves of books on my other side. Those where I sat were filled with volumes of poetry, essays, Wilkie Collins' *The Woman in White*. There were old, worn, leather bound books, some in sets, including Proude's *Short Studies*, Motley's *Dutch Republic*, Shakespeare. There were several books by Robert Lynd, the collected poems of Peacock, Thomas Hardy, John Cowper Powys' *In Defence of Sensuality*, Hazlitt, Marcel Proust, Henry Fielding. In the adjoining shelves the poets spread out, Cowper, Chaucer, Swift, Goldsmith, Richard Church, Dylan Thomas, Edward Davison, Ralph Hodgson, Robert Bridges, Lascelles Abercrombie, G. K. Chesterton, Wordsworth, Longfellow, Tennyson, Robert Browning, Siegfried Sassoon, John Dryden, Walter de la Mare. There was John Drinkwater's *A Pageant of England's Life*, books by Rose Macaulay, Nietzsche, C. Day Lewis. There was *Don Quixote*, *Pilgrim's Progress*, and Lesage's *Gil Blas*. If I was kept a long time I would observe them again and again, fascinated to see what volumes he chose to keep about himself.

He said, "The first world war was a terrible war you know. It wiped out a whole generation of fine young men. I lost many of my own friends in it." His voice carried a weight of immense sadness. "The world has never been the same since. How could it be when the men who should have been building it up into a better world had gone?"

I agreed with him, said it was an appalling war, at which he changed his tone and smiled at me.

"How do you know? It was way before your time?"

"We've all heard and read of it, the trenches, the awfulness of it all. You have only to look at a war memorial to think what a slaughter it was. Once you have children of your own you begin to understand what it must have been like to lose so many in a generation; not only the terrible loss of young lives but the grief of the mothers and wives and families who were left behind."

"Women," he said, "don't have an easy time. I often feel sorry for them." In between his sentences he puffed away steadily, his eyes often seeming to be looking beyond or inside himself. "They depend so much on men. It's their main job in life to find one, to get a husband and keep him. All those women left manless after the first war – that was a bad thing! The world lost its men and the women lost their men. Nobody gained a thing."

The war had left a great melancholy in him. He referred to it often, grieving for the loss of life then as he grieved for it now, feeling the immense tragedy and waste. He spoke of the dark years that followed it, the way attitudes changed and people grew harder. He said that a generation with fine ideals and the vigour to carry them out had been lost, the ideals and vigour lost with them. It was his generation, the one he had grown up with, shared his hopes and youthful dreams with. It had been mown down just as it was about to unfold and he mourned it for the rest of his days. Now he continued,

"When people talk about the Edwardian age as being a golden age, they are mistaken. It was never that, but seen across the dark years that followed it, it seemed to be one."

Again there was a period of thought and then his mood changed and he smiled at me wickedly over the top of his spectacles. "The Edwardian women were a fine lot. They knew what being a woman was all about. They were exciting creatures, deliciously feminine, hiding everything away so that you wondered what was underneath all those layers of petticoats. Far more exciting than any of these girls lying on the beach wearing next to nothing. They're making a mistake there, leaving no guesswork about themselves. Mystery is far more tantalising to a man."

I said, "It must have been a bit restricting for them though! All those corsets and uncomfortable tight things."

"Buttoned up to the neck and down to the wrist," he said with satisfaction. "There was the excitement of undoing the buttons and lacings, like unwrapping one of those parcels that has layer after layer of paper around it! What curves they had! They didn't go in for slimming then. Wait till you read what they ate! I've been looking at some of the lists of food they got through at a sitting. It was quite incredible! No wonder they had such huge fat thighs!" For a moment he pondered on the ample flesh, then added happily, "I like big thighs and those Edwardian women certainly had them – great marmoreal thighs!"

I wondered how he came to be such an expert when they were so well concealed, but it was good to know that somebody liked fat thighs. I felt I had an attraction.

"King Edward had a bigger appetite than any of them," he said. "He'd have lobster for tea! A huge breakfast, kidneys, steak, eggs, sausages, toast and marmalade to follow, perhaps a bit of porridge to begin with, then an enormous lunch with course after course. There'd be a vast dinner in the evening, eight or ten courses, every kind of meat, rich sauces, elaborate puddings, and yet if he didn't get his lobster for tea there'd be hell to pay!"

I expressed amazement, while Mr Priestley, warmed to his subject and eager to enlarge on it continued:

"They'd have those gigantic meals and afterwards it was in and out of the bedrooms. They think they know all about sex now, but believe me, they're not up to anything that the Edwardians weren't up to. The only difference was that it was done secretly then. Hostesses had to make sure they knew who was having an affair with whom and put them into the right bedrooms so that they'd be near enough for visiting. The houses must have been full of moving figures at night! By day they'd be changing their clothes all the time. If they didn't wear the right thing for each move they'd be OUT." His forefinger stabbed to emphasise banishment. "There was morning dress, afternoon dress, evening dress, riding dress, something suitable for shooting, another change for a game of tennis. It wasn't such an idle life as you might think. They were kept very busy with all that changing and eating and hopping about from bedroom to bedroom."

"The women had such elaborate hairstyles," was my contribution.

"Their maids must have spent hours on them."

"I didn't live like that," he said, although I never imagined he did. "We were ordinary people. That kind of life was for the upper classes and while it was going on there was appalling poverty among the working people, men unemployed, children in the streets in winter without shoes, unable to go to school because they'd nothing to wear. No old age pension then – people just had to manage somehow."

Our conversation was there when I came to type the first section of the book for him. It was June and he was away in Yorkshire when I settled into the silence of the house to begin on it. He brought the period powerfully to life so that you immediately got the feel of it, and every now and again he was there himself, a young man flitting about the pages, lively with youthful memories. There were the things he had talked about, the king's lobster teas, the darkness of war. It was as if our talk had never stopped and was never going to because here it was, ready to go to print. He may not have lived in it, but he painted a clear picture of Edwardian high society, its rich glow menaced by the impending shadow:

"...So the rich scene is set. But it is transformed into (I quote a publisher) 'the now fabulous Edwardian age' by the autobiographers who look back not only at their own youth but also at a scene all the more radiant because it is on the other side of the huge black pit of war. They are remembering the time before the real wars came, before the fatal telegrams arrived at every great house. The Edwardian was never a golden age, but seen across the dark years afterwards it could easily be mistaken for one. When it dined and wined, laughed and made love, it had not yet caught a glimpse of the terrible stone face this world can wear."

His portrait of Edward VII was good and perhaps he felt that they had things in common. He wrote sympathetically about the king's pleasure-loving enjoyment of life, and certainly Mr Priestley liked his food, his drink and a good cigar. Something he wrote made my lips twitch, for it reminded me of the caution I used when teasing him:

"Even when he was off duty and at ease it was dangerous to take advantage of his smiling good humour, to forget that the stout elderly gentleman with his glass and his cigar was also His Majesty King

Edward the Seventh: the purring cat suddenly growled like a tiger. This may have been a deliberate policy, a part of his cleverness in handling people. In point of fact, Edward as a man was tolerant and good-natured, never out of temper long, never vindictive."

There were distinct resemblances. Many times he pointed out to me "I'm a very tolerant man, an easy man to get along with. You'll never see me lose my temper and I'm never vindictive." There was truth here for he was indeed never vindictive, never flew into a rage, although he could be a shade querulous but that was seldom. He certainly knew how to handle people when he set his mind to it, but if displeased he also could growl like a tiger.

He spoke of the working classes with sympathy too, of their hard conditions and shockingly low rates of pay. It seemed therefore rather strange to me that his own staff were paid well below the going rate, but then that tends to be the way of things.

Late in July I took my summer holidays, returning on 11th August to find the second section of the book completed and the third already begun. At that point it was still being called *The Edwardian Years*, for only when the manuscript was finished did it become *The Edwardians*. As if I had been missing for months he was waiting anxiously with a list of necessities for me to fetch from Stratford. There were sleeping pills, Benemid for his gout, three packets of Crampex, books for his research to be collected from the library, Steradent for cleaning those of his teeth that were not his own. There was no need, I felt, to draw my attention to them with so much pulling about inside his mouth, and I looked down firmly.

"Do you think Steradent is any good?"

"I've never had to use it, but I believe it's excellent for getting stains out of decanters."

"Decanters! Really? Where did you learn this interesting use for it?"

"In a magazine."

"Is that so? Well, I find it good enough for my teeth and that's what I want it for. Do you think they look all right?"

I did not like to say that when he opened his lips like that his teeth put me in mind of a horse, so I informed him that for a man of his age they seemed quite healthy. There was a good deal of wiring in his mouth, attaching teeth to other teeth, and I was not at all sure how many of them were his own and how many manufactured for him. As inquiries might have led to demonstration I did not mention this.

"Tobacco," he said. "I shall need some more."

We had to go through his tobacco drawer then, inspecting the contents of tins, rattling them and he, unable to open them, handing them to me and watching closely, with immense interest, my struggles with coins and penknife until I managed to get the lids off. Latakia was settled on, and pipe cleaners, which had to be the long ones, and some flints for his cigarette lighters. There were many of these, for friends who observed his lack of success with them sent him the "infallible" kind, "never known to fail". Each was seized with happy anticipation and in his hands each, eventually, sputtered and died. Sometimes the cause was his attempts to put more gas into them, for when I filled them they leapt to life, occasionally with such vigour that my eyelashes were in danger of being scorched. Then I knew that he had been adjusting the flame again.

When I returned from Stratford he was there, waiting to take the books and start going through them immediately. Mary Anne Norbury had sent him three more from the London Library, but they arrived too late. Roaring ahead of everyone he had already done the section they covered and he wrote to tell her so, ending:

"Mrs Batten, who has been away on her holidays, will now begin to complete her copying of Part II and I hope to be able to let you have it within about a couple of weeks."

By now I knew perfectly well that he might talk cheerfully of two weeks but that he would expect completion within two days or so, telling me that it was only a brief job and would involve no particular efforts on my part, to be fitted in here and there in a moment or two between accounts and correspondence and all the other occupations with which I amused myself.

A reminder from his dentist that it was time he had an inspection brought on a further study of his teeth. He wrote saying that he was well aware a visit was overdue, that he was in urgent need of repairs, but that he could not spare the time to come to London. An appointment would be made as soon as it could be fitted in however. The places where repairs were necessary were pointed out to me with a good deal of pulling about and prodding.

John Hadfield telephoned offering to lend Mr Priestley *Edwardian Friends*, but like everyone else he was not keeping pace with JB who no longer felt the need of this volume. He was now so near the end of his book that he was able to tell his daughter Mary that he was "moving towards the end of *The Edwardians* and it will not get easier but more difficult." He hoped to get it finished before his birthday celebrations and then to have time for "idling and painting" for a while. By 29th August I had finished copying Part II and sent it off to Mary Anne. Then, while the Priestleys were away in Breconshire, I settled down to typing the final part. Again it brought back much of the talk we had had. There was the sinking of the *Titanic* and hubris; the first time I had heard the word.

"It was a fearful thing," he said, his voice carrying a weight of doom. "Hubris! They were all so sure of themselves, sure that the *Titanic* was unsinkable, boasting about it. One of the crew even told a woman passenger that God himself couldn't sink this ship. Bad!" It was a long drawn out 'bad', full of foreboding. "They took no account of hubris."

Gleaning that it had something to do with fate, I looked it up in the Oxford Dictionary afterwards, discovering that it was insolent pride or presumption, overweening pride towards the gods, leading to nemesis. It was a word he seldom used but the sense of it was with him always. I noticed that he never said "We are going to..." It was always "We hope to" or "We plan to" or "If all goes well we should..."

His section on the suffragettes was fascinating. Perhaps it was because of his sympathy with women. Later, when the book came out, it was even more fascinating to see so many of them, household names, now with faces to them, for the illustrations were excellent.

The section on ragtime gave him some fun as he wagged his finger with cries of "Hitchy koo, hitchy koo!" and played old tunes, dancing the odd step to them. Ragtime carried him back to the days of young manhood, the dashing fellow in the flowing tie and peg-top trousers living it up at the Bradford Empire. He quoted his own words from his autobiographical *Margin Released*:

"...what we were hearing for the first time was *Alexander's Ragtime Band, Waiting for the Robert E. Lee* and the rest, not forgetting, though its title has gone, that intoxicating refrain which went 'Fiddle up, yiddle up (BOM) on your violin'."

Later a reader informed him that it was *The Ragtime Violin*, words and music by Irving Berlin, and sent the chorus. At the end of the book he returned to that terrible war:

"In that war we lost the better part of a fine generation of young men. This is not sentimentality, no uprush of self pity: the facts bear it out. During the earlier time of voluntary enlistment our young men of greatest promise, the future leaders in everything except making money quickly, became junior officers, and it was the junior officers who were mown down..."

The final illustration at the bottom of the last page is a photograph of the British Cemetery at Bayeux. He did not, however, end on a note of hopelessness, for his closing words were:

"Edwardian England is a time and a land seen across the vast dark chasm of war. Over there the afternoons seem to linger in the mellow sunlight, the nights are immediately romantic. There is illusion here, of course, but it is not all a cheat: something *did go*, something *was* lost, but survives in those of us who grew up as Edwardians and went into the war and came out of it. There is, I think, behind our grousing and grumbling a kind of optimism, not large and wide and one huge smile, almost tiny but very compact and somehow indestructible. It encourages us to engage in all manner of doubtful ventures – as, for instance, trying to huddle Edwardian England between the covers of a book."

They returned from Breconshire on Saturday, 18th October, and activity was resumed almost immediately for he had an engagement in Hemel Hempstead on the following Monday. On Tuesday, when he lunched with John Hadfield in London, he handed over the typed copy of the final section. This was not the end of his involvement of course, for there was yet to be a good deal of consultation about illustrations and the choice of cover. Early in the following year, 1970, he returned from a visit to Ceylon and immediately spent the afternoon at Albany with Mary Anne Norbury going over the paste-ups of the illustrations with her. The design for the jacket took some time to settle, just as the title had done. John Hadfield liked the notion of a reproduction of Robert Bevan's *Cab Yard, Night 1910.* JB considered that there was nothing Edwardian about this, though admitting that it was a charming picture, but he thought it rather subdued and melancholy for a cover. They discussed the possibility of getting an artist to design something, Mary Anne suggested that a hat might be suitable, the Edwardians being noted for their millinery. The idea appealed to him, but he thought that a number of hats would be better still. Hats it was then, an attractive array of them. When the book came out Hatchards, the London bookshop very close to The Albany, filled their window with hats. It was a gesture that pleased him enormously.

The next stage was the proofs when he altered the blurb, for with him nothing was left to chance and he took the keenest interest in the presentation of his work. After going through the proofs of the colour prints he pointed out to Mary Anne that some of the colours were too dark and some of the pictures had not come out well. They were all as they should be in the final version and were highly praised.

The Edwardians came out in October and was received with enthusiasm. In his review for *The Sunday Times* of 18th October Frank Swinnerton said, "The illustrations to *The Edwardians* have been chosen with genius. They brilliantly adorn a brilliant text." Letters of admiration began to arrive and went on coming in for years. I thought it was perhaps the best of his illustrated books. Going so firmly to his roots that was as it should be, with himself weaving in and out of the pages with personal memories and a strong sense of the period.

He had hardly got to the end of this work before he embarked at full speed on another about the Victorians.

AN ACTIVE YEAR

The speedy writing of *The Edwardians* was impressive enough for a man of seventy four, but it must not be supposed that that was his sole occupation for it was only a part of it. In that first year I was amazed at how much he accomplished, attending to his correspondence, being guest of honour at various functions, tossing off articles for several newspapers and journals, receiving visitors, and on top of this giving a good many interviews for radio, television and many different newspapers.

February 1969 may have been limited by flu, but it was not an entirely fruitless month for it was then that he wrote an article for *The Saturday Book* and also that Susan Cooper's collection of his essays was published in England by Heinemann under the title *Essays of Five Decades*. It had been brought out in America the previous year by Atlantic Little Brown and covered, as the title made clear, pieces he had written during fifty years. Reading them was rather like having a long conversation with him, full of hope, indignation, humour, enjoyment of life, pessimism, compassion and down-to-earth common sense. In his review of the book in *The Sunday Times* of March 9th Robert Hughes said:

"His essays are unforced, discursive, addressed to an audience with its boots on the floor and its rump in an armchair... Yet there is a passion in these essays, which makes them so easy to read and the best of them so well worth reading: a broad, heavy decency, a preoccupation with freedom, a distrust of ideological solutions."

Malcolm Muggeridge, writing for *The Observer*, referred to a particular essay which had been taken from JB's *Delight*. Called *Early Childhood and the Treasure* it is short enough to quote in full:

"I can remember, as if it happened last week, more than half a century ago, when I must have been about four and, on fine summer mornings, would sit in a field adjoining the house. What gave me delight then was a mysterious notion, for which I could certainly not have found words, of a Treasure. It was waiting for me either in the earth, just below the buttercups and daisies, or in the golden air. I had formed no idea of what this Treasure would consist of, and nobody had ever talked to me about it. But morning after morning would be radiant with its promise. Somewhere, not far out of reach, it was waiting for me, and at any moment I might roll over and put a hand on it. I suspect now that the Treasure was Earth itself and the light and warmth of the sunbeams; yet sometimes I fancy that I have been searching for it ever since."

As indeed he had, questing, waiting, hoping. He waited for it all his life, watching the post for it, listening for it, dreaming of it, that strange, magical event that would put into his hands this glorious Treasure. Malcolm Muggeridge wrote:

"There *is* a Treasure which we are aware of, which seems just within reach; which, if we are lucky, we never quite lose sight of, but of course never find, never hold in our hands – not even when we think we've firmly got hold of it; perhaps especially not then."

He went on to express respect for Mr Priestley's *oeuvre*, admiration for his craftsmanship. If JBP had any feelings about these reviews he did not voice them. He was not a collector of criticism and when, occasionally, a publisher sent him some cuttings concerning himself he generally pushed them aside. It was I who cut out reviews, if they were worth preserving, and carefully filed them away.

Bradford was occupying him at this period because it was the Fortieth Festival of the Bradford Playhouse in June. He had been its first President, a position he held for over quarter of a century, and his sister Winnie was its first Secretary. The inaugural meeting, in 1929, had been in his parents' house. In the following years the Playhouse had put on many productions of his plays and there was to be a short run of *When We Are Married* as part of these Festival celebrations. He had decided to attend the first night and had agreed to give a talk at the Theatre on the Sunday evening, as well as an interview to Yorkshire Television. With his usual attention to the details, he wrote to Roger Suddards[11], who was chairman of the Festival Committee:

"Many thanks for your letter of 14th March and I think you heard from my secretary that we were away in France, and have in fact only just got back here.

I suggest the following arrangements. We drive up on Saturday 7th June and stay at the Victoria Hotel until Wednesday morning. Perhaps you will be good enough to book us either a suite, which I seem to remember I have often had there, or if that is not feasible then a bedroom with two beds and a bath. I do not know how you feel about this, but in view of the Sunday night talk, for which we think we should charge admission, the Playhouse might take care of these hotel expenses. But if there is any difficulty about this, then I will take care of them myself.

Our plan is to drive up to the Dales on Wednesday and stay for about a week at the Red Lion in Burnsall and perhaps you would be kind enough to book us a room with two beds and a bath (this is more easily done from where you are than where I am), and of course this is entirely my financial responsibility.

I am glad to know that my sister is definitely going up to Bradford and we might possibly be able to give her a lift. I will get in touch with her about this and imagine that when she gets there she will probably be staying with friends.

You will of course have gathered from the above arrangements that we intend to attend the first night of *When We Are Married*. If there is still anything about which you are not clear then perhaps you could give me a ring here one evening."

Donald Baverstock of Yorkshire Television was written to with the same detailed attention and with the suggestion that an alternative to the programme already planned would be a discussion between JB and his old friend Phyllis Bentley.

It was while he was attending to this correspondence that he also wrote to his friend Sir William Emrys Williams who would be coming for a week-end that summer:

"...I look forward to having some talk about the Theatre with you. I now regard it and its dramatic critics with such despair that when managers and actors begin to suggest revivals of my plays, as they do, I find it difficult to work up any enthusiasm."

There was an aside to me about this. "When you write about the Theatre in the sense that I am talking of it here, always use a capital letter for it. It deserves one." The subject caused reverie. Eventually he emerged from it and sighed. "It's not what it was. You won't remember all those fine productions. Do you go to the theatre often?"

"Not very often."

"You should do."

It was all very well for him to speak. He had a staff to take care of things, money to pay for them. I explained that I could not get babysitters, refrained from mentioning the financial side in case he thought I complained.

The next stage in his visit to Yorkshire was in April when he wrote with concern to the Red Lion in Burnsall:

"Dear Mr Webb,

Mr Suddards, of the Bradford Playhouse, forwarded to me your letter to him. I know the Red Lion of course and have had two or three excellent meals there. The fact that you have no room with a private bath does not worry me very much, what does is this idea of having two sittings to lunch and to dinner, especially dinner as we would probably be out all day. If you stand by this rule then reluctantly I must cancel Mr Suddards' arrangements for the week beginning 11th June."

Reassured by the reply he was able to write again:

"Thank you for your letter of the 21st, and in view of what you write we will let the booking stand.

If the weather is fine at all we should not be in for lunch but will be roaming round the Dales looking for something for me to paint. As we shall be taking a packed lunch, then you can put us on full board. I am sure we ought to be able to work out the dinner situation on the spot."

Besides giving his support to the Bradford Playhouse Festival he was to be Patron of the Hemel Hempstead Arts Festival in October. On April 29th, after seeing Mrs Priestley off on her Swan's Hellenic Cruise, he attended a Dvorak Concert at Hemel Hempstead with Mr Owen, the organiser. There was dinner first, and for companionship his daughter Sylvia. Returning to Kissing Tree next morning he wrote at once to Mr Owen:

"Thank you for the very pleasant evening my daughter and I had last night – the fine concert, nice people, good food.

I look forward to hearing the New Philharmonia in the same excellent hall. I wonder if you could persuade the conductor to end the concert with Schumann's Symphony No. 4 in D Minor? It is a great favourite of mine and is such a perfect finale that it always arouses great enthusiasm – that is why it is good as a final item.

I hope you will forgive me if I do not attend the performance of *Johnson Over Jordan*. The point is that I have such a glowing memory of our original production, with its superb cast and lighting that I have always refused to attend any other productions of the play for fear of disturbing this memory of it. There is one point you may like to raise with the producer. In the first Act, you may remember, two examiners question Johnson and of course the questions they ask in my original text are now thirty years out of date. Therefore I suggest that the producer or you or somebody brings those questions up to date – using exactly the same kind of questions but on topical subjects."

For him to want any alteration to bring a play up-to-date was most unusual; normally he wanted a play to remain entirely in its own period even to minor details. When asked whether changes could be made to make his plays more contemporary he generally replied that the play must be left as it stood, that he knew what he was doing when he constructed a play and did not want anybody interfering with it. In the present case the change was merely to prevent the questions being irrelevant. He also agreed, on hearing that the New Philharmonia concert was to end with *The Eroica*, that there was no need to change it for the Schumann.

While his wife was away, as well as getting on with his work, he did some entertaining which included having a woman friend to tea. This was Jean Young who later became Lady Young on her husband's knighthood. He told me what a pleasant person she was, and intelligent too, that he was fond of her. He must have done some thinking about it because on the day before she was due he came into my room with an air of pleased conspiracy and announced that he wanted me to meet her. Not liking to disappoint him I refrained from mentioning that I had done so some time previously, and in any case it was only briefly and I did not suppose that she would remember me. A fresh introduction seemed simple enough to me but he had other ideas.

"We'll have to devise a plan," he said, and paused for thought. "What we'll do is this. I will buzz through for you. You come to the study and I will say that I am expecting a call from John Hadfield and has he telephoned today. You reply that he hasn't and I will ask you to make sure that the 'phone is switched off'. You bend over and fiddle with it and tell me it's all right. Then, as you're still in the room, I'll be able to introduce you. We must both be very casual about it so that Jean doesn't suspect we arranged it. I'm sure you'll like each other."

If I had been with him longer and grown comfortable with him no doubt the plot would have gone smoothly. As it was I was nervous and tense and three rehearsals on the following morning reduced me to a state of terror.

"Casually now. Come and show me how you're going to do it. I will press my bell and you will come in and say 'Did you want something?'"

Mrs Young duly arrived, was shown to the study by Gertrude and some time later my telephone buzzed. Rigid with self-conscious lack of confidence I approached his door. We went into the opening routine.

"I was expecting a call from John Hadfield. Has he rung today?"

"No," I bleated.

"Let me know as soon as he does." Pause with perfect timing. "While you're here would you make sure that the telephone is switched off."

As I bent over the switch and pronounced all well he leaped to his feet eagerly. He, after all, enjoyed dramatics. His face gleaming with pleasure he took my arm and led me to Jean Young.

"This is my secretary, Mrs Batten, Jean."

She rose to take my hand but my role was something of a disaster. I may have managed to make suitable remarks but my voice shook, my breath came gasping. Seeing my lack of ease Mr Priestley turned away and became deeply interested in a bookshelf in the corner, while I, as soon as possible made my escape. If he was disappointed at the failure of his plan he did not mention it, but it was the last of our attempts at Theatre.

Soon after that, as we were going over the mail, he suddenly announced, "I like having you about. You're a very nice person."

At a loss for a reply I looked at my knees and smiled. "You've got very nice knees!"

This was astonishing. I edged a little away from him and pulled my skirt down.

"Not many people have good knees." He leant more towards me and briefly patted one of them.

I moved the chair a fraction away from him and looked in bewilderment at that perfectly ordinary part of me. It was a time when skirts were horribly short.

He laughed at me over his glasses and said, "When I was a lad I used to be a success with the girls."

Hands folded firmly on my knees I smiled belief at him.

"I was never good looking you know."

"You've got a very nice face."

"Not a handsome one though. Nobody could call me that. But that was no drawback." Pipe in hand he put his face closer to mine. "Because I knew I wasn't good looking I had to work hard at it. Some of my friends were handsome chaps, but I'd steal a march on them let me tell you. I could charm the girls and did. A good many of them."

There passed between us a flash of amusement. I said, "I bet you did!"

"Still can."

With an expression of content he puffed his pipe, his mind I supposed on huge Edwardian thighs and giggling girls in petticoats. Presently he picked up a letter from his morning pile and began to dictate a reply.

Mrs Priestley was due to return on Tuesday, 13th May, and her husband was to meet her at the airport.

"It isn't every husband who would travel from here to Heathrow to meet his wife," he said.

"No, it isn't."

"So you see, I'm a very good husband."

"Yes indeed!"

"After all, it isn't much fun to go to an airport. Airports are not my idea of a pleasant outing. Are they yours?"

"No."

"Some people seem to enjoy them, but not me. Do you think Mrs Priestley will appreciate my meeting her?"

"I'm sure she will."

It was arranged, and much arranging it took, and bustle and fuss and excitement. The morning came and he left with Miss Pudduck at 8:45 to catch the Paddington train, for there was business to attend to in London. It was late afternoon before he was collected and taken to Heathrow to greet his wife and they spent that night at Albany, returning the following day to Kissing Tree House, Mrs Priestley well satisfied with her Hellenic cruise, Mr Priestley well pleased with himself in the role of husband.

The rest of the week was quiet, but after that activity was resumed and he wrote a piece for *The Times* on Kenneth Clark's *Civilisation*. In acknowledging a letter about this from the editor, Harold Evans, he remarked that the fee of £75 was acceptable by contemporary standards but in the 1930s he had written a series of articles on subjects of his own choosing for the Sunday papers and had been paid £75 for each of them. This meant that there had been no increase after all these years he pointed out, a shade reproachfully.

In the middle of the week Lord Snowdon came to photograph him for *The Sunday Times Magazine*, the pictures to accompany an article to be written by Susan Cooper for his 75th birthday. We were amused to see him posed in the shrubbery, looking not too pleased about it, but the results delighted us. Something of his impish quality was caught, even if it was a rather oversized imp, and one of these photographs, head and shoulders under his big black beret, was used for the cover of Susan Cooper's book, *J. B. Priestley, Portrait of an Author*, and again, several years later, for John Braine's *J. B. Priestley*.

There was entertaining then, his son Tom coming to spend the week-end and the Robert Robinsons. They were joined on Sunday in time for lunch by Marghanita Laski and her husband John Howard. Lord and Lady Redcliffe-Maud were overnight guests on the following Thursday. Visitors tended to come in clusters and then there would be intervals of work and recuperation.

Plans were well in hand for the visit to Bradford and the programme had grown to include a visit to the university and the central library. There was to be a civic lunch on Wednesday and after that they would be free to leave for their holiday in Burnsall. Always eager to include his family and to demonstrate to them that he was in demand and busy he wrote on 28th May to his sister Winnie:

"We are driving up on Sunday morning, the 8th, and I have made no arrangements for that day except giving my talk at the Playhouse at night. Monday I shall be fairly busy because I am doing a 45 minute programme with Yorkshire Television and that will take most of the day, and then at night we have agreed to dine with the Suddards at Tong Hall, but Tuesday is really an empty day except for the play at night and we mean to spend it getting out a bit with the car and if you felt like it you could join us then."

June turned the rose that had scratched at the wintry window into a mass of golden centred crimson blooms, but he did not remark on them. His views were wider than mine, up and out and beyond. He would admire a tree, the great beech spreading over the lawn with its coppery coat that turned gold in the autumn, the oak, sturdy as an English bulldog, or the white-cream blossoms of the chestnut trees. Flowers were scarcely ever mentioned, except by me, although he would speak of their scent sometimes. An unusual cloud formation would cause him to rise from his seat and stare through the glass as a child might stare at a kaleidoscope. A flock of geese skimming the sky on their way to the river would hold him attentive, listening eagerly to the cry they made, the swish of their outstretched wings against air. He would call me to watch a squirrel swinging from branch to branch of the cedar, or a hedgehog crossing the lawn on its matchstick legs. Hedgehogs made him laugh sometimes.

"They can run quite fast," he said.

"I know, I've seen them."

"You've seen hedgehogs running!"

"Certainly."

"Where did you see this sight?"

"When we were camping in Scotland, but I've seen them run several times since. They get quite tall when they stretch their legs out."

"Running," he cried, bulging his eyes, his arms waving wildly as if he were trying to get somewhere quickly. "So Mrs Batten has seen a hedgehog running!"

Soon after I came he had asked what I wished to be called and I replied, "Mrs Batten". Convent educated I drift into formality easily, and besides there was risk that they would use my Christian name and expect me to use the formal address, which would offend my easily offended dignity. In time it became almost a joke between us. He would shruggle his brows and wobble his chins and say, with his face close to mine and his eyes twinkling, "How is Mrs Batten today?" If we were alone sometimes it gave him a satisfying sense of sin to use my first name.

"Ssh! Ssh! When there is nobody about I shall call you Rosalie. It will be something we keep to ourselves."

He waited expectantly, but to me he was by then settled as Mr Priestley, JB occasionally. Eventually he became "Himself" when I spoke of him and I addressed him from time to time as "Yourself". Himself seemed to suit him because he was himself. Himself filled the house and made things happen in it.

He said, "They are going to reissue my book on Dickens next year, which is the Dickens centenary year." He was holding a letter from Thames and Hudson.

"That's appropriate."

"It's a small book, but that doesn't stop it from being a good book. I hope that you'll read it some time."

"I'm sure that I shall."

"And that you'll enjoy it."

"I dare say I will," peering at him over the top of imaginary spectacles, for I could do a little teasing of my own sometimes.

Teasing could be uncertain and I approached it cautiously. If it was Himself who teased it was in his eyes invariably funny, but if he was being teased he might fail to see the humour of it. Never totally sure of his mood I would venture delicately, watching to see that all was well. He might roar with laughter, or smile, look unamused or, horrors, his face might begin to darken and I would spring back like a scalded cat and at once resume earnestness. My vigilance saved me from ever annoying him that I was aware of.

This time all was well; he peered back over his own real spectacles and said, "I trust that you will, Madam."

I said, "*The Bradford Telegraph and Argus* will be telephoning you this morning. They want to talk about the arrangements for your visit there."

Preparations for Bradford assumed a major key and he began to sort out his painting things, to lay quantities of paper on the billiard table to be sorted through, to huff and puff over his ties and supplies of tobacco, reminding me to cancel the newspapers, sending me out to buy shaving cream, soap, indigestion pills, throat tablets, razor blades and all the other commodities that might never be discovered in Bradford. They departed on the Sunday and when I came in on Monday there was complete silence. The domestic staff were on holiday too, and there was only the echo of him, a faint scent of tobacco, a calm that was tinged with expectancy as if at any moment the front door might be flung open wide and he appear in the hall. Settling to type *The Edwardians* I was always aware of him.

He returned lamenting the changes in the city which he did not feel were any improvement, regretting the replacing of fine old buildings with glass and concrete, the destruction of character. Nevertheless Bradford had been a success, his talk had gone well and he had enjoyed the production of his play. The Dales had also gone well and they had travelled from the Red Lion at Burnsall to the Black Swan at Helmsley, he painting contentedly while his wife explored. Now he spread the results on the billiard table and beckoned me to come and see.

The paintings were all of views, wide skies puffed with cloud, distant hills, long stretches of green. Some of the clouds were bright with sunlight, others storm dark, purple grey where they touched the horizon. The hills rolled and ascended, darkening at the menace of dark cloud, glowing where the sun warmed their slopes. His trees were sometimes a shade too solid, but his water was lively, full of reflection and sparkle.

"What do you think?"

"Your skies are as good as any I've seen."

The answer pleased him. "You have to do them quickly – that's the secret. If you stop and dabble about you lose them."

I asked him how he achieved such vigorous clouds and was told that he did them with his fingers, dipping them into his gouache and spreading them swiftly. It was hard to see how this dashing about with fingers could make that soft, fluffy wispiness at the upper edge, the folds and hollows, the rosy streaks, the rain-filled heaviness of dull days, but I took his word for it and praised.

"You could sell them and become well-known as a painter as well as a writer."

He shook his head. "I've stood in the market all my life for my books. I'm certainly not standing there for my painting."

It surprised me to learn that he felt like this, that he stood in the market. He seemed to be so strong and certain, so very rock solid. He never appeared to have the smallest doubt about his work and its value, had not suffered the countless rejection slips that come to most writers. In any case, to judge from his mail, the market was forming a queue for his favours. *The Telegraph Magazine* asked him to do a piece for them; Penguin Books announced that they were bringing some of his works out in paperback, there were requests for his plays, the proofs of the Chekhov book awaiting approval and the advance copy of his first big illustrated volume, *The Prince of Pleasure*. Henry Moore was staying that week-end and took the book to bed with him, loud in its praises. His agent wanted to know if he would consider writing a short story for the BOAC magazine, *All Aboard*; the Canadian Broadcasting Corporation requested an interview. As he was going to attend the Lord Mayor's Banquet in London at the end of June he arranged to see them there.

On 9th July he wrote to his agents, Peters, agreeing to the BBC doing a radio version of his play *Mr Kettle and Mrs Moon*. The letter requesting this had arrived after lunch and afternoons being more leisurely he took his time about it. Sitting beside him in the study I watched his face crease with amusement.

"Have you read the play?"

"It's one that I haven't heard of."

After further contemplation and a few chuckles he went on, "It's broad comedy – a bit of sex – might shock you!" A prospect that delighted him. "Mr Kettle is a highly respectable bank manager living a proper and dreary life in a dull provincial town, but one morning he suddenly decides that he's had enough and throws the whole thing up. Mrs Moon is a respectable woman, very severe and proper. She is married to an extremely dull man. A lot of men are dull. Don't you agree?"

"Some are."

"Especially the middle-aged ones. Something seems to happen to men when they get older; perhaps their jobs paralyse them. They lose their sparkle, turn into business machines – nothing much in prospect except their work. Women are much better at keeping their sparkle. They're interested in everything – want to know what's happening. They age better than men because they've always got something to occupy them, even if it's only knitting. The kind of man who has been totally preoccupied with business doesn't know what to do with himself when it's finished with him so he goes mad with boredom, boring everybody else in the process, or else he dies. Don't you think so?"

Having doubts about this I was non-committal.

Returning to the play he said, "Mrs Moon comes to see Mr Kettle on business and finds him at home determined to have nothing to do with business. He's busy being rude to the bank's clients, playing with a game he's bought and listening to some splendid music. He declares himself to be in love with Mrs Moon." He slapped his legs in delight here. "She's in love with him too and they end up by going off together into the unknown."

This seemed to me rather to contradict his usual desire for people to be there doing their jobs properly, running things smoothly to make life civilised. Indeed he said more than once to me, "People should rest on holiday. They shouldn't go dashing about doing things. They need to rest so that they can go back to their work with renewed energy." He felt the same about week-ends, that people should spend them sitting about recovering from their week's effort and be fresh for Monday. It may have been his own staff that he had in mind here and I used to listen glumly. In view of all his rambling about on the moors or buying tobacco in Swan Arcade when he was a young clerk and should have been at work I thought his view strange! Perhaps he lost hope of ever converting me as he eventually ceased to recommend this way of life. The play itself, when I read it, was not one that appealed to me and I found its humour forced. Reading is, of course, very different from seeing a play on the stage when I suppose it could have seemed hilarious.

If *Mr Kettle and Mrs Moon* failed to stir much laughter in me, the man himself could fill me with it. The door of my room would open, his face appear in the gap, cautiously, his chins would wobble, for he knew that this was the move that never failed to fill me with mirth. Then he would enter the room and take on whatever role suited the moment's mood. He might be Charlie Chaplin, Harry Lauder waving his stick and singing, a fat, ponderous man, a self-important small committee man or an aged, tremulous, pathetic one looking for his pen, cigarette lighter, a misplaced letter, or simply some extra attention from his secretary. He would roll his eyes in desperation miming his need, while I, equally desperately, proffered things. Sometimes he would come in very solemn, stand and regard me earnestly, then suddenly break into the chin wobble, delighting in its effect on me.

Peters next wanted to know if he was agreeable to an American publisher reprinting his forty year old *The Balconinny*. They enclosed a photocopy of the request from the company concerned and he noted that they had made the error most likely to displease him, leaving out the e in Priestley. "I am not an adjective," he said. "If people want something they should take the trouble to get my name right." The result was that he replied:

"...I feel I should know rather more before I sign this contract. Who are these people (who cannot spell my name properly) and what do they propose to do with my book? Do they want it as a paperback or some kind of cheap school edition?

The suggested advance of $150, and royalty of 10%, and the statement in clause 5 that the publisher will supply me with one free copy of his edition, all suggest that this is anything but a generous and prosperous business and unless you can tell me more I do not feel inclined to let them reprint a book of mine 40 years old."

All was smoothed out, however, and having received answers that satisfied he signed the contract the following week.

Gollancz, who had just brought out Daphne du Maurier's latest book, *The House on the Strand*, sent Mr Priestley a copy of it. He wrote to her to explain that he had begun to read it in bed, but that because of having to read so much for his present work it would be some time before he finished it. Perhaps to show her that he did enjoy her writing despite this slowness he added:

"Did I ever tell you how much I value your life of your father? It is in my opinion one of the best biographies of the century and if I find I have to consult it, writing about the Edwardian Theatre, then I know very well I shall go on reading it all over again."

Late in July I took my summer holiday, listening in silence to talk of how inconvenient it would be to be without a secretary, how much work there was. I returned on 11th August and heard talk of busyness and things piling up and what difficulties holidays made for society, but he relented enough to hope I had enjoyed myself. He had himself answered much of his mail.

September was largely taken up with the celebrations for his 75th birthday, following which they were to take a holiday in Breconshire before the Hemel Hempstead Festival. Colours were changing in the garden now and he called me to look at the copper beech outside my window. Huge and spreading it was fired by the sun to burnished gold.

"Have you ever seen such a sight!"

Later, Gertrude, standing by the dining room window, made almost the same remark.

There was a last rush of correspondence before departure for Breconshire. He wrote to thank Moura Budberg, one time mistress of H. G. Wells, for a letter, suggested she might join them for a meal when they were next in London. To me he said, "H. G. Wells had a very high pitched voice, you know. It was always a surprise when he spoke because it was not at all what you expected. A high up treble." Happy recollection made him smile.

Twenty of his paintings were to be shown at Hemel Hempstead and we set to work to label them. *The Black Mountains in Breconshire; View from Hong Kong; Marrakesh, South Morocco; Meteora, Thessaly, Greece; Port of Spain, Trinidad; Mayan Temple in the Jungle at Tekal, Guatemala.*

To Mr Owen he wrote:

"...I enclose my little introduction and the material for the catalogue and all the pictures properly numbered. All will be ready for you here on the 10th, but as about four of them are not framed in glass I suggest you bring with you a certain amount of packing material to make sure that these pictures are not damaged in transport (I must add that this whole business has taken far more time than I wish to spare and I can only hope the result will be worth the trouble.)

I would have thought that six was a bit too early to be sitting down to dinner on the 20th, but in spite of the rush hour we will try to be with you about that time, if only to drink in your company a very cold and very dry Martini cocktail, which I think we all like. Wine I must leave to you because it really does depend on the dinner. I tend to keep off brandy myself, but possibly my wife might like some. We shall not be dressing of course.

I also imagine that you do not want me to be wearing a black tie for my talk on the Tuesday night, though of course I can if you prefer it.

I have arranged with my daughter Sylvia and her husband, Michael Goaman, to drive us up and back."

Finally, there was a letter to a Mr Thomas in America:

"Thank you for your letter of the 21st, which I was glad to have even if, like so many Americans, you leave out the second e in my name – it is ley and not ly."

They returned from Breconshire on Saturday, 18th October, and almost immediately had to be off again for a programme that might have exhausted a man twenty years younger than he was; he did not flinch at it. There was the journey to London, the dinner and concert that evening, lunch with John Hadfield on Tuesday when he handed over the final part of *The Edwardians*, and that evening his talk at Hemel Hempstead. On Wednesday morning he gave an interview and then a lunch party attended by John and Diana Collins, Norah Smallwood of Chatto and Windus, L. P. Hartley and Moura Budberg. In the evening the Priestleys were taken out to dinner at the Café Royal.

They returned to Stratford for a few days rest and then, quite suddenly, decided to go to Amsterdam to see the Rembrandt Exhibition. They would fly from Birmingham Airport on Tuesday, return on Thursday. Birmingham, he said, was a small and comfortable airport, not gigantic and impersonal like the others. He said, "I don't usually like air travel, not because I've any objection to flying but because of all that airport business. If we could always go from small places like Birmingham, in pleasant surroundings and not hours of travelling before you can even begin, I'd be a much more enthusiastic traveller than I am." Perhaps he was risking hubris here, for they set out in total hope planning to have an hour and a half at the Exhibition and then lunch. In the event a fault in the aircraft meant that another had to take its place and there was a two hour delay. There was only just time for lunch at their hotel and Rembrandt had to wait until the afternoon. He returned full of enthusiasm and wrote a piece on the Exhibition for the *New Statesman*, talked of some of the small brush-drawings of people as "little miracles of observation and technique". The later self-portraits drew his greatest admiration. He praised their realism, the way the artist faced himself without illusion.

"The more you look at them," he said, "the more you see. He takes you deeper and deeper into what those wise old eyes observe, showing beyond the realism a sense of mystery. It's no good rushing past; you have to stop quietly there with him, discovering more and more of what the man's telling you."

I told him of my visit some years previously to the Rijksmuseum when I had been able to sit for some considerable time before the Rembrandts there, how the light in the pictures had affected me.

He spoke softly. "Emerging from darkness into light, fading into darkness again." There was a pause and then, "I am older now than he was when he did those portraits."

"You don't look old like that though. Your skin is so smooth."

"Madam, are you flattering me?"

"No."

He ran a pleased finger over his face and agreed that perhaps it was not too bad for a fellow of 75.

After that he dashed off a piece for *The Sunday Times*, accepted an invitation to a Foyle's Literary Luncheon for Kenneth Clark and, in view of the piece he had written about *Civilisation*, later agreed to take the chair at this. He was asked for his choice of speakers for the occasion and suggested Lord Snow (C. P. Snow), Sir Mortimer Wheeler and John Betjeman, pointing out that nobody should be expected to speak for longer than five minutes. There was a brief visit to London when he visited Roy Jenkins at 11 Downing Street to talk about income tax. In the evening he attended a reception at number 10 and the following morning went to his dentist. During all this he was also making arrangements for a longish trip to Ceylon, pausing to write a piece about Tony Hancock whose widow now wrote to thank him for it. He replied that her husband made such a fascinating subject that he would like to write about him again some time, and if he did he would get in touch with her.

To me he said, "It's a terrible strain, being a comic, and Tony Hancock was a very good one. He drank to relieve the strain of it. A comedian often has a nature that is truly melancholy."

We had some discussion on this and then he said, "Drink, if you let it take charge, can be a bad thing. The secret is to regulate it. I like my drink, but you will have noticed, I hope, that I never have a drink before lunchtime. And after lunch I don't drink again until the evening. It's drinking at odd times, without any discipline, that's fatal. Terrible to see it get hold of someone. And if it does, the husband or wife of that person often drinks too, just to keep pace. Then it's two lives ruined."

Having disposed of this unhappy subject he turned to Roy Jenkins, sending him a copy of the Regency book. He referred to their talk, hoped that Mr Jenkins would be able to do something about taxing aged authors, saying "it would enable elderly professional men to escape being harried during their last years by the tax man." He felt that people over retirement age should not have to pay tax, having contributed enough during their "working years", but although he was listened to with sympathy he could never get the administrators to agree with him.

Receiving news of Stephen Potter's death, he felt that he ought to write to Mary Potter, even though that marriage had ended a good time previously:

"...The news came as a great shock to us because we had not known that he was ill and now it appears that he had been ill for some time.

It is years since I last ran into him and I never at any time saw a lot of him. But I always enjoyed his company just as I did his work, and I think that like an enormous number of other people I am going to miss him.

We have a fair number of guests and visitors who come into this study of mine and sooner or later take a good long look at your portrait of Jacquetta, and it has been very much admired."

It was December again, with Christmas looming. The Prime Minister's wife, Mary Wilson, had received *The Prince of Pleasure* from her husband as an early Christmas present and wrote to say how much she was enjoying it, having always been fascinated by the Regency period. She thought the book beautifully produced and illustrated and, touchingly, ended "Yours with respect".

It was the season for him to lament the passing of Bradford days, to describe nostalgically the Yorkshire hospitality, parties, games, songs round the piano, gathering of characters, the talk and warm welcome everywhere, the unending activity, the pantomime, and "none of the sitting about with nothing happening that you find here.

Christmas in Yorkshire in those days was something to celebrate," he said, and settled himself, disgruntled, to endure the present one.

I had been with him a year now. Sometimes it seemed as if I had known him for a lifetime. No one else could share a conversation as he did and it had no limitations. Not out to impress anyone, not false about a thing, he listened intently, spoke his thoughts without any coyness, went to a deeper level, did not shrink from emotions, either his or yours. That was his private face. In public, perhaps he was more reticent.

"I'm a forgotten man," he used to say occasionally. "Nobody wants to know, nobody thinks of me now." Reflecting on the year's activities, the work produced, correspondence attended to, the daily requests for him to be a guest of honour, judge essays, attend plays, to write, to read, to speak, I wondered what it was like in the days when he was remembered.

INTERLUDE FOR A SMALL DOG

The dog in question was my own; a small cream Pekinese whose toes ended in tufts that curled up like Siamese slippers. Her nose was black, her eyes deep brown, enormous and heavily fringed by eyelashes. Her ears made me think of the bunches of ringlets that framed the faces of girls at the Restoration. Thinking myself very original I had called her SuSu, making a play on Tzu-hsi, that last Great Empress of China. After that of course I discovered that similar names were almost universal. This delectable dog had been a Christmas present from my husband, though I had pointed out anxiously that I might possibly take a job and what of the dog then? In the event a friend had taken her for a walk each lunchtime, but for the rest of the day SuSu lay in her bed chewing her tail and waiting for me. Although I knew my predecessor had brought a dog to work it took nearly a year for me to pluck up the courage to request this privilege for mine.

"A dog you say?"

"Only a small one." I regarded him anxiously.

"A dog!"

I explained that it was lonely for a dog to be left all day, that they needed companionship.

"Is it well behaved – this dog?"

I assured him there had never been so angelic and gentle a creature, but I expect he thought that I exaggerated.

"A Pekinese you say?"

"The prettiest I've ever met. Her teeth don't stick out like some do. She has a lovely face and is very good-natured. She smiles a lot."

"Smiles!"

"And walks for miles. She's come all over the Welsh mountains with us."

"She is obviously such a remarkable animal that I shall have to meet her."

I thanked him tremulously.

"I don't really care much for dogs," he said. "They are like drunken men, pestering you, pawing you, putting their faces close to yours and refusing to go away when you suggest it to them. Dogs are not my idea of company."

This did not sound too good a start and I produced SuSu nervously, held my breath as she approached him, proud of her movement for she walked superbly with her head well up, fronded tail curled up like a question mark, feet high, fringed fur flouncing. Wherever I went people stopped me to admire her.

He said, "She looks exactly like Mrs X. Her face is just like that!"

Mrs X used to visit the Priestleys with her husband, but although I knew Mr X I never met his wife and do not know if she really did have a face like a Pekinese, only that the comparison was made at any mention of her name.

"Hello DOG," he said, making it sound so like a growl that SuSu halted, wrinkling her forehead in bewilderment. "HELLO, DOG!" His voice was generally deep but when he addressed her it tended to drop into his boots. "She doesn't seem to like me."

To suggest that it was the way in which he spoke to her might have been unwise, and besides I was too frightened to, so I merely told him that she was a little shy. After that she accompanied me each day, went on her lead with me into his study, sat at my feet while he dictated to me. Occasionally he would speak to her. She would rise immediately, go to look at him, as cautious as I was in approaching him. If he sounded encouraging she would stand to place her paws on his knees, resting her chin on them. He would say, "She likes me you see," or "She looks like Mrs X," or "That's enough DOG," more sternly so that she retreated hastily. Sometimes he patted her head, not lingering over it but well intentioned. She was a small dog and he was not entirely sure how he should treat her, but he grew fond of her, called her a nice little dog, inquired after her health, expressed concern if it did not go well. If he met her free of her lead in the long hall he might call to her so that she went bounding eagerly to greet him, but then he sometimes did his boot voice again and she became uneasy. Disappointed he would again remark that she did not seem to like him, but she was a flatterer and given a chance told him that she thought him wonderful.

The years advanced in the house and age took its toll. Little more than a puppy when I first brought her, SuSu remained sprightly until she was around fourteen. Then she grew old suddenly, became slow and ponderous, sighed deeply. Her sight dimmed and her hearing grew faint, but her spirit never failed and she accepted her handicaps with courage. When she was young Mrs Priestley had explained that they did not want her running in the garden; now she was allowed there and would walk slowly by the side of the rose bed. Author and dog used to meet, their thoughts almost tangible. "You too!" they seemed to say, he heavy on his stick, she unable to run in case she should throw herself against a rose bush. It had happened once, agonisingly, for even half blind she had bounded like a little rubber ball. As he sat on his chair in the hall at that half-way resting point, with his fingers curled round his stick and his head down, brooding, she and I would come down for our coffee break. I led her slowly as far as the hall steps, lifted her down towards where he sat, let out a sigh of sympathy. He would look at her and at me and words were unnecessary.

She died at sixteen. When it was clear there was no hope the vet came to our house and, with my hands clasping her paws in love and gratitude, as is right at the end, she was eased instantly and painlessly from life.

Himself seemed to feel her departure, spoke sympathetically of her as of any close friend. Mrs Priestley too was sad and spoke kindly to me.

CEYLON

In earlier days it had been his habit to travel far and spend some time away. With age he had developed a reluctance to leave his home so that Gertrude would sigh and say impatiently, "Are they never going to go away?" It was not that she wished to see the back of them but there was always house-cleaning and while the Priestleys were in residence she and Miss Pudduck were unable to make a full attack on it as it would disturb him. Ceylon and New Zealand were the only major expeditions that were made in my time.

Ceylon seemed to be the fashion that year for several of their friends were either there or going to be. With winter closing in on them the Priestleys began to consider where to go for warmth. They generally did go to some milder region for that gloomy period at the end of winter, but this time they were considering spending Christmas abroad and Ceylon seemed appropriate. As Angus Wilson and his friend Tony Garrett were there already Mr Priestley wrote to ask them for advice:

"We have read a lot of tourist stuff about Ceylon and cannot help wondering what it is really like. If it is as warm and humid as Bangkok or Singapore, then it is out as far as I am concerned because this kind of climate leaves me feeling permanently exhausted. And then what is the accommodation really like? I gather from one booklet that it is limited and that early bookings are desirable.

If it were much nearer then we would take a chance, but it is, after all, a long way and costs a great deal. But we must make up our minds very soon where we want to go. I realise you will not know the island well yet, but even so, if you would airmail us at once giving us a candid account of it, this would be of great help."

Evidently the plan was very serious as even before a reply came the Priestleys had been given their first inoculation against cholera. Mrs Priestley wrote to ask a friend who had lived there for her opinion of it, and when they learned that John and Diana Collins were also going to Ceylon the decision was as good as made. Their hope was to find a fairly quiet place to settle down and to do some work there, and Kandy seemed suitable, high up so that the climate should be healthy and the heat tempered.

Having obtained the name and address of the British Council representative in Colombo, Bill McAlpine, Mr Priestley wrote to him:

"Many British Council representatives, from Chile to Trinidad, Delphi to Athens, have given me a great deal of friendly help during the last ten years and in most instances I have been able to repay that help by holding press conferences or giving a lecture or two. So I won't apologise for troubling you.

The situation is this – that my wife (Jacquetta Hawkes) and I are thinking of flying out to Ceylon arriving at Colombo in the early afternoon of December 22nd, perhaps spending Christmas there and then moving on to Kandy – that is, if we can find suitable accommodation. We should then stay in the Island probably well into February, making it more or less a working holiday.

So far we are finding it difficult to get exact information, both about the climate (we dislike hot and humid places like Singapore and Bangkok) and about suitable accommodation. Incidentally, if the latter is good it need not necessarily be cheap. We usually require a room with two beds (or two single rooms close together) with, if possible, a private bathroom and some sort of balcony. Could you please let us know about all this by return airmail, or if that for any reason is slow – and I have not had a reply yet from Angus Wilson to whom I wrote eleven or twelve days ago – then please reply by cable.

Finally, it is more than likely that one or both of us will be writing something about the island."

This letter sent, Angus Wilson's reply came almost immediately, but as Mr Priestley was by then in London I had to read the gist of it to him over a line that constantly crackled and faded intermittently. The message was that Mrs Fonseka, at the Chalet Guest House in Kandy, could provide a large bedroom with two beds, an attached modern bathroom, a comfortable private sitting room and a balcony with access to the garden. It was exactly what he had in mind and I was instructed to send a telegram reserving it from 27th December. He intended to fly out on 22nd December but to spend the first few days in Colombo. On his return from London he wrote at once to Angus Wilson with details of his plans, saying too, that on the 18th he had sent an airmail letter to "McAlpine at the British Council in Colombo asking for some advice and help, but up to this time of writing I have received no reply". It was useless pointing out to him that nine days is a pretty short time for an exchange of mail over such a vast distance. Nine days, so far as he was concerned, might just as well be nine months.

"Only nine days," I said, trying to reconcile him.

His reply was, "That's a hell of a long time," in a tone that rebuked me for speaking out of turn.

In no time at all, it seemed to me, the letter arrived and the arrangements went forward. The doctor called to give the Priestleys their second injections and then they went off to London for the Foyle luncheon he was to preside over. That evening they gave a large dinner party at Albany, on the following morning he saw Mary Anne about illustrations and had A. D. Peters to lunch. In the afternoon he gave an interview then went on to attend a farewell cocktail party for Karl Meyer, London correspondent for the *Washington Post* who was returning to America. A cocktail party at the *New Statesman* was followed next evening by dinner with friends.

They returned to make their final preparations and I was sent to get sleeping pills, a box of Meggesons Lozenges for his throat, three boxes of Crampex, Benemid for gout, shaving cream, toothpaste and Steradent. He said, "We'll be flying first class," and paused. "That is not because I think myself superior to the people who fly second class."

I agreed that this was understood.

"It is because I am a very big man. When you are big you need more space." His eyes were round with earnestness. "That is the ONLY reason I travel first class. The seats are wider."

The point appeared to haunt him as whenever they travelled first class the reason was given to me and he wrote an article about it some time later.

Anxious that I might be idle while they were away he began to think up tasks to keep me occupied. I was to make fresh copies of his biographical notes and bring them up to date. These were sometimes asked for so we kept a pile of them ready to be handed out. I was also to collect and put together all the manuscripts of his books ready to be sent to Texas when he got back. The Humanities Research Centre at the University of Texas had all his original manuscripts. The list of these is prodigious. They also have most of the letters to him from well known people, many photographs, his portrait in oils by Henry Carr, done in 1950, and bronzes by Jacob Epstein and Maurice Lambert done in 1931 and 1948 respectively, the first a bust, the second a study of his head. I gathered up everything from recent years and labelled them, only to be told to put the whole lot away when he returned! Another holiday task he left me was to go through all his drawers and sort out the contents, making lists of them. Finally, having been asked by Ira Morris, an American writer living in Paris, to write an article he dashed this off and sent it on the Friday before his departure saying:

"…we are due to fly to Ceylon on Sunday and may be there for a good many weeks. I am not very clear how you wish to proceed, but I have left the top copy with my secretary here, Mrs Batten, and if you will let her know she could send the article to Peters, my agent, at any time you wish. I refuse to try to mastermind these arrangements from Ceylon…"

Ira Morris accordingly telephoned on Christmas day, but as I was, amazingly, at home then, left a message with the gardener's wife. When I returned from work and he rang me again from Paris, I politely refrained from making any comment on his first choice of day. Perhaps he did not notice Christmas! It seemed to be unpopular with authors.

Ceylon was not a huge success, partly because it rained there. I sent them copies of the mail that I thought might be of special interest. I told them how the house was gleaming from the great clean, that the first aconites were to be seen in sheltered parts of the garden, that the viburnum was in flower and the air was scented with it. Back came their news of the unseasonal monsoon weather that had caused mildew to cover Mr Priestley's hat as it lay in the cupboard. Hour after hour the rain fell in torrents until indoors seemed to be as damp as it was outside and their clothes and bedding felt moist from it. They had enjoyed Colombo well enough, though they had been so caught up in its social life that there had been small time left for sight-seeing. They had visited the zoological gardens there, finding them good and full of lush vegetation. Also in Colombo they had eaten the Lindt chocolate that I had given them for Christmas and had much pleasure from it. Then, both very tired, they had arrived in Kandy and, while the rains cascaded, were able to rest. Flooding elsewhere had been desperate although they had seen no sign of refugees where they were. Outside their windows there were monkeys and birds and flowers. They had made some expeditions to high tea plantations where there were marvellous views all over the surrounding mountains. Later, visiting two temples in the jungle Mrs Priestley, walking through the green of it, had found herself hung with leeches.

I sent lists of queries to JB, receiving NO to all of them. No to two radio programmes, no to writing for a magazine, no to a newspaper. Someone wanted to know his favourite flower for an anthology she was writing and Mrs Priestley answered for him that it was the freesia, because they bring a good smell and spring-like quality in winter. He wrote that the rain had stopped now and they had just returned from a trek up North to see the ruined old cities. He did not sound enthusiastic. Mrs Priestley, however, found them fascinating and the surrounding countryside appealing. He said it was warm by day now, cool at night, that they planned to drive up to Nuwara Eliya which is over 6,000 feet and would be cold.

The next letter was the last. They proposed to leave Kandy for Colombo on February 5th to stay with the McAlpines till the 9th when they would fly to London. I was to let Peters' office know and arrange a car for them. After this a cable announced that they would arrive in a VC 10 at 22.55 on Monday on flight BA 793. I was to telephone BOAC Skyport 5511 to check. Finally I received a telephone call from the Flight Captain, from the air, to say that all was well. There were advantages in being J. B. Priestley!

Soon he was back, turning the echoes in the house into reality, walking slowly round the billiard table, settling again into his place. Ceylon, he said, had been a curious mixture, striking in its beauty sometimes, but often he had found it boring, though he thought the weather could have caused this. He had managed to do some writing and as usual some painting, strange pictures of jungle scenery, distant domes, the huge rock at Sigiriya with its towering steps, long bare trunks of trees tufted at the top with enormous leaves so that they looked like slender handled shaving brushes. Everywhere he had put in small dark figures dressed in saris; they dotted the steps, walked in line, dozens and dozens of little matchstick people. Mrs Priestley had enjoyed the jungle, but he had felt there was too much of it. She had delighted in Anuradhapura and Polonnaruwa. He would have been just as happy to have read about them, although he had enjoyed seeing the huge reservoirs known as tanks there. He described Kandy's situation as magnificent, at just the right height and surrounded by distant mountains, though the town itself did not particularly appeal to him. The nearby Peradeniya Botanic Gardens he found admirable, the trees there extraordinary and wonderful and he thought it must be one of the finest arboretums in the world.

"There were ants," he said.

"Ants?"

"All over the place, and in my bedroom. Some of them got into my bed and walked across my face." He puffed with indignation. "I'm too old now for the insect game. When I go on holiday I like to be able to relax and not have to worry about mosquito nets and tropical diseases. All the fuss there is about the water. In fact, let me tell you, Madam, I've done enough travelling. It's good to be home again."

He often spoke about being done with travel but, due to my own thirst for distant places, I was always faintly sceptical. Possibly I may have been wrong there and he really did now want to settle in his own familiar place.

"It was supposed to be the dry season there and we got torrents of rain!"

"That was hard."

"There were caterpillars too. Hundreds of them. They drowned on our balcony, penetrated our bedroom!"

Where men considerably younger than he was might have taken a few days to recover from the journey he moved straight into the thick of it, attending to business affairs in London immediately after the flight, and at Kissing Tree giving thought to his next book *Victoria's Heyday* as well as working on the play which he had started in Ceylon, *Island Incident*. Perhaps the effects of Ceylon touched even his writing, for although it is difficult to judge from typing a piece, I felt the play was not quite right. On his next visit to London he took a copy of it and left it for his agent to read; he also left a copy with Ralph Richardson[12]. Alas, their feelings coincided with mine and with the utmost tact and kindness A. D. Peters wrote to tell him that the play was not as good as he thought it was. His reply filled me with admiration:

"...I fear that you are right and that I was wrong. Obviously there is an instinctive feeling about the Theatre that tends to vanish with age, and must be taken into account. I shall write to Ralph and say that you have told me what he was too polite to tell me."

If the play was a disappointment to him the book was not, and there were many more books to come yet before Time caught up with him. *Victoria's Heyday* came out for his 76th birthday, since birthdays were a time for publication.

BIRTHDAYS

It was in the first year that I discovered the importance of birthdays.

"This year," he said, giving some weight to it, "I shall be seventy five!"

I looked impressed.

"A good age, don't you think?"

"A splendid age."

"But I don't feel it. You know, as you get older and your body ages it seems to have nothing to do with you. You stay young inside, impatient with the old chap who's collapsing round you with his ache here and his stiffness there."

It did not seem to me that he had too much to complain about in the aches and pains line, being quite remarkably healthy. Nevertheless I nodded sympathetically, for with his spirit I could understand that any physical limitations at all must be a trial.

"Anyway," I said, "you don't look seventy five so why think about it?"

He thought about it a good deal; not the being older part but about the birthday, for birthdays meant much to him, were a highlight in his year. Writing is a lonely business, shutting yourself away to get on with it, having none of the terms of reference that somebody working with colleagues has, having to make all the decisions for yourself, hoping in this cell of solitude that you are producing something that will reach people. Birthdays made a break from it and gave him a period of special recognition, congratulations pouring in and signs of affection. Also, although he would never have admitted it, he enjoyed the importance of occasion – providing that it was his kind of occasion.

"Have you ever heard of the little girl who wanted to be in the importance?" he asked, and repeated over the years for it caused him particular amusement. A smile from me was enough to make him continue, his face creased with merriment. "A little girl was asked what she would like to be and she replied that she wanted to be in the importance. I know exactly what she meant, don't you? It's a lovely phrase, so descriptive of the fuss and consequence that would make the little girl feel that she was important." He slapped his knees and raised his head in acknowledgement of an applauding crowd. "Do you want to be in the importance?"

"Not really."

"Nor do I. Don't give a damn. Couldn't care less."

I thought my thoughts, knowing how he responded to fuss, drooped if there was not enough of it, but perhaps we both fooled ourselves. He had a great need of the warmth of special attention when he emerged from that solitude of work. Birthdays were an important time and he was eager that people should know about them, writing in replies to letters from strangers that it was his birthday soon, or had been, and if their letters coincided with the date, that they had written on his birthday.

"All this stir is nothing to me," he said. "It's only another birthday."

But he would begin quite early to plan for it, waiting to see what his publisher would offer this time, thinking with pleasure of a family gathering for he saw himself as very much a family man, was proud of his five children, told me how he had a good relationship with all of them, and with his stepdaughter too.

"No quarrels and disagreements. We all get on."

"That's as it should be," I observed with warmth.

"I'm a good parent," he said very solemnly. "Never interfere. The secret of being a good parent is to give affectionate neglect. Let your children develop in their own way, not the way that you impose on them."

Seventy five was one of the major birthdays and Heinemann were giving a special dinner at the Savoy with friends coming from as far away as America. This was to be on Monday 15th September; the actual day of the birthday, Saturday the 13th, was being reserved for the family party. On the Sunday between, John and Diana Collins were having a small gathering which would be attended by Susan Cooper, who was coming from America to join the festivities. There was nearly always a book brought out in the birthday month and for this one it was to be *The Prince of Pleasure*. We had all been asked for our opinion on the striking jacket, all been delighted with it. It showed a head and shoulders reproduction of Sir Thomas Lawrence's richly colourful portrait, The Prince Regent in Garter Robes, crimson velvet, white satin, jewelled and enamelled gold chains. The final choice of jacket was something that was shared with his household, our approval, when it was an especially handsome one, coming as an accolade at the end of his labours. We, with our opinions sought in this way, shared a sense of involvement, as if we had some part in the design.

His birthdays, particularly the five year ones, usually brought interest from the media. This, being one of the special ones, caused activity to start early in the year with television recordings, interviews, requests for photographs to be taken, for brief statements of his thoughts and memories. By the time September loomed activity was hectic.

Pleased, he said, "The telephone's gone mad."

"People want to know about you," I replied.

"Don't suppose they'll even bother to read it."

He made a dismissive gesture with his hand, but his face betrayed his pleasure and he moved with the energy of a man who is at full steam with business to attend to, knowing that what he is about is in demand. What man would not feel satisfaction in being told at seventy five that he is appreciated and sought after? The attention gave him fresh impetus.

On September 3rd he was to take part in a television interview in Birmingham with Patrick Harvey of the BBC and, at Mr Priestley's suggestion, Gareth Lloyd Evans, lecturer, biographer, drama critic of *The Guardian* who, while writing *J. B. Priestley The Dramatist* in 1964, had become a close friend. Appreciating his great sense of humour and sharp mind, JB was always happy to take part in any programme with him. This one had been planned since March, but at first he was not entirely satisfied with its form and wrote to tell Patrick Harvey:

"I am afraid I am not at all happy about the skeleton programme you have sketched to Lloyd Evans. There seems to be a terrible shortage of recordings of me and my work (I sometimes think there is a man at the BBC who goes round destroying all recordings connected with me) and the stuff from Joad (Professor Joad) and Agate (James) seems to me to be mere padding. May I remind you that this period also includes my farcical comedy *When We Are Married*, which has always been extremely popular - is there no recording of that?"

Problems were overcome, the participants gathering at Kissing Tree House for lunch, when they had finally settled the ultimate form the programme should take. Duly, on the morning of the 3rd, JB set out for Birmingham armed with copies of *Margin Released* and *When We Are Married,* noting that while there he must go to Rackhams for some picture frames. These were for his own paintings. He returned at teatime completely satisfied, for the recording had gone well and the frames were exactly what he had in mind. Unfortunately for me though he required my help in placing the pictures in them, and we spent many hours sorting, re-sorting, testing various mounts, he asking my opinion, impeding my attempts to get the paintings straight. I in turn tried to avoid taking too much responsibility for I knew whose fault it would be if the results were not entirely right. Happily we later discovered an excellent picture framer in Stratford and, with encouragement, Mr Priestley sent his future paintings to him.

That week-end Stratford was celebrating the jubilee of David Garrick. The Priestleys joined in, attending the Jubilee Banquet at the Town Hall on Saturday night, a special lunch on Sunday and in the evening a concert at the Royal Shakespeare Theatre with a party afterwards in the foyer of the dress circle. Then it was back to the birthday with more interviews, more requested, the telephone jingling steadily. JB remained bent over his typewriter, the cotton wool firm in his ears, emerging in the afternoons to attend to it all and take his regular walk around the village. Jane Bown came to photograph him for *The Observer;* the BBC made a further recording for radio. Cards began to arrive and letters of good wishes. "What a fuss," he remarked basking in it.

The family party was to be held at Albany and would include all five of his children, their spouses and those of his grandchildren who had reached their teens, but with consternation he realised that he had omitted to give his sister her invitation. He sent a telegram immediately:

"Can you attend family party Albany Saturday night? I provide fare Sylvia or Barbara bed. Love Jack."

The acceptance also came by telegram and he was quick to send a detailed letter:

"It has now been arranged that you should spend Saturday night at Barbara's and I suggest you give her a ring – telephone number is...

I imagine that your best plan would be to take a train from Bristol in the morning and then be met by either Peter or Barbara, but you can discuss all this on the telephone.

We are very much looking forward to seeing you on Saturday night."

It did not seem to occur to him that as his sister was in constant touch with the family and visited them regularly she would be sure already to have such details as he gave her. His one anxiety was to smooth the path and be the man in charge of things.

The Sunday Times Magazine were currently running a series on *1000 Makers of the Twentieth Century*, the entry on Priestley being in the issue of August 31, 1969, together with a nice smiling picture of him, shrewdness in those eyes behind the cheerfulness:

"John Boynton Priestley (British, b.1894): writer. J. B. Priestley is perhaps the last of the great literary all rounders. His prodigious output of novels, plays, essays *et alia* represents the central tradition of English Literature – that of craftsmen who simultaneously entertain and criticise their own time. Born in Yorkshire, he is an essentially English writer who has given a fiercely humanitarian concern for society by the abrupt end of the glowing Camelot years of his Edwardian youth. His early best-seller *The Good Companions* is less typical of his major works than more complex novels like *Bright Day* and *Lost Empires* or the reflective curiosity of *Man and Time* and *Margin Released*, and though his world-wide popular reputation has alienated some critics he has always been a lively experimentalist with an uncompromising literary integrity. The English radical conscience which led him to attack Depression politics before the Second World War, and to spark off the Campaign for Nuclear Disarmament after it, also illuminated the wartime broadcasts which made him a national hero during the London Blitz: his fundamental concern has always been the condition of man. This, and the life enhancing quality of his work, have made him a symbol of permanence in our shifting century. S.M.C."

I do not know who S.M.C. is, but Mr Priestley seemed pleased with his entry and it must have added to the good feelings of that time. In September the same journal published a specially commissioned tribute by Susan Cooper (could she have an unknown M?)[13] under the title *That's J. B. Priestley For You*. It carried a full page presentation of Snowdon's delightful picture of him sitting among the shrubs with a background of glistening ivy leaves and a few swords of iris. Wearing his black raincoat, stick grasped in one hand, pipe in the other, he smiles from beneath his black beret, perhaps faintly bemused by his position. Writing afterwards to Lord Snowdon he was able to say, "*The Sunday Times Magazine* photograph was undoubtedly a very great success and I have never met anybody who did not like it."

Harper's Bazaar sent a photographer and the *Radio Times* had an interview which, when it was published, was headed with his own description of himself as having "a face like a glowering pudding!" There was a letter from Ralph Richardson about a television programme which was to mark the birthday. In reply Mr Priestley wrote:

"Many thanks for your letter. I am very glad to learn from it that you are doing Johnson for this birthday programme. This was intended as a surprise for me so I have never really known what it consists of or who is in it. But I look forward to seeing it on the 14th and to seeing you on the 15th. Copies of my Regency books have just arrived and so I am sending you one through the parcel post.

Two or three months ago I had to take part in an anniversary of the Bradford Playhouse, of which I was the president for many years. They did *When We Are Married* … I still found the play extremely funny. I have now been asked many times to agree to a revival of this play but have always refused in the hope that you would play the photographer, with which you could have a marvellous time. And I have the nucleus of a very good cast in my mind."

Unfortunately Sir Ralph's plans to attend the dinner had to be changed because filming took him to Yugoslavia for the crucial date. He wrote explaining this and sending a gift of tobacco "put up by a neighbour of yours in London." This was presumably Dunhills in the Burlington Arcade. He wrote:

"Dear Jack,
It seems tonight, that we shall
not be able to come to your

dinner on Monday the 15th
because I have just been told
that I must go to Split, in
Yugoslavia not later than
Sunday 14th – this is to take part
in a film about the (last) days
of Napoleon.
I am so sorry to have to miss
this chance to see you – a
sight of Napoleon will not be
half so good.
Happy Birthday to you,
dear friend
under separate cover a
little smoke, of a kind which
I have liked; put up by a
neighbour of yours in London
EVER
Affectionately
Ralph
I am enjoying reading your
Regency book so
much – every night, in bed!"

There was also some birthday correspondence with Richard Church whose *Over the Bridge* JB considered to be one of the best autobiographical works of his generation and he dipped into it often. It was a habit of his to read small parts of books, enjoying their pleasant familiarity as one enjoys a few words with close friends. Taking them out of their shelf he would sit turning the pages until he found some particular place he was looking for, when he would fall back comfortably and sink into contented silence. He read his own work too, and was particularly fond of *The Image Men*, for having spent so long creating Professor Saltana and Dr Tuby he parted with their company reluctantly. He has written about how much he looked forward to joining them each day in that corner of the study where they were waiting for him. Perhaps they waited for him still, went on to new adventures as he read again what he had said of them.

Richard Church wrote:

"Heinemann have sent us an invitation to the dinner for your 75th birthday and we plan to come. I feel guilty at not having accepted the invitation from you and Jacquetta to come down to Stratford again, where I have had such delightful visits, but I too grow old and am not particularly capable of physical exertion, though I try to keep up with this strange occupation of ours.

I thoroughly enjoyed your recent collection of essays (*Essays of Five Decades*) and wrote a piece in *Country Life*. You really are a master in this branch of our trade and will take your place with Hazlitt and company..."

In spite of seeming so unlike, as well as admiration JB and Richard Church had real affection for each other. JB was the younger by a year and it was not the first time that his friend had joined his birthday festivities. Writing to announce his marriage to Dorothy Beale in 1967 Church had gone on to refer to Mr Priestley's sixtieth when he lived at Brooke, on the Isle of Wight:

"Browsing today in the Diaries of William Allingham (they are quite enchanting in their 'close-ups' of the Victorian giants), I met this passage, 'Ap.10. 1864. Walked over to Brooke, Mr Seeley's, with one of the Camerons, and saw Garibaldi in the drawing room, who, understanding me to be a poet, called me 'mio caro', and shook hands heartily.'

That would be your drawing room, where you and I 'shook hands heartily' on your 60th birthday, when Catya and I came for a delightful week-end. A nice bit of historical sequence, don't you think; and a peg on which to hang a reminder of our ever-dear friendship?"

Miss Pudduck had been doing a good deal of cooking for the family party and on Thursday the 11th she and Gertrude went ahead to London to make their preparations, the Priestleys following on Friday. Afterwards I heard it was a great success with games and good food in abundance and "plenty of drinks". Brought up on Yorkshire hospitality with its huge high teas, its rollicking supper parties, games and determination to have a good time, this was the kind of thing that JB loved. He arranged little competitions with prizes, indulged in all the jovial play-acting that was so much his forte.

At John and Diana Collins' gathering on Sunday evening they settled to watch the BBC's television programme which honoured the occasion. There were the usual tributes from his friends, the usual recollections, and then the extract from *Johnson Over Jordan*. Susan Cooper has described it so well in *J. B. Priestley, Portrait of An Author* that I give it here:

"But then, like the moment Priestley once celebrated 'when suddenly and softly the orchestra creeps in to accompany the piano', the magic that one had been hoping for all along suddenly came filtering through this television programme; for the part of Robert Johnson was being played here by the man for whom it had been written some thirty years before, Ralph Richardson, and Richardson and Priestley between them, actor and dramatist, magicians both, wrought a spell that produced, despite all handicaps, the real thing. Time had made one of those curious spiralling turns, for Richardson had grown older to meet the play, and fitted easily now into the role for which he had once had to draw in an extra couple of decades on his face; he played it without a false move or a marred inflection, and by the time he turned to walk into infinity, Everyman in a bowler hat, leaving one dimension for another unknown, I had forgotten the deficiencies of the small screen and could indeed hardly perceive its outlines at all. I had never seen *Johnson Over Jordan* in the theatre, but it had always moved me even as a written play, and I had never expected to have the chance of seeing Richardson act the part which had been subtly tailored to his talent and voice. Now, however inferior his surroundings, I had. I blew my nose rather hard, and glanced across at Priestley ... Priestley sat silent for a moment, gazing into space, looking unusually small in a very large armchair; and then he rubbed his eyes. 'I shed tears,' he said, rather gruff and low, 'not for what I have seen, but for what I have been remembering.' Then he hoisted himself up and was his proper height again."

In my Warwickshire home I too watched the programme, with much pride, happily aware that I was now part of the life that revolved around him.

Monday, of course, was the Heinemann dinner and again was a great success. His relationship with his publishers was a good one of very long standing and they seemed to be almost part of the family, even on minor birthdays generally giving a buffet supper party for him at their London building. On this occasion speeches were made by Kenneth Clark, later Lord Clark, Robert Robinson, Iris Murdoch and Norman Collins. JBP, who wore the plum velvet jacket he favoured for formal occasions, replied, and I have no doubt that his speech was good, that it warmed the hearts of his listeners and that it was short. The man who had made such a mark with his wartime broadcasts that people still wrote frequently to tell him how well they remembered them, knew well enough how to hold the attention of an audience. He had spoken to me about how to make speeches.

"Leave them wanting more," he said. "Let them be sorry you've stopped. Never go on until they begin losing interest. A speech should be short."

Some years later when I was president of a local society and had to make several speeches I expressed my terror to him, and to anybody else who would listen to me.

"There's nothing to be afraid of," he said. "Always remember that the audience is on your side. They've no wish to be critical, they're ready to laugh if there's anything the least bit funny. You don't hear of audiences attacking people."

I explained that I knew this perfectly well, but that nothing would abate my terror, that I shook most horribly even though I managed to say, somehow, whatever I had to say. This troubled him, he listened with concern and shook his head, said that he was sorry for it. It was so clear that he meant it that I felt even greater regret for my fear and wished I could make a wonderfully confident speech just to please him.

When he returned to Kissing Tree it was not the end of the festivities. There were endless letters to write for he had received greetings from all over the world and it took the rest of the month to reply to them. Among the telegrams was one from Noel Coward in Switzerland, adding that he was enjoying the Regency book. Evelyn Ames, a friend from America, returned with them and stayed for several days. There were trips to the theatre for *A Winter's Tale* and *Twelfth Night*. Sir Brian and Lady Alice Fairfax-Lucy came for lunch, then Ian Richardson and Gareth Lloyd Evans to dinner. They went to tea with Elsie Clifford in the Cotswolds; she always gave him homemade gingerbread as a birthday gift. It carried on into the following week when Mrs Priestley's son and daughter-in-law brought their baby for a visit. The Michael Foots lunched that week; there were drinks with friends on Saturday, supper with others on Sunday, tea at Charlecote on Monday, and Tom for an overnight visit.

Birthdays were so much on his mind that he made a point of noticing those of others, writing to Robert McCrindle:

"I noticed on Saturday morning that it was your 75th birthday and made up my mind to send you a telegram but then, as often happens when one's secretary is away, I was caught up by a lot of other things and so failed to send a telegram. However, do please accept our belated best wishes and let me add on my own behalf a welcome to the glorious club of 75s and over..."

Later in the month there was Noel Coward's 70th. He was staying at the Savoy Hotel and was sent a telegram:

"Welcome to borrowed time and warmest good wishes."

Presently I too began to attend his birthday parties. My husband and I used to call at Albany to give a lift to Miss Pudduck, and on one occasion Mrs Priestley's son, Nicolas, in a year when his wife could not come. It could have been awkward, for we used to stand and wait in the little hall, the door between us and the drawing room wide open, Mrs Priestley entertaining Nicolas and Rosalind to drinks there. JB, however, removed that awkwardness by coming to stand outside and talk to us in his most genial host style until Miss Pudduck appeared.

Just as when he had guests at Kissing Tree he seemed to like to break off from the entertaining, join his secretary for a moment's respite, everyday conversation, silent if he wished to be. He would call me over for an instant at his parties, wink, nudge, mutter something slightly wicked, make a joke about a friend, murmur, "All this fuss!" Although I enjoy parties I am occasionally seized with a spasm of nervousness, as happened once at his. He beckoned me instantly, patted the seat at his side, leant close, nudge, wink, and spoke in 'just you and me' tones.

"Too many people here for my liking. Let's have our own little party together, you and I!"

I giggled happily, mentally clutched at the familiar presence, ceased to be nervous.

It was one of his favourite quotations from Wordsworth. "We live by Admiration, Hope and Love." He wrote of this quotation in *The Moments*, saying "I believe this statement, I trust in it, absolutely. I would be ready to make it the test of any society. When and where admiration withers, hope vanishes, and love is hard or impossible to find, the mental hospitals are overcrowded, the prisons and detention camps are packed, and plans are being made for atomic and biological warfare." He quoted it again in one of his last television interviews, when his voice had lost some of its strength but none of its power. "We have to hope," he said then, "because despair is useless. We have to love. Love is very strong, very enduring and can last many, many years. So if anybody wants a short guide to a decent life, let me offer this. 'We live by Admiration, Hope and Love.'" The message was much the same at that birthday party, finding its target in a least one heart and lodging there. They seemed to me three qualities which he gave most generously.

THEATRE

All through the years ran Theatre. It renewed his energy, gave him fresh impetus, and besides, as he pointed out with satisfaction, his plays brought money. With the cost of running that enormous house this meant much to him, but he was not prepared to sell at any price. If the cast, the company and the general attitude were not right for a play then he would not agree to its being performed.

He was frequently approached about *Time and the Conways*, a work that was of particular importance to him. In 1969 Stephen Mitchell[14] wrote, eager to produce it. Mr Priestley replied that he felt the difficulty would be in casting this, especially the part of Kay. Whenever anybody wanted to do this play he would speak of the need for someone very special to take the part; indeed there seemed no actress living who was suitable. Kay had been portrayed in the original 1937 production by Jean Forbes-Robertson. She, clearly, had made an enormous impression on him and he used to talk about her with infinite regret in that slow, deep, thoughtful style with many pauses, many puffs at his pipe, searching with his eyes to the very depths from which he drew out his memories.

"You won't know her of course?"

I shook my head.

"She came from an acting family. Her father was Sir Johnston Forbes-Robertson, her mother Gertrude Elliot, actress and manager. She herself was an actress of very rare quality, quite unlike any other actress of her time." He sighed. "She was also very beautiful."

We both fell silent, he remembering, me waiting for more. "Off stage she was unlike any actress I have ever met. She never wanted to talk about acting, never carried the part she was playing into real life. When she was on stage she had a spiritual quality that was never carried into ordinary life. That was extraordinary. The actress and woman in her were wide apart, a rare thing with actresses."

There was another long, searching pause, and then,

"Whenever she took the part of Kay in my *Time and the Conways* she was a marvel to work with." His voice lingered on the "marvel" as if he still wondered at it. "She was quick and sure, instinctively made the right moves. She *was* the part."

It was rare for him to talk at length about anybody. Now he

continued in a voice that was full of concern, "Then she began to change. It was as if it was all too much for her and she could not go on any longer. She began to drink too much. Something had gone wrong for her somewhere. It might have been a love affair – I don't know. Something was lost from her, the fine edge of her work blunted. It was a sad thing to see. She drifted out of the theatre altogether in the end and when she died in 1962 she was a forgotten woman. It was tragic! Jessica Tandy played Kay later in New York, and played it well, but there was never anyone to touch Jean Forbes-Robertson. She had a quality like spring, so fresh and lovely!"

He never did find anybody else whom he felt so right for Kay, just as Ralph Richardson remained his Johnson. Whenever the play was brought up he became evasive, although he denied that he did not want it to have a revival. A possible cast would be presented, weighed and discarded for the process to be gone through again, and perhaps again. Always he returned to the outstanding qualities of the original cast, the impossibility of casting Kay. He did, however, agree to see Stephen Mitchell when he was in London the following week and they were still corresponding about a possible production of the play two years later.

That same year he was asked to perform a short opening ceremony at the Richmond Theatre who were producing *An Inspector Calls*. As there was a chance he might be abroad at the time he declined, but made some helpful comments:

"…May I point out that it is essential to the success of this play that the Inspector must be played as naturally as possible, avoiding any staginess of tone and any lapses into sentiment or melodrama. In short, apart from two or three speeches, including the last one, the part should be underplayed rather than overplayed, which is what Ralph Richardson did with it in the original Old Vic production…"

In the following year, 1970, E & B Productions proposed a revival of *When We Are Married*, which had its first performance at the St Martin's Theatre in 1938. The new production would open at the Yvonne Arnaud Theatre in Guildford and then go on tour, with the hope that it would reach the West End. The idea appealed, and he had no sooner agreed to it than Laurence Olivier wrote to ask him if it might be available for the National. I began to see how much the

Theatre meant to him. He was full of enthusiasm for the planned production, enjoyed the theatrical contact, talked about it, mentioned it in letters to friends, and made me think of an excited schoolboy with his first computer. He had for some time thought about this play because he was eager to have Ralph Richardson in it in the role of the photographer. He had brought it up when he wrote to his friend about the Ceylon play:

"Having now read *Island Incident*, Peters, backed by his assistant, has said what you were too polite to say – that the play simply won't do. I accept this verdict and will put it aside, possibly using some of it as material for a TV play. It is clear to me now that with age one loses an instinctive sense of Theatre very active earlier. Please let me have the script back at your convenience.

Two points I feel I ought to make. As you probably know they are now casting what looks to me a very promising revival of *When We Are Married*. Nothing has been settled yet about the photographer. You would of course be absolutely superb in this part. The other point is this – that when we were lunching the other day you spoke rather wistfully about Lawson's performance in *I Have Been Here Before* and the part itself. Now a year or two ago when we were considering a season of these plays, I gather – because you did not say so to me – that you felt you were too old to play Ormund. I do not want to persuade you to play it but I must certainly make the point that in my view you are not too old, because Ormund is presented as a middle aged man and you can certainly pass for about 50 or so on the stage."

Now, with the enthusiasm spilling out of him, he wrote again:

"As you probably know from Peters, about three months ago Chichester said they wanted to do *When We Are Married* and I had to tell them that I had already given permission to revive it to E & B Productions.

Now a few days ago I got a long letter from Larry (Olivier) asking if there was any possibility of the National Theatre doing it, and promising me his three leading ladies and himself playing. Again I had to say that I had already committed the play elsewhere and it was already being cast ... the only thing is that we all want you to play the photographer ... (In fact I remember quite well, after you had seen the play, you told me how you would do it).

All the signs suggest that this production will play to very big business both at the large Number One theatres, which have already been booked, and then afterwards, coming in well before Christmas, in the West End. For my part I would love to see it at the Haymarket and I am certain that it would have a long and very successful run there."

Alas though, Sir Ralph's commitments did not leave him free to take the part.

E & B Productions, like so many people, were not used to the speed at which JB worked and failed to keep up with him. He complained of their slowness with correspondence, became agitated when a letter he sent them was not answered immediately, wrote to tell Peters that there seemed no point in his writing to them as they did not reply. This posted, a reply came instantly and eventually a satisfactory exchange was maintained. He met the producer, Laurier Lister, and felt he would get on well with him. The cast began to take shape, including Peggy Mount, Renée Asherson, Freda Jackson, Daphne Anderson, Frank Thornton, Hugh Lloyd and Fred Emery, who was to play the photographer.

This was the year for *When We Are Married* as it was now being produced in Australia as a musical. It was also, to Mr Priestley's barely suppressed horror, set in Australia. He agreed to this provided it went nowhere else and afterwards told his play agent, Anthony Jones that he did not want to know the details about it because he could not imagine it with an Australian setting with music and did not want to. He was told that the company had obtained top Australian stars but was too unfamiliar with the country's Names to recognise them.

There was one of those sudden unbelievable bursts of heat that we get in this climate. He had intended to call on his publisher during a two day visit to London, but there was not time. After keeping an appointment with his dentist immediately after arriving he entertained the Howards to lunch (she being Marghanita Laski). That evening he dined with the Collins and almost the whole of next day was spent with Laurier Lister at the Globe Theatre auditioning for the play. After that he told his publishers that it was too hot to do another thing; until the evening when he took two of his grand-daughters to a concert at the Festival Hall. As usual he gave them detailed directions to go up to level 5 on the green side, enter the auditorium by door 5B, and the actual box number was 22. Afterwards there would be supper waiting at Albany. Clearly enjoying being grandfather giving a treat, his voice lingered on the supper so that I could sense feast.

The opening night of *When We Are Married*, originally planned for August, was advanced to September 8th. He attended a read-through rehearsal in London, kept himself informed of progress, enjoying it all enormously and showing distinct signs of sensing importance. Presently he wrote to Laurier Lister to say that he would be visiting rehearsals at Guildford at the end of the month, travelling by train:

"This is just to complete our arrangements for seeing a rehearsal or two on Monday August 31st and possibly Tuesday September 1st. I do not want to come down on Sunday night again as the train is slow and liable to be late, so I propose to come down from here in the morning of the 31st and go straight from Paddington to Waterloo and then catch the first train to Guildford. And with any luck I ought to be with you at lunch time. I would then see the afternoon rehearsal and then we could discuss notes and then I would go back to London.

If it should be necessary I could then come down for a morning rehearsal on Tuesday 1st September and return here that afternoon. But if things seem to be going well on Monday I would not bother coming down again on Tuesday morning. Meanwhile, you might let me have your details of the arrangements for September 7th and 8th so that I do not come down until I am really wanted, though of course I must attend the dress rehearsal on Monday night.

If it would not be too much trouble I should be very glad if your secretary could let me have the times of trains between Guildford and Waterloo excluding all those earlier than 9 am but then giving me all the times right up to the latest trains back to Waterloo."

He was as meticulous in his arrangements as he was in the constructing of his plays.

It was also in late August that Sybil Thorndike and John Carroll, who were to give a poetry recital in Stratford, came to spend a week-end so that there was again a flurry of dinner and lunch parties for their entertainment. My husband and I attended the poetry reading, delighted that it included *The Owl and the Pussycat* read by Dame Sybil. Afterwards there was to be a party given by Dr Fox of the Shakespeare Birthplace Trust.

Mr Priestley, who was keeping a watch for us, beckoned me as we were leaving and presented, very gleefully, a scheme.

"You'd like to come to the party, wouldn't you?" I was given a jolly dig. "There's to be a little gathering given by the Birthplace lot. You and your husband come along. If Dr Fox asks about it, you tell him I invited you both."

Being the last person to attend a party uninvited I could only look at him in horror and explain, stumbling over it, that the children were expecting us.

His face fell. "You'll enjoy the party. It's sure to be a good one with plenty to drink and worth-while company."

I could only stand in obstinate silence so he tried again.

"I'll speak to Dr Fox."

The idea of standing about while he asked Dr Fox to invite us did not appeal to me at all and I would still feel like a gatecrasher. I explained again that to stay was impossible and began to edge away, he looking after me, rather forlorn. Sometimes he used to tell me I was puritanical!

Dame Sybil was still at Kissing Tree when I arrived for work on Monday. She was a lovely, warm, generous spirited woman who took the greatest interest in everybody. Her beautiful voice filled the house like music and we were all completely caught in the spell of her. She was then in her eighties, like a golden summer day descended on us. When she had gone and we were again settled to our business, Mr Priestley said,

"You should have come to the party on Sunday."

I remained mute.

"It was a pleasant affair and you'd have had a good time. A fine woman, Sybil. She and her husband (Sir Lewis Casson) were in my play *The Linden Tree* in 1947. Each of them gave a memorable performance." The recollection obviously pleased him. That play had won the Ellen Terry award, a silvery statuette that lived on the chimneypiece in the billiard room.

It was pointless to discuss my failure to stay for the party any further, so he turned to sending copies of Susan Cooper's book about him to his friends. Newly published they had just arrived. He wrote to Ralph Richardson:

"As you pop up several times in this book, I think you had better have a copy of it.

I hope you opened well at the Apollo – a theatre I have had once or twice but never liked because when you look down at the stalls you think it is an intimate theatre, whereas in fact it is about a mile high.

Your film programme the other night on TV offered me one of my favourite scenes of all time, the Charlie Chaplin pawnbroker..."

It was Sir Ralph's role at the Apollo Theatre that had prevented his taking the part of JB's photographer.

As the opening of *When We Are Married* drew near he sent Duncan Weldon of E & B Productions details of his movements up to the event in case he should be wanted, saying that he proposed to attend the dress rehearsal on 7th September and then stay on in Guildford, "As there may be a good deal of last minute work to do." He stated finally that he never sat in an audience himself on a first night, but that he would need tickets for his family and staff. Miss Pudduck and Gertrude were to be in on this, while I, like Cinderella, stayed at home. Someone had to be around to answer the phone and deal with all the correspondence. My turn came though, for when the play came to London he gave me four tickets for myself and family, lending us his flat in Albany for the night so that we should be comfortably near. It was a kindness that gave us all delight, both in the play and in our accommodation. Albany, so close to Piccadilly, is an oasis of incredible silence in that roar of traffic.

The Guildford opening was quite a family occasion. Barbara came with her daughter Sadie, Michael (Sylvia's husband) with their daughter Karen, Mary and the daughter of Angela, Catherine. Himself was given an office at the theatre where they could gather together for drinks. The excitement reached to Kissing Tree where telegrams arrived full of good wishes. The telephone hummed, letters poured in, the activity embraced us all. It was like that with him, he the instigator, we the sharers. On his return he wrote to tell Duncan Weldon that they had had a good strong cast, especially the three couples who he felt would be even better once they had settled into their parts. He warned that the production should be watched to see that it did not become more and more farcical as, although he had called it originally "a farcical comedy, it is still a comedy and not a farce." At the end of the Guildford run he thanked Laurier Lister for all his courtesy and hospitality, adding that he hoped to work with him again in the not too distant future, a hope that he repeated to his agent.

It was clear now that the play would be moving to London, but before that it would appear in Leeds, which was close enough to Bradford to be home territory. He told the manager of the Leeds Grand Theatre that he would be attending the opening performance and would like the box he had used there on several occasions. He also announced his intention of inviting a few friends to join them, among them Donald Baverstock of Yorkshire TV, with whom he had worked during the Bradford Playhouse Festival the previous year.

The play opened in Leeds on November 2nd and the Priestleys made an early start for he had a busy day ahead of him. The programme, for a man of seventy six, was that they were to be called for by the local car hire people at 7.25 in the morning so as to catch the 8.35 train from Birmingham, due to arrive at Leeds at 11.30. At noon he was to have an interview with the *Bradford Telegraph and Argus*, and another at 12.30 with Radio Leeds. There would be lunch then after which he would proceed to the Television Studios for another interview. No afternoon rest for him! Apart from watching the performance in the evening there were the friends to entertain, but here he was in his element. It was the kind of atmosphere that made his circulation flow.

After a night at the Queen's Hotel he returned to Kissing Tree in high good spirits, pronouncing the play to be in wonderful shape, the cast even better than in the original production. Wishing to tell E & B Productions how delighted he was, he asked me to get them on the telephone. I was to ask for Mr Elliott and then ask him to telephone JB in the afternoon. This was one of his regular methods of keeping his telephone bill under control, and it always worked for him.

Here Laurier Lister suggested a revival of *Dangerous Corner* at Guildford. Mr Priestley was against this because it had been done recently on ITV in what he considered a particularly good production, well cast and well acted. If it were put on now he felt it would prevent some more suitable play of his from opening in that theatre. He had already told Peters what a splendid launching pad Guildford was for a play and how good the figures had been there.

As the London preview of *When We Are Married* drew near there was the customary series of press interviews, many telephone calls and that sense of expectancy that presaged the event, a sense that was generated by JB on these occasions, expanding to reach the entire household. The actual opening at the Strand Theatre was on 17th November with a gathering of family and friends. There was much discussion about seating and in the end Edith Evans was put next to Basil Dean in the centre of the second row, with various publishing friends nearby including A. D. Peters and his wife, George Rainbird, John Hadfield. There were the usual get-togethers in the intervals and at the end a speech from JB. I heard about it afterwards but knew well enough how it would be, that the speech would be a short one, that the evening would be a happy Theatre one, for he was satisfied with the production and in his element with the occasion.

The reviews were cheering. Felix Barker in *The Evening News* described it as "a warm, undemanding, thoroughly old-fashioned and delightful evening", saying that the cast had reason to thank the author for he had "written good, showy parts for everyone". Milton Shulman in *The Evening Standard* reported that "Fortunately, from the perky arrogance of Gretchen Franklin as an impertinent char to the formidable, matronly bullying of Peggy Mount, the cast last night caught perfectly the dour, narrow, intolerant, spirit of a Yorkshire community at the early part of this century". Peter Lewis ended his review for *The Daily Mail* with, "And by the end, when Fred Emery, as the drunken photographer, had rolled his raffish bulk round in circles like an enormous soppy dog, we were all hooting happily. Give the piece time and it still works a treat."

The Priestleys returned from London, still with an air of celebration, to a pile of enthusiastic letters. Encouraging mail continued to arrive. Lord Snow (C. P. Snow), thanking Mr Priestley for "a characteristically interesting and generous letter" about his latest book, went on to end with, "We shall all go to see *When We Are Married*. I saw it long ago and it is time that the young saw it too." Allan Hill, of Heinemann Educational Books, wrote in November, "The revival of *When We Are Married* is splendid news – the funniest play I have ever seen. I am taking the whole family on the Monday after Christmas." He expressed a wish to publish the play in their Hereford Plays series, which already included *An Inspector Calls*. This was agreed to, "If you think it worth it."

Early in December the cast held a Christmas party in the Green Room Club, where the Priestleys joined them. There was always a good deal of warmth in the Theatre when a play went well. JBP generally sent a telegram for the opening night, the cast returning the compliment, sending him birthday greetings too if he had a play on then. There was a family feeling there it seemed, just as there was with us. Warmth of spirit was needed soon for the company of *When We Are Married*, as it was at that time that we ran into power cuts and they were obliged, in a period when the theatres would normally be crowded, to play to audiences reduced in size by being plunged into darkness and cold. At Kissing Tree the author wrung his hands in dismay over the falling profits, complaining about the greed of the power workers and their lack of care for the harm they caused. He was concerned too for the company.

The welfare of the actors was important to him and he once took me to task because I was unable to recall the names of some of the cast in a television play the previous evening.

"You should always remember an actor's name," he said. "Note it and see that it stays with you, because it is their livelihood. If their name is forgotten then they are forgotten, and to be forgotten is the worst thing that can happen to an actor."

I replied that I did not mean to forget, but that I found it quite impossible to remember everything. I was quite good on the names of authors, knew most of the big names in Theatre, but could not know all. But he shook his head and spoke most solemnly, telling me that I should always try for it was serious. It was all part of his love of Theatre, a love that began in his youth with the Bradford music halls that crept into his writing repeatedly even when he was away from the writing of plays. The world of Theatre was for him the embodiment of the magic that lay in him. He had only to hear the word for his face to light with interest. It served him well in his age, for there was never a time when work of his was not appearing all over the world, and seldom a time when some major production was not being put on at home. He would point this out to me, saying how well his plays lasted, how well they were constructed, as if he needed the reassurance of affirming this. But it must not be supposed that he had not other occupations!

OTHER OCCUPATIONS

All the time he was dealing with *When We Are Married*, and interviews, recordings, business and all the other work that goes with being a writer of novels, plays, essays, critical studies and biographies, he was also, naturally, producing new books. He had no sooner completed the Ceylon play than he turned to a story for children, *Snoggle*, although he described it as being suitable for "Anyone between 9 and 90". Published the following year, 1971, it was about a visitor from space, with attractive illustrations by Margaret Palmer.

He was also making plans for the Victorian book and had decided that it should cover the 1850s, being the middle of the century and offering the Great Exhibition, the Crimean War, the Indian Mutiny and a great deal of literature. Seeking a researcher he was disappointed to learn that Mrs Jervis (née MacMahon), who had been such a great help with *The Prince of Pleasure*, was not available at present. At Mary Anne's suggestion he wrote to Nicola Lacey who replied that she could only take on the task on a part-time basis. After a meeting at Albany it was agreed, for as he did so much reading himself he felt he could manage on these terms. They worked well together, although at the start he found her slower than he had hoped, but she soon caught the thread of his thought and provided him with the kind of material that he needed. Remembering my own early days I wondered if in his opinion anyone was anything but slow when they began to work with him. When the time came for her first payment, ignoring the fact that she was accustomed to dealing with her affairs, he gave kindly advice:

"I think it is time you had some money so here is a cheque for the first £50. Please sign and return the receipt on the lower half of this sheet. While you are liable to tax on this money, please remember that as you are selling the research material to me you are entitled to do this on Schedule D and in that category you can claim various expenses."

It was a sign of the satisfaction that she gave him that she was included in a letter to Mrs Jervis, who had just asked him to give her a reference. "I shall have to think of a book for which you three girls do all the work and I sit here at home occasionally blaming or praising". The third of the three was Mary Anne, and as they were all acquainted with each other he had referred to a "grapevine of Priestley researchers".

Inevitably time began to press on him so that he expressed alarm over Nicola Lacey's holiday plans, but had to adjust to them, for they were already agreed, and he himself had indicated that they should take a few weeks' break. When she undertook to work part-time she had no means of knowing his sense of urgency for he always initially agreed to "fitting things in". Now his concern was indicated with:

"Your various holiday arrangements would have suited me perfectly if I had kept to my original plan but ... not wanting to do anything else at the moment and having soaked myself in the subject I have been pressing on. However, the fault is mine and not yours."

There was not the slightest cause for alarm as John Hadfield had already told JB that Heinemann were in favour of publishing the book in July 1972, which would make it necessary for him to finish the text early in 1971. He asked if this was feasible, a question that already amused me. The book was finished ahead of any date originally projected, which was what I had come to expect. This did not prevent him from writing to Nicola Lacey after her holiday to point out, rather peevishly, that he was sorry to notice that she had reviewed some novels for *The Observer* when he had received nothing from her. He asked for some solid material instead of scraps. At the time he had a lingering cold and was out of humour. She replied with the greatest tact explaining that she was planning to send a lot of material in the immediate future. This did not prevent him from asking me to telephone to tell her that he was waiting for the Crimean War and the Indian Mutiny and nothing else. He could not get on without this material.

Victoria's Heyday was finished on 10th November, and knowing perfectly well that its end was only days away he wrote to send the final cheque saying:

"This brings our association to an end as I can see no point whatever in going on. You began well but you have lost interest or have too many irons in the fire."

Completely disregarding their original agreement, he was still annoyed that she had done a book review when he felt she should be concentrating on his work. She was not so easily put down, and replied with spirit:

"Recriminations are futile – I should merely like to point out that I have by no means lost interest, you have finished writing, leaving me with no more to do. Nor do I have other irons in the fire – I told *The Observer* I was busy until at least after Christmas. I may add that the only reason I did the long review to which you took such exception was because you said we would take a few weeks break and it seemed a relaxing thing to do in the intervals of house moving. So now I have been left in the lurch, and am very bitter, more especially because I would not have dreamed of accepting the research had I known it was a matter of five months work instead of the year I had been led to believe. I am sad to end it on such bad terms since, albeit you do not wish to admit it, I believe I was of some use to you. Please let me know if you want a list of book references…"

If he replied to this I was not told, but he did express gratitude for Nicola Lacey's help in his Preface to the book. It was always the same with him, urgency overtaking plans, and it is likely that he had genuinely forgotten his initial approach, the leisurely speed anticipated, the willingness to fit in with his researcher's arrangements. It was his habit to conceive a book, talk of taking his time over it, believe that he was not in a hurry, but once he began there was no holding back, the impetus of writing forcing him on so that he invariably finished before the date previously set. Researchers had a hard time.

It was a year since he had received galley proofs of his Chekhov book and as it had still not appeared he wrote to ask what was happening. A week after this he received his copies and wrote again immediately to express his pleasure in them, although he had some reservations about the illustrations and pointed out to friends that he had no responsibility for these. Ralph Richardson sent his thanks in a letter that evokes a pleasing picture:

"It was very kind of you to

send me your little book
on Tchekov – a little
while ago – I have been
a bit busy lately but
today had my first
'day off'.

I took my bicycle and
some paints and your
volume – I had a
very nice bottle of wine in
a pub – with your
book propped onto
the sugar bason and
I had a fascinating
time – I did not know
much about Tchekov
before – I had a different
idea about his background
and what you told me
in your wonderfully easy
non-informative style
gave me so much pleasure
I thank you.
Afterwards I took my byke
into a beautiful part
of Hertfordshire – the
rising ground above
Eaot – St Laurence
Do SHW – you know where!
I did some water colour
sketches – they shall be
buried full fathom deep.
But I thought of you and
your gouash – you do
so well with that.

There is not much news with
me – I work like a rat

I struggle, I curse, but I
have some happy times,
like the burgundy in the
pub and your book!
Thank you
EVER
  affectionately,
Ralph"

The spelling here is reproduced from the original!

Monk Gibbon also wrote to compliment him on the book, sending a copy of his own recent novel *The Climate of Love*. Replying, Mr Priestley complained that he had seen no reviews or advertisements for Chekhov, and indeed it seemed to live a life of remarkable secrecy, soon disappearing altogether. He enjoyed *The Climate of Love* and after reading it made a gift of it to me, elated to have something to bestow that cost him nothing! It was a good book and I was glad to have it.

It was a habit of his to make small presentation of things like stale chocolates or with centres that did not appeal to him. Whenever he unearthed a sweet from the depths of his pocket or a drawer I tried not to look at it suspiciously and told him I would eat it later. Once he gave me, with an air of great generosity, some of his tubes of oil paints saying that since he always worked in gouache now he would not be needing them again. I thanked him cordially, keeping my thoughts to myself, and sure enough when I got them home found them completely dried out and useless. This made it all the more impressive when he bestowed on me some of his gift of smoked trout, for that was something that he prized. Indeed, there was a year when Chris Rookes, his local wine merchant, failed to send his customary Christmas gift of this commodity. In consternation JB wrote to tell him so, making the point that as this welcome gift came annually he felt something must have gone wrong this year and he was sure Mr Rookes intended him to have it. It was despatched immediately!

In between writing the Victorian book and attending rehearsals he found time to sit for his portrait to Michael Noakes. Henry Carr, who had painted him many years previously, wrote that he would like to do so again, but Mr Priestley declined, saying it would be a mistake. He considered that if he sat for another portrait it should be for a painter of a younger generation which might show him from a new angle. Mr Carr, he suggested, should reverse this by showing what younger people look like to a painter of an older generation. By coincidence he was approached almost at once by Michael Noakes, who sent photographs of some of his work, including a sketch of Ralph Richardson. Providing that it was not regarded as a commission, and that no more than three or four sittings were required, Mr Priestley agreed. As he was so busy in Stratford he asked Mr Noakes to write again in two months' time when he might be able to arrange some sittings in London. However, this proved too difficult and instead Michael Noakes arrived in June to paint him at Kissing Tree House, staying overnight to do so.

Immaculately dressed, he looked more like a lawyer than an artist, but this did not prevent him from painting, to the sound of classical music, three extremely good portraits. When he asked his subject to sit up a little as his suit was getting rumpled, he received the reply, deeply delivered and typical,

"I *am* rumpled. I've been rumpled for years."

The two of them established a happy relationship and the suit came out looking comfortably settled about him, as Mr Priestley liked it to be. He pronounced the portraits the best that had ever been done of him and his publishers gave a cocktail party to show them. Afterwards Michael Noakes presented him with a smaller one, a head and shoulders version. Mr Priestley hung it in the study and, highly delighted, nudged me roguishly as he stood regarding it and said,

"That man doesn't give a damn! He doesn't know and he doesn't care!"

He was so pleased with this observation that he repeated it to other people when they admired the painting.

Soon after this Michael Noakes' wife, Vivien, brought out her excellent biography of Lear. Having read it with keen interest JB wrote to tell her,

"…how much I have enjoyed your *Lear*, which is astonishingly well done for a first book. You are a clever girl! He cannot have been an easy subject if only because his miseries and tears must have made him seem at times both monotonous and tiresome. One thing you bring out strongly always surprises me – that the amount of travel there was at a time when a great deal of travel was slow, difficult and even dangerous. Somebody ought to do a book about it and about the various colonies of English scattered around..."

It was also in June that he went up to London to propose 'The Immortal Memory' at the Dickens Fellowship Banquet, the following morning opening an exhibition of Dickens stamps where he decided that those designed by his artist daughter, Sylvia, were "easily the best". Later he and his wife went on to Heinemann's to meet Monica Dickens who was over from America for these Dickens Centenary celebrations. In July he dashed up to Bradford to receive an honorary D.Litt. from the University.

As well as all this he also wrote pieces for various journals and a letter to *The Times* protesting about the encroachment of conifers into the English landscape, having just learned with considerable horror that 600 acres were to be planted in Upper Langstrothdale, "so destroying its stark magnificence". This led to a request from *The Daily Mail* for an article on the subject and he gave them *Let's Raise Hell*, an outcry against these trees which:

"...look, at a distance, as if a green fur rug had been draped over the hills. Their fascinating shapes vanish. The play of light and shade and colour on them can no longer be seen. Their old enchantment has gone."

These two items brought him a lot of mail and a request from *The Ecologist* that he should write something for them. He replied that time was forever pressing on him and suggested that they should reproduce *Let's Raise Hell* if *The Daily Mail* agreed.

He made further protest against the destruction of England in a Preface he wrote for the new *Shell Guide to England*. In a previous Introduction he had done for the 1935 edition he had perhaps regretted the factory scenes in the West Riding, for he now said that it was not the old mills and the steep Victorian streets that offended his eye, but the occasional new factories and blocks of flats, "all glass and glitter and California ... so many swaggering invaders". The thirties he described as the most tasteless decade of all, leaving a "mountain of trash". He regretted the pulling down of charming old houses or rows of cottages to make way for motor roads. Describing the road from Brighton to Portsmouth he said, "I do not think any other people in Europe would have done what we have done to that coastline." Having made his protest he went on to write of the happier side, the astonishing variety of scene and landscape in small areas, so different from bigger countries where you can travel for hours without any change. He extolled the beauty of the Lake District, but above all of the Yorkshire Dales, "...which I believe to be the most rewarding, the most satisfying countryside in the world."

It was no wonder that he was obliged to speak of shortage of time and pressure of work, so that when Iris Murdoch hoped that he would be present at the opening of her play in Greenwich he replied with apologies. He went on to say that if she wanted a friend to stand by her then he would be there, but if she was merely inviting him to a special occasion he would prefer not to come because he was behind with his work, by now believing it. Invited by Mr Owen to attend this year's Hemel Hempstead Arts Festival, whose patron was to be André Previn, he was again obliged to refuse. He added that he had met the conductor when he was in Florida with the London Symphony Orchestra writing *Trumpets Over the Sea* and had found him "not only a very accomplished and versatile musician but also an extremely pleasant fellow", and he was very sorry indeed that he could not attend the Festival. Asked by Richard Crossman to review Asa Briggs' *History of Broadcasting* for the *New Statesman* he declined, beginning his letter in response to Mr Crossman's with:

"Since when have I been 'John' to you? I am only called John in places like Russia and Chile and I have been Jack to you for at least a quarter of a century."

Another piece of writing that failed to materialise was a new edition of Bill Brandt's *Literary Britain*. This had been discussed when, on their holiday in Vence the previous year, the Priestleys and the Brandts met. The idea that then formed was that Brandt should take some new photographs for a fresh edition and that JBP would write a text for it. John Hadfield liked the suggestion, but wanted it to be a world book rather than just an English one, and felt the American literary scene should be included. Brandt was totally against this, preferring to work in surroundings that were familiar to him. While the plan was still being discussed he came to Kissing Tree to photograph Mr Priestley and a year later, when asked why a copy of the result had never been sent to us, replied that this was because he thought JB would not like it, as his sitters never did like their portraits. However he now enclosed it. His thanks was:

"Dear B. B.,

Thank you for sending me a print of my portrait. It is quite horrible. It makes me look like a Chinese murderer in an Afa film of the early 1920s. It might be called *The Photographer's Revenge*, though for what injury I cannot imagine. In your conscious mind I may figure as a fairly nice chap, but from the evidence here your unconscious hates my guts.

Kindest regards to you both."

The description of the photograph did not exaggerate.

The *Olympians* appeared on the scene now, and through it all there was woven a possible visit to Ireland for a painting holiday, planned and postponed for months.

EXPEDITION FOR PAPER AND PAINT

Although long planned, the Irish holiday was an on and off affair until the early summer of 1971 when Mrs Priestley at last finished her book and returned from a visit to America where she had lectured at the University of Washington as John Danz Visiting Professor. While she was away JB wrote to Mr Kelly of Aer Lingus who were to provide their accommodation, flight and car. In return he was to write for the Aer Lingus magazine, *Cara*. Having been provided with a pile of brochures he now sent his selected list of hotels and their proposed itinerary, adding with some concern:

"…I believe I am right in thinking that none of these hotels has a dance band, cabaret etc., as we do not want to go to the West of Ireland looking for nightlife."

Reassured on this point the bookings went ahead and he began to think about his painting things, for it was to be a painting holiday and he had told me that he considered the Irish countryside among the most beautiful in the world. Presently he urged me to go and see it for myself, saying "It has the most magical countryside I know."

In his wife's absence he arranged, in his usual way, a modest round of social activity, which included a visit to London where he stayed with his daughter Barbara. She, an architect and artist herself, took him to her local art shop to replenish his supplies of gouache and it was arranged that they should be sent to him at Kissing Tree. When the parcel arrived, however, there were several colours missing and he wrote immediately to Barbara:

"…I have just undone the parcel from the art shop and find I have no record of the paints they have not got and for which I have already paid. I should be very much obliged if you will keep in touch with them because I shall need to have those paints before about Monday week and parcels seem to me incredibly slow … as many of the missing colours are very important ones, if there is any likelihood of a delay longer than a week from now, then please ring me or ask them to ring me here and I will try to buy them locally. As I ought to be able to get good paper in Leamington, as I did before, then I think I had better not risk ordering the paper from your shop as it is not easy to send through the post and does it no good..."

So it was decided that I should drive him to Leamington Spa in my small and rather elderly Austin A35.

He was not at all used to small cars and had a poor opinion of them as transport for himself, explaining that he was a large man and would be cramped in a car that was short of space. Possibly the thought of expense put him off hiring a car for the trip, as he seemed to have forgotten all about size and cramp, announcing firmly, "We'll go in your car," before disappearing to prepare himself.

Like a small black beetle the car stood ready in the courtyard. Like a large and pleasing black stag beetle he emerged through the back door and stood watching with an expression of contented interest as I opened the door for him. He was wearing his black raincoat and above it his big black hat with the brim that swept over his face. He held his pipe ready and I hoped that he was not going to smoke it in *my* car. Feeling that if he did it himself it might possibly fall off, I gripped the door firmly and closed it for him. He settled into the seat, largely, and did not complain. Indeed as we drew away he remarked, "It's a nice car," saying nothing at all about the size of it.

We drove along the country road with an agreeable sense of companionship. I was relieved to note that he did not seem to intend to smoke the pipe, merely to put it to his lips sometimes as if the fragrance of it lingered on the stem. He gazed out of the window, noting the passing scene, and occasionally looked at me, smiling.

"You're a good driver," he said, in dulcet, honey tones. "You're sure and steady and I feel quite safe with you. That's more than you can say for a lot of people."

Pleased as a cat having its fur stroked in the right direction I accepted his praise. My pleasure, however, did not prevent a slight suspicion that he was planning future expeditions in my car, or, worse, that he wanted me to drive him to London as previous secretaries had done. A sight of my alarm in city traffic would soon cure that! My driving was steady enough, but I did not see that it called for admiration. I was careful, certainly, for in my view cars were lethal and had to be handled with more caution than firearms were. It was possible, though, that he was just being pleasant. I gave him a small glance from the side of my eye and saw him squashed into his seat, the picture of benevolence. The car, very much aware of the unaccustomed weight in it, chugged along like a rather stout lady who has just eaten a large portion of Christmas pudding but does not intend to let it defeat her.

"I was never any good at driving myself," he said. "Things got in the way or the car would go wrong. I seemed to be constantly visiting garages or stuck in some remote country road, possibly with the nose of the car resting against a tree trunk."

In one of his essays he wrote:

"...I would go on so merrily that after a time I would begin to think about other things, and when I did return to the matter in hand I was always a few seconds too late. I was too late at High Wycombe, when I bent the front axle; at Ealing when I hit the tram; at Northwood when I ran into the oldest Ford in the world (it belonged to a bill-poster and smashed my radiator); at Newport, that horrible November afternoon when I cracked the electric standard and gathered round me all the people of Monmouth."

He went on, "In the end I gave up any attempt to drive and I've been a much happier man ever since. There's no point in doing a thing when it is made quite clear to you that you were not meant to do it. It became clear enough to me that cars and I would never get along together."

We arrived in Leamington and I was lucky enough to find a parking space reasonably close to the art shop. We walked together along the street, he with a suggestion of shuffle, his hand on my arm, pointing at objects of interest with his walking stick, I swelled with pride at having brought him safely to our destination. At the door of the shop he paused and peered, examined the window, pointed some more and considered things carefully. Shopping for him was a rare occasion, not to be rushed over. When we went inside he took a good look round, inspected some paintbrushes and eventually approached the counter, where we waited with the necessary patience.

The young girl who served us clearly considered that elderly meant stupid. Gouache paints were brought at his request, and a pile of paper. He began to go through these, important about it, with a touch of fuss as was his way. The paper was not quite right and he asked to see more. The assistant looked at him as if he were an idiot and fetched the paper. As he fingered it, commenting on the various colours and textures, she gave me a conspiratorial smile and met frost. All the time he was choosing his paints and paper the girl continued to act in a way that made me simmer with indignation. He showed no sign of noticing this and when we left the shop and I glanced at him I saw eyes that were alight with humour.

We returned to the car and made a great business of stowing his purchases on the back seat, then he settled himself with the same satisfaction that he had shown on the outward journey.

"I should like to try watercolours some time," he said. "It's a much more difficult medium than gouache – you have to be quick and accurate with watercolour. Have you tried it?"

I assured him that I needed a medium that could be corrected and could not imagine ever working in watercolour. I stayed with oils, just as he, after long consideration of watercolour, remained with gouache which he found suited his method of painting.

After that we made several excursions in my little car. He never once complained of its size, although when I suggested he should have a smaller car than the big Mercedes he always explained that he was a large man and needed plenty of space to fit himself into.

APRIL 1985

There is a sense of loss in the house, and yet there is also a sense of presence. When I came downstairs a moment ago it seemed for an instant as if there was a shadow there, at the foot of them. But there was nothing. He would wait sometimes, just there, hold out his hand to take mine and conduct me solemnly into the study. "We have work to do Madam!" First though, if he was in that kind of mood, he would sing a short snatch of song, still holding my hand, and dance a few steps while I endeavoured to follow him. We would settle then as if there had been no interlude.

Faint mist today is lit by pale sun that casts soft, silver light over all that it touches, making a fairyland. He would have loved that. It was his land, the land where the magic is. The light glows against the dark of the cedars, falls on the church and on the great white Georgian house that is the Youth Hostel. It is all there from his study window, the window at which he used to stand in awe of the world.

"Look at that sky!" or "Look at that sunset!" His face would be bright from the gleam of the window. "Look there at those clouds! What clouds! What marvels!"

Old he might be, but not too old to feel the wonder of life, to let it pour in and replenish him. Grumble he might, "I'm old and forgotten, who wants to read me, who bothers?" The grumble was only an unimportant surface thing and did not restrain him from holding out his arms, metaphorically, and letting the strength pour in to him to be passed on.

Nobody now says, "You've got a new shade of lipstick today," in tones of approval as if some great treat were being provided. Nobody says, "That dress suits you very well," or "You look nice today," or "I like your knees." Nobody now nudges me roguishly, plays Harry Lauder for me, wobbles his chins. Nobody peers at me with close concern, asks if I'm happy, takes my hand for an instant, gently and tenderly, offers support.

"Are you all right?" he would ask anxiously, as if he meant it. "If ever you need help, I'm here."

"I'm here. I'm here," the house seems to echo now.

When some pompous, self-important person comes to the house there is no longer anyone, when that person is gone, to throw out a stomach already prominent and strut, pouffing importantly, waving a hand in disdainful acknowledgement. "Pouf, pouf!" ready to burst with importance. Nobody now to wink behind a visitor's head, nudge and smile in wicked conspiracy. No-one to come into my room, close the door, settle into the far corner of the sofa, sigh with relief and fall into a comfortable silence, looking, smiling, coming to peer over my shoulder, going to drop ash from his pipe all over my nice clean letters on the billiard table.

"There is no malice in me," he would say, anxious that it should be understood. "Nobody could accuse me of doing anything deliberately hurtful. I don't bear malice or hate, don't wish to cause harm to anyone. Malice is negative and bad."

I would agree that this was so; there was only an impish sense of fun, no spite. He could be rude, but there was no venom in him.

On the subject of hating, Frank Muir once approached him for examples of this for a book he was writing and was told:

"...In my own novels, plays, essays, I laugh at a great many people, but I doubt if I actually display any hate. Probably, especially in talk, I am always beginning sentences with 'I hate', but I am not really much of a hater and I think I have this in common with most English people. But Hazlitt was a good hater and you might look at his views on Gifford in, I think, *The Spirit of the Age...*"

He would point out to me too how I had never seen him lose his temper or shout at anyone, and again I would agree.

One afternoon when I entered my room I found him bent over the billiard table, reading from a book. Having studied it for some time he beckoned me over. "Hugh Walpole wrote this about me. Read it." I read:

"Strange man! ... so sensitive and vain, so sure of his uniqueness, his power, his wisdom – yet with a marvellous control of his real nature (he is peevish and complaining, but I have never known him once in all these years lose his temper), so pessimistic, but with a gorgeous sense of humour. So penurious about little things and yet so generous-minded. He is so gruff, ill-mannered, and yet how sweet he was to Mrs Brown on Sunday. He can be an admirable critic. But through all and everything there is a deep sweetness that pervades his whole nature – which is why I love him."

I was instantly filled with recognition. That one short paragraph summed him up perfectly.

"What do you think of it?" he asked presently.

I replied that it seemed to me quite right, which was perhaps not too tactful.

"It isn't all good about me," said JB. "There are some pretty unflattering things there."

Carried away by my delight in the description, I said, "But they are all true."

This made him thoughtful. He returned to his study and brooded on it, but when I went in later and found him regarding me I got the impression he was pleased with me. From that time on his courtesy towards me never failed.

After his death I spent a long time looking for that quotation. All I knew was that it had been in a fat green book. Having sought in all the likely places I had a sudden urge to look somewhere that seemed quite improbable, a glass bookcase on the landing. There was Rupert Hart-Davies's *Hugh Walpole*, a volume of biography published by Macmillan. It was thick and green. I took it out doubtfully and almost at once found the quotation, which was taken from Walpole's journal.

The daffodils are in bloom now. There are thousands of them making a great golden river at the side of the meadow. Unlikely to comment on a single flower, the flow of daffodils was so immense that he would catch his breath at them, take my arm and draw me to the window to look. I stand alone now and see them like a golden sea, stretching beyond view all through the copse. On his walks in the garden he would stand at the edge of it and watch them, his face alight with joy. They were one of the good things to be admired each year, waited for from the moment when the sun caught the first promise of them in a yellow mist.

Many things were not good, for he took a gloomy view of the modern world and complained that each year looked like being worse than the last one had been. There was tax, the bomb, cruelty, the political situation, strikes and delays with the post and travel. Travel delays he took as a personal insult, and in the matter of post he was convinced that somewhere along the line something very important to him was being held up and kept from him. Cruelty was ever

The front of Kissing Tree House, 1960. Priestley can be seen on the bench front right of the property. (Photo Mark Gerson)

The rear of Kissing Tree House, 1960. (Photo Mark Gerson)

Priestley at the rear entrance to the house in 1961. (Special Collections, University of Bradford)

Below: A misty view of the house from the south east. (Special Collections, University of Bradford)

A summertime shot of the garden, 1969.
(Special Collections, University of Bradford)

The whole of Kissing Tree House photographed from Kissing Tree Way.
(Photo Rosalind Pulvertaft)

The second entrance in the mist. The house had two driveways both accessed from Kissing Tree Way. (Special Collections, University of Bradford)

Priestley welcomed many famous figures to his Alveston home. Here he is in the company of three other great Yorkshiremen: Sir Leonard Hutton, Henry Moore and Fred Hoyle in 1969. (Special Collections, University of Bradford)

Priestley with Susan Cooper, 1969. He 'kept Susan Cooper's own letters clipped together in his working desk; for her he had a deep affection.'
(Special Collections, University of Bradford)

Below: Susan Cooper and Gareth Lloyd Evans join Priestley to celebrate his 75th birthday at the Savoy Hotel, 13th September, 1969. (Photo Tomas Jaski)

Priestley and Iris Murdoch on the drive in 1969. Murdoch and her husband John Bayley were frequent visitors. Priestley helped Murdoch dramatise her 1961 novel, *A Severed Head*; it ran in the West End for two years from July 1963.
(Special Collections, University of Bradford)

Diana Collins and John Bayley outside Kissing Tree, 1969. In 1994, Diana Collins charted and celebrated her friendship with Priestley and Jacquetta in her memoir, *Time and the Priestleys: The Story of a Friendship*.
(Special Collections, University of Bradford)

Kissing Tree had a garden summer house which Priestley used as a studio for painting. He is pictured here in 1967. (Special Collections, University of Bradford)

An image taken inside in the early 1970s. Priestley and his granddaughter Sadie are with Gertrude Jones (left) and Miss Puddock (right).
(Special Collections, University of Bradford)

The Priestleys' drawing room in the 1970s. (Special Collections, University of Bradford)

Priestley and Jacquetta Hawkes, early 1970s.
(Special Collections, University of Bradford)

Below: Priestley at the time of his honorary degree from The University of Bradford, with Harold Wilson and E.G. Edwards, July 1970.
(Special Collections, University of Bradford)

Priestley replying to the conferment of his honorary degree in the Great Hall at The University of Bradford, July 1970.
(Special Collections, University of Bradford)

Priestley, characteristic pipe in hand, in the study at Kissing Tree House.
(Special Collections, University of Bradford)

Above: Two shots of Priestley sketching during his visit to New Zealand in 1973. (Special Collections, University of Bradford)

Right: Priestley around the time he was granted the Freedom of the City of Bradford in 1973. Shortly after this honour the city commissioned David Hockney (another famous Bradfordian) to create a drawing of Priestley. In return, Priestley made a gift of two of his own paintings of the Yorkshire Dales (pictured) to the city. (Special Collections, University of Bradford)

Priestley, with a mischievous smile, in his office, 1978. (Photos Sheri Bankes)

Two images showing Priestley sporting a fedora in 1978. (Photos Sheri Bankes)

Priestley and Jacquetta outside, 1978. (Photo Sheri Bankes)

Enjoying the sunshine in the garden at Kissing Tree, late 1970s.
(Photo Tom Priestley)

Once more in the garden. This time in the early 1980s. The fedora has been swapped for a beret.
(Special Collections, University of Bradford)

John Collins, Jacquetta Hawkes and Priestley, Nicolas and Corinna Hawkes in the grounds of the Grinkle Park Hotel, Saltburn, Cleveland circa 1980.
(Photo Camilla Hawkes)

Priestley and his eldest daughter, Barbara Wykeham, in the library at Kissing Tree in the early 1980s. Barbara was a very talented architect and painter. (Special Collections, University of Bradford)

A late colour image of Priestley, inscribed to his son Tom. (Special Collections, University of Bradford)

Priestley with daughter Sylvia Goaman and son Tom. Sylvia gained an international reputation in the specialised field of postage stamp design; Tom became a leading British film editor. (Special Collections, University of Bradford)

Priestley's half-sister, Winnie, alongside Jacquetta and Sylvia Goaman in the early 1980s. (Special Collections, University of Bradford)

Rosalie Batten, pictured here in 1986 at the time the memoir was written.

Jacquetta Hawkes stands below the statue of her husband in 1986. The work was commissioned by Bradford Council and created by Ian Judd. Priestley forever casts a protective stare across his beloved city. (Photo Yorkshire Post)

present, there in the newspapers each day, tales of monstrous behaviour by parents to their own children; tales of terrible things done to animals. They wrenched his heart. "Children," he said, with anguish in his voice. "When you are a child things seem to go on for ever and ever and you can see no end, so that when a child is mistreated it thinks it will be like that forever, that there will be no escape, no end to the pain. An adult knows that things will end eventually. What an enormity it is, to abuse a child! And it can do nothing back! Nothing back!" His finger stabbed at the last words, which he repeated in tones of such pain that it seemed as if the suffering world were gathered about us, there in his room. "There is more of it now." He shook his head, whether in horror or to deny it, as if denying would cause it to end, I do not know. "Every day I read something that appals me." He pointed to the newspaper. "Here – a father who systematically burned his child all over her body with a lighted cigarette and beat her until he broke some of her bones. What that child must have gone through! The agony! The despair! Day after day of torment! What makes anyone want to torture a child?"

I shook my head.

It was at such moments that you felt the spirit of him, the enormous care.

There is such a strong sense of him in the study that I feel I have only to turn and he will be there, seated at the end of the sofa or browsing through the ranks of books, ready to ask me to climb to the top of the library steps and reach up to a high volume. He will hold my ankles, imagining that he is keeping me steady! I put my hand on the sofa, bend to the place, but it is empty. And yet he is there somewhere, surely?

DIFFERENCES

We had a falling out once, he and I. At least I fell out with him, holding my head high against the upset of him, while he, who never wore dark glasses, sought out a pair and kept them on all day. It was strange to see him looking at me through those dark orbs, like someone I did not know. He was full of remorse, but I remained unrelenting for he had offended me grievously.

The cause was the funeral of my husband's cousin Daphne. She was a lovely person. We heard of her death late, with the funeral particulars the evening before when there was no time left for formalities. We would go, of course. I telephoned Kissing Tree House, discovered the Priestleys were dining and left a message with the housekeeper explaining that I would not be there next day and the reason why.

My return on the day after that was a terrible shock, for feeling distressed I expected sympathy. Instead he was waiting by the study door with a face like thunder.

"What do you mean by taking a day off to attend the funeral of some distant relative? We need you here."

It came like whiplash, left me silent, a silence that perhaps he took for guilt.

"Just an excuse for a day off," he said.

"I was extremely fond of her."

"A remote cousin of your husband's – what was that to you?"

His tone was almost too much for me and I fought back tears, replied through lumps, "I wouldn't have gone if I hadn't cared."

After that we both went our ways abruptly. I was hostile, he, possibly edged on by a sense he had gone too far, was haughty. I do not know if it was that afternoon or the following morning that I gave him my notice. All I recall is that long day of this American gangster figure in glasses coming in and out of the room, hovering, watching, retreating from stone. He asked me to stay. I said, "No."

"I did not realise that this cousin meant so much to you."

I made no reply.

Mrs Priestley said that he had asked her to give me his apologies, asked me again on his behalf to stay, but I stood unmoving. He had offended my dead, my deep feelings. Besides, I was tired of doing more than I had ever wanted to do, missing so much of my children, such short holidays. It seemed to me that I gave and gave and got no thanks for it. The present insult was the last straw.

He came that afternoon and stood close to me, peered through the smoke of the glasses, apologised for himself. It did not occur to me that there was anything remarkable about this, but I suppose there was. If he had expected a sudden breaking down, reconciliation, he was disappointed. My dead were sacred to me and I spoke politely, acknowledged his regret, said that I would still prefer to leave. Afterwards Mrs Priestley asked if there was anything that would persuade me to stay and I answered there was nothing. It was only next day that I began to soften, and presently we agreed that I should henceforth have a day off a month, a week off at Christmas, a week at Easter, three weeks for the summer holidays and leave at 3.30 on Fridays. Riches indeed, but always a battle to have them! The Fridays caused such prolonged upset, such awkwardness, that in the end I voluntarily yielded them.

It was the only real difference that we ever had, and a puzzle to me for he was the first to give sympathy when there was cause for it. Perhaps he thought back to his days in an office in Bradford and judged me on the memories. I do not know. After that, although I was cool for a time, we seemed to grow more comfortable and close as the last of my nervousness gradually faded away from me. At least where he was concerned it did.

MORE THAN IRELAND

On those small, neat feet he shuffled into the study, smiled that innocent, friendly smile that was one of his ways of communicating, and settled onto the sofa. Pulling his dressing gown about him he began to study the mail. Richard Church had sent his recent book of essays and he now acknowledged it:

"I have been reading the essays with great interest and pleasure. You are very much at home in this form, if only because you have – in the old-fashioned phrase – a well stored mind. My one complaint is that in your talk there is a certain sharpness of judgement and phrase that I miss in the essays. However, they are very good indeed."

He sat and mused for a while and I sat and looked at his feet. They troubled him in winter. Pushed into leather slippers they were bare, and bare, pale ankles rose above them. There were draughts about and sometimes the outside door was open to admit fresh air.

"Aren't you cold?" I asked, unable to endure the sight of those ankles any longer.

He raised his eyes to peer at me over the top of his spectacles. "I'm never cold."

As he grew older, and again older, my alarm increased. Fearful visions of hypothermia rose and I would fuss a little, but to no avail. Later I was forever sneaking into his room to switch on the electric heater, or to check that it was already on, for Miss Pudduck was diligent. "Hot in here," he would say. "Turn that fire off." He was ever mindful of electricity bills. In early days it was he who would check the heaters and the lights in my room to see that they were not running up his account. Then, I did not need electric heaters because the central heating was on for a longer time. Presently though, Mrs Priestley decided on economies so that it was off from about 11.30 in the morning until after I left for home. She decided too that the radiators in my room should be turned off when I was not in it, so that it never warmed up properly and I was obliged to switch on the electric fire all day. By then it was he who fussed about my heat, so that we had an exchange of anxiety. "You are warm enough in here?" he would ask. "Come into my room if you like. Turn on the fires here.

Get another if you need it."

Riches indeed were offered.

He smiled again, still the innocent smile. Sometimes his smiles were villainous or calculating.

"Do you enjoy essays?"

"I'm enjoying yours very much indeed." He had recently given me a book of them.

He looked at me hard to make sure I was not flattering him.

"I never sit and read through them steadily, but every now and again I dip into them and perhaps read one in bed."

"That's how essays ought to be read," he replied, approvingly.

It was the turn of the year again and 1971 was to contain a good deal more than an Irish holiday. At the end of the old one he had written a piece for *The New Statesman* which Richard Crossman had reserved for the 1970 Christmas issue. Entitled *Falling Backwards Down An Escalator* it was about a recent occasion when he had done just that and people's reactions to it, from which he concluded that the English had a need for drama. He described how he had shifted his foot and lost his balance, falling backwards against the upwards movement of the escalator, finding himself "quite helpless, in a worse mess than an upturned beetle." There were screams and shouts and he wondered what was to become of him. Then somebody switched off the machine and fellow-passengers rushed to assist him. It was all good natured friendliness for the English were rising to the occasion, united in concern and helpfulness. He urged politicians to consider this. "Not every day do people see a bulky elderly man bumping backwards down an escalator. My accident aroused immediate interest and then sympathy because it was *dramatic*." He went on, "...if people seem to behave badly ... it is because the national scene presented to them does not encourage noble thoughts of the commonweal." He wrote of ill-will and hate in the world. "Everybody is so busy tearing the world in two that sometimes when I can't sleep I think I can hear it screaming. Empathy is becoming as rare as alchemy." Finally, after the contemplation of national discord, he said:

"Any great disaster shows that much of this is false. But it is itself a disaster, and we English, born grumblers, not haters, should move away from it. We can use our imagination, instead of sneering and jeering. We can lend each other a hand. We can ask ourselves, still using our imagination, not what is wrong but what is right with us English. We can ask our political leaders to remember that we are easily bored – even by five economists wrangling round a table – and long for the dramatic and the heroic, events not smaller but larger than life, such as the arrival at the Treasury of some gigantic charlatan of economics. With prices steadily rising and our purchasing power bumping down and down, we may well feel we are all falling on an escalator – but look what happened to me!"

This was written, of course, at a time of galloping inflation.

Most men of 76 who had fallen backwards down an escalator might have felt that a period of rest was due to them, but not JB, and having written his piece on the event, and sent off the typescript of *The Victorians*, he went on to consider the piece he was to write, at the invitation of John Hadfield, for this year's *Saturday Book*. The subject was to be Tobacco, which would involve a visit to his old friends Dunhills who would supply samples for him to try and think about. Eagerly he made this visit in the middle of January and the result was *The Art of Smoking* which began:

"It is now over sixty years since I first began smoking a pipe. I smoke when I am working, smoke when I am thinking or pretend to myself that I am thinking, and rather too often smoke when I am talking. (The point here being that a pipe and a rumbling lazy voice sometimes make me inaudible. But are my hearers missing much? Probably not.)"

He enjoyed writing about tobacco and had done so before. It had a way of creeping into his books and whole essays had been devoted to it. He spoke enthusiastically of cakes, flakes, Navy Cuts, rolls and twists, of full rich mixtures with plenty of Latakia in them. From time to time he used to give me talks on the stuff, holding out his leather pouch for me to sniff the contents. It was always pleasantly fragrant and equally so when he smoked it. He asked me to buy Latakia for him regularly. For him it was the rich, black 'seasoner' that he sought, for me a vision of the East and mystery. He blended his own tobacco, taking a little from one tin, more from another, gently stirring it into his pouch, sniffing and adding a little Perique or Cavendish until he achieved the desired mix. Then he would fill his pipe and light it, gleaming joy at me through the resultant spiral of smoke.

"You should try some," he said.

I shook my head.

"Mrs Priestley loves my mixtures – smokes them regularly."

He held the tobacco pouch towards me as if it were the apple in Eden, but I was firm. Enjoying the fragrance he produced I had no wish to spoil it.

When the proofs of this piece arrived there was almost disaster, for the E had been left out of his name and there, in big black capital letters under the heading, was BY J.B. PRIESTLY. It was enough to make him tear the whole thing up and banish it, but the day was saved by a big E in the margin and a strong line after the L to draw attention to it.

He might be an expert on pipe smoking, but he continued wholly inadequate with the lighters he used for igniting them. Two were returned to Ronsons for repair with the complaint that they had cost him a small fortune in lighter fuel and he understood that the valves were at fault. I, with an eye to escape from the almost daily task of inserting new flints, fuel and attending to screws, adjusting the flame and having my efforts undone almost immediately, suggested matches, tapers and anything that would get him away from machines which disintegrated in his hands no matter how well made they were. But he would persevere.

It was now that he was approached by the actor, Leslie Sands, a fellow Bradfordian and an admirer of Priestley, who made a proposal for a Priestley evening. It would consist of extracts from JB's plays, novels, essays, and would be treated exactly like a play. There would be a cast of four, an older and a younger pair and Leslie Sands and his wife, Pauline Williams. Well known for his part as Cluff in the BBC television series, Mr Sands was currently playing Toby Belch with the Royal Shakespeare Company at the Aldwych Theatre and was to appear in David Mercer's *After Haggerty*, due in the West End the following spring. Mr Priestley had a high opinion of his acting ability and took up the idea with interest. An exchange of letters was followed by a visit from the Sands, who arrived in time for lunch on Sunday, 21st February, and stayed for the night. It was the first of many visits. Leslie Sands had written six stage plays as well as a novel, so that he was no novice to the task of setting things out. The idea began to expand, a backer was found, and the younger couple, Keith Drinkel and Cherith Mellor, was settled. Under the title of *Open House* the evening opened in Leicester at the Phoenix Theatre in February 1972. Later, with a revised script, a new young couple, Derrick Gilbert and Judy Loe, and its name changed to *The World of J. B. Priestley*, it toured the country, beginning at the Alhambra Theatre in Bradford and ending at the Alexandra Theatre in Birmingham. For the Bradford opening JB had written a programme introduction:

"While I knew – and much appreciated – various performances by Leslie Sands in the Theatre and on TV, I didn't know him personally. It was as a stranger but a 'fan' that he first wrote to me, explaining his idea for an evening's entertainment consisting of excerpts from my plays, novels and essays. I welcomed the idea and then, shortly afterwards, the man himself. Since then, though a pair of obstinate and opinionated Bradfordians, we have got along splendidly and at this time of writing are good friends. (It is a fine thing in your later 70s to form a new friendship with such an attractive couple as Pauline and Leslie Sands.) But though I have responded to queries and made a few suggestions, so far as *The World of J. B. Priestley* is an entertainment, something for the Theatre, it is his work and not mine. On the other hand, if you dislike what you hear, blame me, not him.

And two points are worth making here. If you think a Theatre evening of this kind looks all too easy, you are wrong. In fact it makes unusual demands on the director, Stephen MacDonald, and his four players, far more I would say than most ordinary plays. Finally, if it works and pleases, it will have done something rather important. It will have enlarged the scope of the Theatre, and it will have done it without undressing the cast, using shock tactics with exhibitions of violence, rape, sodomy, making the players jump down into the audience to shout at them and even manhandle them. It aims to entertain, to please, without keeping to a familiar level of triviality, but making some attempts to convey some genuine thoughts and feelings about this difficult life of ours."

The production was given a favourable reception, *The Colchester Express* saying, "Nothing of the essential Priestley – his wit, humanity and gentle humour, which millions have learned to love – is missing."

Two years later Yorkshire Television screened a version of it for JB's 80th birthday celebrations.

He was at present in the process of considering possible subjects for his next book, his first idea being Tom Moore. Thomas Moore was a famous Irish poet and a friend of Byron, and a great favourite of Whig Society in the London of the Regency. He left a voluminous diary from which Mr Priestley had, in 1925, extracted the best passages to form a book which was published by the Cambridge University Press. He thought it might make a suitable illustrated volume to follow on the social histories, and there was an exchange about it with John Hadfield. Eventually it was concluded that the appeal of such a book might be too limited to justify the high production costs. A month or so after this letters fairly flew between himself and Mr Hadfield on the theme of an illustrated autobiographical social history which they decided should be called *The Times of My Life*. In this his own recollections would entwine with the social history of various decades and he said would bring in some of his travelling, pointing out that this had been extensive and would provide good material for illustration. At first he became increasingly keen on this idea, planning to bring in theatre, films, radio and television and some of the literary figures of his day, but then something went wrong with it and he began to come up against his custom of not keeping a diary, so that he had no detailed records of his personal activities. The plan was abandoned, but by then he had already made a start on *Over the Long High Wall*.

In the meantime he accepted the Booksellers Association's invitation to be one of the judges for the newly instituted Whitbread Literary Awards which were to offer £1,000 in each of three categories, Biography, Fiction and First Book, for writers who had lived in Great Britain or Ireland for five or more years. The other judges were to be Margaret Drabble and Anthony Thwaite, and it was arranged that JB should be chairman. Naturally he was then inundated with books to read. Not wanting to get behind with the necessary reading he wrote, before he and his wife left for Ireland, instructing the Booksellers Association to continue sending them while he was away, "as Mrs Batten will be here". This doubtless settled his anxiety that I should always be fully occupied during his absences. The Awards were to be presented at a lunch in Whitbread's city cellars in October. Writing about the arrangements in September gave him an opportunity to mention an important date:

"Thank you for your letter of the 13th, which incidentally was my 77th birthday.

I have only one change to suggest in connection with the lunch and that is that instead of my doing all the speaking, my two colleagues, Margaret Drabble and Anthony Thwaite, should speak briefly about one of the awards, so that all three of us will have a chance of describing briefly one of the three awards..."

His own choice of winner was Gerda Charles for her *Destiny Waltz*, in the field of fiction.

Safe from the threat of dancing and cabaret they flew to Cork and travelled to Shanagarry to stay at Ballymaloe House chosen for its fine food. Then it was on to County Clare, where with the pink of its limestone rock terraces, *The Burren* defeated his attempts to paint it. Connemara was his favourite region and here they stayed at Renvyle, a remote place where surgeon and poet Oliver Gogarty's old country house was now an excellent hotel. They spent three days at Sligo where he did some of his best painting on the trip, saying this was because it was Yeats country, and Yeats inspired him. In his Bradford wool office he had kept a copy of Yeats' *The Wind Among the Reeds* in the drawer of his desk, reading it when he should have been writing business letters.

Painting was not going well on this holiday, for they had some rain and mist and then when they reached Donegal he found it too hot and cloudless to capture in gouache, which refused "to melt and dissolve as the landscapes do". He felt that it called for oils or watercolours.

If the painting was disappointing the food was not and he talked of it in glowing terms afterwards.

"You could get food in a little Irish grocer's shop for a picnic lunch which was as good as any you would find in France. We bought beautiful, freshly cooked ham and new bread and butter. With Guinness to drink you couldn't do better!"

Picnics provided by the hotels were also excellent, cold collations so good "you could almost make speeches" over them. Wherever they stayed, and it was mainly in hotels that had once been large country mansions, they found the accommodation good, the dinners and breakfasts delicious. There was a pleasing lack of commercialism, and he liked the pretty girls at reception desks who were ready to greet him like a "favourite long lost uncle."

Having so much enjoyed Ireland previously, and Kissing Tree was full of paintings of it, he had feared disappointment, but instead liked it as much as ever and hoped to return there.

They arrived back at Kissing Tree on 9th June where, in early July he received a visit from an Italian nun, Sister Domingo, who brought a party of twenty girls with her. They all took tea with him.

It was the year of A. D. Peters' 80th birthday and JB took the chair at the celebration dinner in the ballroom of the Savile Club. Writing to thank him for his speech and gift of one of his paintings, Peters said that the party would not have been the same without,

"…you who have been a friend for so long as well as a keystone of this edifice. We have worked together since the day more than forty years ago when we were both beginners and what is more we have heard the chimes of midnight in many a city in England, in New York and in Hollywood."

The painting was of Marrakesh and JB, hearing later that Peters had never been there, wrote to suggest that as this painting was a favourite of Mrs Priestley's Peters should look out for another, "no worse artistically" and they would do a swop!

His own birthday followed within days and after the usual party he wrote proudly to tell Rachel who was living in Aden that "Tom was undoubtedly the beau of the party, all the women asking who that handsome, striking looking man could be." Another guest he much admired was Peggy Ashcroft, a friend of many years who used to dine when she was staying in Alveston.

My offering to him that year was a book by my father-in-law (H. Mortimer Batten), *The Singing Forest*. It was in *The Sunday Times* list of 100 best books for children and is quite suitable for adults too, particularly as JB thought adults would enjoy his own *Snoggle*. This, however, was one of the occasions when he gave me cause for umbrage, expressing horror that another book should have been brought "into this house which is full of books." Having had little success with previous presents, I gave him honey on future birthdays, and at Christmas eventually settled on a big box of Thornton's

Continental Chocolates for both the Priestleys. He rather liked small toys, and was delighted when two visiting Polish girls gave him a pair of fat little wooden men with Dali moustaches and curving swords, their hands holding aloft wooden beer tankards. He kept them on the chimneypiece. Another successful gift came from Sylvia, when she produced a little steel see-saw with figures at either end which rocked for ages when you touched them. When I entered the room they were often bobbing up and down, and if I was there alone when he returned they were sometimes active! He also admired a little glass seaweed tree with fish swimming through it which came from Rachel. He told me they represented the third dimension.

In the previous year Sir Arthur Bliss had written to say that there was to be a concert performance of *The Olympians* in the Royal Festival Hall at some future date. This opera was the outcome of a collaboration between Sir Arthur and JB which began in 1945 and took two years to complete. In his autobiographical *As I Remember*, published by Faber and Faber, Sir Arthur revealed that the seed of the opera was sown during a talk he had with JB at the Cheltenham Festival in 1945 and that he could not have chosen a better collaborator. He described Mr Priestley as a quick thinker, prolific of ideas and with an enviable experience of the theatre, saying that he found him both generous and sensitive, that they had got along remarkably well, Priestley deferring to his opinion as a musician, he accepting the other's opinion on stage matters. The music was mostly composed in the peaceful music room which had been specially built for Sir Arthur in the woods of his Somerset house, Pen Pits, while the libretto was written in Mr Priestley's study at Billingham Manor on the Isle of Wight. *The Olympians* was accepted by Covent Garden in 1947 but not produced until 1949 in a production that was beset with difficulties, including a clash of temperament between the producer, Peter Brook, and the conductor, Karl Rankl. There were such late decisions on the choice of singers that Sir Arthur did not get his principal tenor until ten days before the first night. A final misfortune was the opening of the dress rehearsal to the critics so that they saw a well-rehearsed and produced first act, a second act that still needed some work on it, and a third act which, as the composer said in his book, "looked exactly, in its raw state, like some village charade". He was filled with such despair that on the first night he sat gloomily in the Garrick Club and only went to the Opera House in time to thank those to whom thanks were due. As was to be expected in the circumstances, the criticisms were very mixed, but there were letters of praise for both the music and the libretto.

Mr Priestley, having told me about the opera, saying how fine it was, acknowledging with satisfaction his own well-written libretto, had replied to Sir Arthur's letter with a suggestion that the best way to give the audience some idea of the plot and dramatic movement would be to have a précis of the three acts, either included in the programme or printed on a separate sheet. He also said that, if it would help the venture, he would be happy to forego any royalties due on the performance.

Correspondence on the subject was resumed now, so that between meetings with Leslie Sands, reading for the Whitbread Award and thinking about projected work, JB wrote in reply to Sir Arthur's latest news that it was hoped the performance would be early the following year. He said that he sometimes wondered "if it would be beyond our wit to devise a second act that would not make such heavy demands as the one we have now." He went on to explain that he did not mean that anything would have to be re-written, but that it might be possible to simplify the staging. He made the same point to Sir Denis Forman, who was then Joint Managing Director of Granada Television and of the Granada Publishing Group, who had recently taken over Novellos, the music publishers who published *The Olympians*. Sir Denis was a close friend of the Priestleys, and in his working capacity was involved with arranging the special prom concert which was to celebrate Sir Arthur's 80th birthday. Mr Priestley informed him:

"It has a magnificent and very tuneful score by Bliss and I have always been told by those who know that the libretto is high above the average. It was produced at Covent Garden in the worst possible circumstances … The result of this was that we had a very well-rehearsed first act, an under-rehearsed second act and in the third act were practically playing charades. I have myself never heard that the opera has been neglected because of the third act. (This point was in answer to a query from Sir Denis.) It has two weaknesses. The first is that it has no dominating role so that no visiting star performer wants it to be done. The second weakness, though this would not apply to Covent Garden, is that it does make very heavy demands – a large orchestra, chorus, ballet dancers, and a fairly large cast of singers.

It is true that the third act is highly dramatic, but it is far from being boring. The ending has, I think, a great deal of charm ...

It is worth noticing that the first act of this opera, which does not demand a large chorus and dancers, is really quite self-contained and so could be performed by itself without an enormous amount of trouble and expense."

He also remarked that he thought *The Olympians*, with some adaptation, would make a superb TV opera.

The performance was in due course firmly arranged to take place in the following February in the presence of H. M. Queen Elizabeth the Queen Mother. In replying to accept his invitation to this and to the supper at the Savoy afterwards, JB told Sir Denis that because Sir Arthur was Sylvia's godfather, she and her husband Michael had attended his 75th birthday party. "That does not mean you have to invite them, but it would certainly be very nice if you did." He expressed apprehension about Proms, not having been to one since the days when he used to stand up in the Queen's Hall. "Are decent boxes to be had?" The hoped for invitation was issued immediately and by return came reassurance about the seating arrangements. Mr Priestley, having thanked Sir Denis, telling him that he looked forward both to the concert and the party, dictated a final paragraph concerning Lady Forman. It was one of the occasions when I found some difficulty in remaining blank:

"The next time you are home (he was writing to Granada's office) will you please take the novel *Such Good Friends* from Helen, then give it to your secretary to post back to me. People keep books not because they want to own them, but because they are too lazy to wrap them up and take them to the Post Office."

"People," he said to me, "are forever taking books. They borrow them while they're staying with us, wanting to finish them at home, and then they forget about them. Do you have your books returned when you lend them to people?"

I told him that generally I did, but expressed indignation about the loss of my copy of our village scrap book to someone who had moved away – a vicar's daughter too!

"How very annoying," he said, his tones as sympathetic as if I spoke about bereavement. And then, after thinking it over to himself, he asked, "Do you return people's books?"

"Yes," I said, virtuously.

"I think that you would do. I do too."

We sat comfortably approving of ourselves. I noted though, that on 23rd August, he wrote to his friends Thane and Elspeth Parker:

"Rummaging through some theatre books here the other day I found this one … which is inscribed to Thane and I cannot think how it got onto my shelves. Anyway, here it is…"

So that even the best of us cannot be perfect!

The Olympians concert was duly performed on 21st February attended by not only the Queen Mother but also Edward Heath who was at that time Prime Minister. Worries about seating arrangements had indeed been needless as JB had three boxes for himself and family. All were there, apart from Rachel who was in Aden, and the party included some of his grandchildren. They joined him first for wine and food at Albany, making it one of the special festivities in which he took such particular pleasure.

All this time *Over the Long High Wall* had been taking shape and by the time *The Olympians* was performed it had reached the proof stage. It began in the summer of 1971 under the title of *The Uneasy Chair*, which it remained until nearly the end when he felt that the new one conveyed more of the subject, sub-headed 'Some Reflections and Speculations on Life, Death and Time'. He felt strongly about this book, which crystallised some of his deep beliefs and feelings. In it he protested vigorously against the attitudes of a society that appears to dislike itself, of technology running out of control. He cried out against *Admass*, a word coined by himself to describe a system which reduced mankind to consumers:

"We are supposed to be Consumers and not much else; surely the lowest view mankind has ever taken of itself. We are televised and advertised out of our senses."

He felt that the balance between masculine and feminine principles, the Yang and its Yin, was wrong, that feminine values were unable to blossom but were being submerged by the masculine, largely as a result of industrialisation and technology.

"Feminist though I am, I feel that women have often been much happier when superficially they have appeared to be altogether too subordinate, but when in fact their whole civilisation has contained a very large element of the feminine, when their essential values have long been recognised and steadily accepted."

Observing that the old Chinese Empire probably endured so long because its Yang and its Yin were so shrewdly balanced he wrote:

"We must not be fooled by those stories of girls having their feet tightly bound to keep them small. A girl will risk cramped feet if she knows that soon she will be rooted in family life and instead of being unwanted as she grows old she will become a deeply-respected grandmother, a powerful matriarch."

He regretted, too, the devaluing of sex, of human relationships, the narrowing of thought and beliefs, the uniformity that is developing from one end of the world to the other. But it was not all protest. He went on to enumerate some of the advantages of contemporary life, television bringing us sights of art and nature that would otherwise be beyond our reach, music being available in our own homes, the vast choices given to us, cheap and speedy travel, books on any subject that might interest us. It was all there to be enjoyed, and "enjoy it" he urged, as he urged throughout his life, even in that last recording he made a few days before he died, for he wanted to share his own deep capacity for joy, for wonder, for the magic that hangs in the seasons, that lies within us waiting for recognition.

"We carry a theatre around with us, and we should enjoy the comedy inside. What goes on in our inner world can soon be turned into an enjoyable comedy if we stop hugging and petting our injured vanity, our jealousy and envy, all our bitter disappointments, our grief."

This inner world was what he was concerned about, fearing that it had been narrowed, urging that it should be given freedom to expand, touching on the wonder of life and going on to consider ageing and death, reincarnation, dreams and precognition, the after-life and eternity, extra sensory perception and Time.

He tried, with great patience, to explain his Time theory to me, but I largely failed to follow it and sat, stolidly Christian, baffled by the idea of it. This Time being in triple layers, constantly recurring, life being lived all over again, on and on, was so different from my own belief. He could only say, as he quite often did, sounding pleased about it and sometimes laughing to himself with delight, "You're so intellectual," or "You've no great intellect!"

On the subject of death in the book he noted that it was seldom referred to, having taken the place of Sex as the unmentionable topic:

"Death was hardly off the stage in the mid-Victorian decade, the 1850's I explored to write *Victoria's Heyday*. The undertaker and his hearse were always arriving. Handfuls of clay fell on coffins, often pitiably small, like constant heavy rain. Funerals would wend their way through school stories..."

and then:

"If an impresario in our day wanted to be really original and quite shocking, he would not bring on more and more nipples and pubic hair, he would stage a revue in which all the sketches and lyrics turned on death, perhaps to be called *Wait for It!* Or *What D'You Expect?*"

The topic might be grave and important to him, but the humour was always there, bubbling inside him, bursting out of solemnity as he laughed at himself and the human predicament with its folly and pathos and clumsiness.

Over the Long High Wall was written with a sense of urgency. It came from his deep concern for modern society, his belief that something was wrong with it and that we were losing touch with our inner selves, contracting instead of expanding the psyche. It aimed to advise us how to readjust our thinking about the nature of time and consciousness, to rediscover our spiritual identity. This sense of urgency, his desire to reach as many people as possible, caused him to suggest to the BBC that he should do a number of broadcasts based on the book. After some discussion about it he agreed to three half hour broadcasts, although this was fewer than he had intended and he felt that such a limited number would not have the effect he wished for. However, he signed the contract in the following March and the talks were recorded in August of that year, in time for his 78th birthday.

Perhaps the theme of the book laid its seed in the young Priestley, for he had written in *The Bradford Pioneer*[15] in 1913:

"'I am afraid you are a dreamer', quoth a correspondent ... And now let me have my say so that I can pass out into the starlit night ... Leave me to my dreams and remember, carping realists, that the splendid dreams of yesterday were ever tomorrow's most beautiful realities!...

Now I know that when the dark curtain falls upon our little drama – comedy and tragedy – here, the dreamers will still sound their music drums in some dim eternal twilight."

One day he came into my room, watching and hovering as he so often did, and then asked me:

"Do you have an inner voice? A voice that carries on above the surface, making comments about you, telling you things, often about yourself, as if you had two selves, one that is living and one that is watching you do it?"

I replied that I did, knowing exactly what he meant, that inner voice with its comments and entertainment.

The reply satisfied him, and we went on to suppose that everybody had such a voice, although we wondered how some of them could hear it above the sound of background music that is so popular in some quarters, which gave him an opening for a grumble about the sound of it in public places, restaurants, hotels, pubs even.

"There is something wrong," he said, "if people are afraid of silence."

I agreed with him vigorously, and he proceeded to pace around the billiard table, deep in thought, pausing frequently for further conversation, watching all the time whatever I was about. It was a habit of his on days when it was too wet or cold to take his usual walk and he explained that this circling of my room gave him some exercise.

It was while he was writing *Over the Long High Wall* that he asked me if I was afraid to die and I answered that I was not.

"Nor am I. Don't give a damn. When it comes I'm ready for it."

I refrained from pointing out that he would not be given an

alternative, but we went on to agree that we did not want any machines keeping us lingering. When death called we wanted to get out as quickly as possible, although it was I who expressed the hope that it would not be too unpleasant. Death was too big a thing for him to make a fuss over and he would accept it with that stoical approach kept for real illnesses.

The book brought him many letters, not in a great flood but in a steady supply right until the end. It was while we were discussing one of these that he asked me to do a particular thing for him.

"When I am dying, will you write me a letter?"

It seemed quite an undertaking, but I replied that I would and waited for him to speak again.

"You'll know when the time comes," he said. "I want it to be a special letter."

I nodded gravely, determined that I would make every effort to give him what he wanted. Sometimes, thinking about it, I felt a tremor of alarm at my own temerity. I had agreed to write a special letter to J. B. Priestley to lighten him on his final way! He regarded me trustfully and I returned the look with some tranquillity, for surely for something so important I could drain from the depths words to comfort him? I very much hoped so. He only brought it up once again, some years later, observing to me pointedly. "You *will* write that letter?" Again I replied that I would. It was a serious matter that I took very seriously. In moments of self-doubt I wondered what I would say, but there were occasions when I felt almost confident about it.

That year Christmas was spent in London, which was a rare event. They spent the 25th with Barbara, went to Sylvia for Boxing Day. He did his Christmas shopping in Leamington Spa first, afterwards having a growl about it. "I would much rather stay at home trying to earn the money to spend on it than do Christmas shopping! It seems to get worse every year, and the odd thing is that no matter how bad the economic situation may be, people seem to spend money like drunken sailors!" He went off to console himself by seeing Jacques Tati's new film, *Traffic*. This was a man who filled him with laughter, whom he described as brilliant, later writing an appreciation of him for *Books and Bookmen*.

1972 began with a visit to Crete and carried him on to a new illustrated book to be called *The English*. It was to be a year of change and, refusing to be kept down any longer, of *The Good Companions*.

THE GOOD COMPANIONS

That exuberant, warm, jubilant book, with all its enduring appeal, was born of despair, and although he might decry it, protest that it prevented his work from being viewed seriously, it remains the book through which many came to know him, giving enormous and harmless pleasure to thousands and thousands of readers who do not need it to be explained to them to enjoy it. It is a book for Everyman who recognises the humanity in it, making lifelong friends of its characters, turning to it as he himself had turned from the trials of life.

Emerging from a war in which almost every friend he had known had been killed, he married, in 1921, a local girl, Emily Tempest, known as Pat. The wedding was at their nearby Westgate Baptist Chapel, the bride, a typist, aged 24, was two years younger than himself. He was then up at Cambridge at Trinity Hall, struggling to make ends meet by supplementing his ex-Army grant with whatever he could earn by writing, coaching or lecturing. While there he brought out, through the local booksellers Bowes and Bowes, his *Brief Diversions*. It was acclaimed by the leading reviewers, including Edmund Gosse, so that, thinking he had achieved instant success, as he said in *Margin Released*:

"...Like a man playing a fruit machine, I cupped my hands for the clanging spill of the jackpot. And nothing happened. So fame, not a hint of it. No sudden big sales, no hasty reprintings. (It took years to sell the small first edition). But didn't publishers and editors write to this new young man whom Gosse and the rest had reviewed? They did not. Nobody wrote a word. Nothing happened. My career began with an enormous anti-climax."

After staying on at Cambridge to do post-graduate research, he decided, after considering various foreign professorships and Extension lecturing, to freelance in London. Clearly he had found a supportive wife, for their total capital was £50 and a child was expected who arrived in March the following year, a second daughter being born a year later, by which time they had moved to Wood Close, Chinnor Hill, Oxford, when his wife was a dying woman. They were hard years for him, both as regards work and emotions, and as he wrote, "...not only did I earn a living but, by doing two men's work, writing day and night, I was able to cope financially, if not emotionally, with my wife's long and fatal illness." The money came from reviews, criticisms, which he did for a wide range of journals, and books which he described as being "on the edge of criticism proper", such as *English Humour* and *English Comic Characters*.

He gave a brief glimpse of his despair in *Margin Released* when he described how he began working on a book on Meredith when he was spending his time between home and Guy's Hospital in London, where his wife was dying:

"I got back to Chinnor Hill, late one afternoon, so deep in despair I did not know what to do with myself. I was nearly out of my mind with misery. Had I been close to a town I might have visited friends, gone to a pub or a cinema, wandered about the streets, but Chinnor Hill was miles from anywhere. Finally, just to pass the time while I was at the bottom of this pit, I decided to write something – anything – a few pages to be torn up after I felt less wretched. On my desk was a rough list of chapters for the Meredith book. I chose one of the chapters, not the first, and slowly, painfully, set to work on it. In an hour I was writing freely and well. It is in fact one of the best chapters in the book. And I wrote myself out of my misery, followed a trail of thought and words into daylight."

He seldom spoke about this time, his very silence about it seeming to indicate depth of feeling. On the rare occasions when it was mentioned it was followed by the stillness that I observed when he heard of the death of some dear friend. It was only recently, when sorting through the box of letters to do with family, that I came across two he must have kept all through the years from his wife, Pat, to his mother who was still living then at 5 Saltburn Place, Bradford. They were full of concern for 'J'. The first, from Chinnor Hill, began with apologies for being a "wretched correspondent", explaining that this was due to lack of either physical or mental energy, that when she was not at Guy's she was in the hammock in the garden. They were trying to find a house in town to be closer to the hospital, and by then they had been obliged to employ a cook-housekeeper. The babies, Barbara and Sylvia, were well, and 'J' was up to the eyes trying to finish another book by the following week. The second letter, showing gentle concern for her mother-in-law, regretted that she had been unable to see the "kiddies", and made the sad comment that she had seen precious little of them herself. She referred to their need to find a house soon as she did not want her husband to have more worry than was necessary.

Soon she was dead, and JBP, left with his two tiny girls, presently remarried.

From all this emerged *The Good Companions*. As he described in *Margin Released*:

"Then, just as life was opening out, there came a period of anxiety, overwork, constant strain, ending tragically. Later, when that time was further away, I would be able to face it, not only in memory but in my work, where it can all be found in one place or another … So in *The Good Companions* I gave myself a holiday from anxiety and strain and tragic circumstance, shaping and colouring a long happy daydream. And because a lot of other people then must have felt in need of such a holiday, so long a daydream, the elephant suddenly turned into a balloon."

The balloon was an enduring one. The book has been printed over and over again, filmed twice, adapted for the stage and television, made J. B. Priestley a household name, for who can resist its appeal from the very first page which carries you into the heart of it:

"There, far below, is the knobbly backbone of England, the Pennine Range. At first, the whole dark length of it, from the Peak to Cross Fell, is visible. Then the Derbyshire hills and the Cumberland fells disappear, for you are descending, somewhere about the middle of the range, where the high moorland thrusts itself between the woollen mills of Yorkshire and the cotton mills of Lancashire. Great winds blow over miles and miles of ling and bog and black rock, and the curlews still go crying in that empty air as they did before the Romans came. There is a glitter of water here and there, from the moorland tarns that are now called reservoirs. In summer you could wander here all day, listening to the larks, and never meet a soul. In winter you could lose your way in an hour or two and die of exposure perhaps, not a dozen miles from where the Bradford trams end or the

Burnley trams begin."

His roots are in that book and we know immediately the feelings, the powers of observation of the young man who, before that terrible war, spent week-ends in the Dales with friends who shared his sentiments. We know the characters who gathered in his father's house, for he has used them here. Written before fame had, inevitably, isolated him, it was a book in which man spoke to man. Later he could hardly go anywhere without being pointed out, and there were constant jovial references to his being a 'good companion' so that perhaps something of his irritation is understandable. He wrote on and on, but there it was, as if it was a little ballooned caption over his head, *The Good Companions*, and he could not get away from it. There came a time, though, when he set up a trust that gave the royalties from the book to his four daughters, before his son was born.

It was a work that seemed to arouse music in its readers, for several times during my years with him he was asked to allow it to be adapted as a musical and refused. Like a volcano that lies quiet for a period before bursting into renewed activity, it began to stir in 1971. At the beginning of that year he had decided against a possible musical version by Michael Ashton and Ian Kellam; in May the BBC telephoned Anthony Jones to say they would like to do the stage version in their 'Play of the Month' series. As there was also interest in doing the book as a BBC classic serial, a project delayed by the fact that filmed television rights were at the time held elsewhere, it was decided that it would be better to wait the necessary three or four years and opt for that. In the autumn there came yet another approach from the American songwriter, Johnny Mercer, who wanted a twelve month option on the stage musical rights. He had recently formed a new production company in New York and wanted to make *The Good Companions* one of his first ventures, hopefully with André Previn writing the music.

JBP was doubtful about the idea because although the novel was popular there he was not sure that the play had been particularly successful in its New York run. However he suggested that Johnny Mercer or his agents should have a good long look at the play, and if possible at the film version. He told Anthony Jones to go ahead if there was a firm offer of money, reminding him that this would not go to him but to the trust for his family. There was then a long silence on the matter, broken the following June, 1972, by the arrival of a letter from Mercer full of praise for a story in which "every character ... is appealing or attractive and/or amusing". There had been some delay over rights and he asked for Mr Priestley's help if he could give any, ending with gratitude for the "jolliest, happiest and most heart-warming story I know".

In the same month Donah Wilson, having learnt that the rights barring a TV version would revert in 1974, wrote to say that he had thought for years that the book would make a splendid serial for television and had submitted the project to Granada Television. This came to nothing due to lack of sufficient financial backing but in the meantime agreement had been reached for the musical to be produced in England, the songs to be written by Johnny Mercer, music by André Previn, with a script by Ronald Harwood.

Other events were occurring now to disturb the easy rhythm of his life, for Hayles the gardener and Gertrude Jones the parlour-maid, who had all been with him since his previous marriage, when he lived on the Isle of Wight, decided to retire. Only Miss Pudduck remained until the end, striving to keep things as they had always been, for to her the Priestley comfort was paramount. Gertrude, of course, was wholly irreplaceable. She who had bustled about, pressing his suits, sorting his linen, scolding him when he went to appear in public in something that was not quite right, for he had said often enough himself that a fortnight's wear by him could make any suit look old and rumpled, was of a kind that no longer existed. Mr Hayles, whose hobby and work had merged so that he often continued in the garden until the light faded, who had produced such quantities of beautiful vegetables that to have four at a meal was commonplace, could have no equal. No one would ever again work such long hours, apart from Miss Pudduck, and although it was his wife who dealt with the domestic arrangements, he could not fail to notice that things had changed. Besides which, new staff expected more pay!

The disturbance did not affect his work, for nothing was allowed to do that. Fate, in her sledge hammer way, made an assault on his health at the same time, giving a good deal of pain and discomfort, unpleasant examinations and time in bed. He who had always typed his own first copy was obliged to dictate a piece he had written for *Punch* from his bed. He was up in time to celebrate his birthday in Bradford, a day which he afterwards described as "murderous", due to the pain and the fact that he did not stop moving around or doing something from ten in the morning until midnight. This included two visits to Leeds for television interviews, press interviews, lunch with the Lord Mayor at the City Hall, when he was presented with a "marvellous rug", and in the evening a performance of *The World of J. B. Priestley*, which was to play all that week at the Alhambra Theatre.

On the day after his return to Kissing Tree the oboist Léon Goossens came for an overnight stay, for the two of them were to give a recital that evening in aid of the Council for the Preservation of Rural England (now known as the Campaign to Protect Rural England). The oboist was a friend from the Isle of Wight days when he used to play at the concerts Mr Priestley arranged at his home, Brook Hill. We ourselves attended the recital in the Guy Nelson Hall at Warwick where spell-binder Priestley, peering over his spectacles, knowing exactly what he was about, read, among other pieces, *Fountains* and *The Grumbler's Apology* from his book *Delight*, the readings divided by the music of Goossens. Between them they produced a memorable evening, Priestley, perhaps with a knowledge of timing picked up in his music hall days, knew exactly how to rouse an audience's sympathy, give that 'You and me' feeling, with a wink and a smile, leaving the rest of the world out there missing something, and that was the joke of it.

At the end of October, still troubled by ill health, he went to London to attend an evening at the Haymarket Theatre in honour of Dame Sybil Thorndike's 90th birthday for which he had written an Epilogue to be read by Ralph Richardson. He told Sir Ralph, "Obviously you must please yourself how you do it, but I would suggest that you memorise it and then pretend to read it." Warmly praised, the Epilogue was afterwards reproduced on parchment in a limited number and signed by JB so that there should be a lasting record of it.

While in London he saw his old London doctor, Dr Hamilton, who advised him to have an operation. On his return he wrote to Mr Savage, his surgeon in Leamington, to say that as he had no important engagements in the immediate future "as soon as you and a single hospital room are available I shall be ready for you." He entered the private block of the Warneford Hospital, Oxford, in November, stoical, armed with the items required of him, his two pairs of pyjamas, dressing gown, slippers, normal toilet requisites, two hand towels and a box of tissues. So as to avoid publicity the whole thing was kept secret except from his very closest friends and his family.

We had expected him to be gone for at least ten days, but after his operation he soon pointed out to the surgeon that the kind of treatment he was having could be done better at home. He was allowed to leave provided it was maintained, for he hated being in hospital, and if there was anything wrong with him he wanted it to be in his own surroundings. The proofs of *The English* were sent to him in case he should like to read them while he was in bed. They were promptly handed to me. This book he had begun in February, at first with the help of a researcher but soon preferring to work on his own, which was surprising as his researcher was one of his favourites and he had worked well with her before. He had told her early that her notes were not very satisfactory but wrote again:

"While many of the details you worked so hard to get down are not much use to me, I have actually found that your notes in general have been much more useful than I said in my last letter."

Nevertheless he continued from then without help.

Soon it was back to *The Good Companions* and by now Ronald Harwood and André Previn had conferred and begun to work seriously. On 27th November JB wrote to Ronald Harwood:

"Many thanks for your letter of the 25th. Since we met in Albany I have been in hospital and have had an operation. I am back home now – if only because I insisted upon getting out of hospital at the earliest possible moment – but I am living an invalidish vegetable sort of life under the surgeon's orders. So there really is no hurry about showing me your Act 1, though I do suggest that you let me see it while it is still in a fairly fluid condition and has not absolutely hardened in your minds. (But let me add here that I have not the slightest desire to impose myself on you and your colleagues, if only because I have left that face behind) ..."

By December he was in London again, lunching on the 12th with his publisher. On the 13th he lunched with Sir Bernard Miles to discuss *An Inspector Calls*, which was to be put on at the Mermaid. Earlier in that year of change they had given up one of their sets of chambers in Albany so that he had to fit himself into half the space. It did not prevent him from carrying out a whole series of business engagements and a conference in his own apartments.

By February 1972 Ronald Harwood had become Ronnie and a firm friend, joining, with his wife Natasha, the circle who received week-end invitations to Kissing Tree. By this time too he and André Previn had done a fair amount of work on constructing and structuring the musical and had called in a director who they described as "a very talented young man". This was Braham Murray. The plan now was that as Previn was to go to New York with the London Symphony Orchestra in March he should see Johnny Mercer there and work on the songs. Mercer was to come to England in April to work with his colleagues and by 1st May it was hoped to have the first draft ready, the final version to be completed by the beginning of August, when the designer would start work. The making of costumes and set was scheduled for November and in early December rehearsals should begin. A possible opening for tour or previews was set for 7th January, 1974 and the London opening for 4th February, but such things seldom work out precisely and these dates were eventually advanced to June and July. Mr Priestley, in the thick of all this activity, was in his element. As well as *The Good Companions, An Inspector Calls* and *The World of J. B. Priestley* there was a production of *Eden End* which the Priestleys had attended when it reached the Malvern Festival Theatre.

Hearing from Ronald Harwood that he would be receiving a step outline for his comments, JB replied that on March 4th he and his wife would be flying to New Zealand and would not return until just before or just after Easter. He thought he might be most useful to them in late April or early May, but that as he would have many affairs in hand by then they could be sure that there would be no interference and adverse criticism for their own sakes. He was assured by Ronald Harwood that they would "*welcome* interference, adverse criticism, comments, advice from you if you are willing to give them," and that the shape and construction of the musical would remain fluid right up to the opening night.

After that there was a longish break before activity resumed at our end. By the end of the year rehearsals had been put forward to the following April and other dates amended accordingly. In February

1974 Ronald Harwood wrote again to say that Previn and Mercer had written a new song for Susie which was absolutely first rate. If JB had a cassette recorder he would send a tape of it. JB, however, did not hold with machinery and although he did have "some kind of instrument" he had "never used it, did not know how to, did not believe that it worked, and had misplaced the instructions". He went instead to Arizona. Afterwards, invited to attend the first rehearsal he declined and sent his good wishes. The cast was led by John Mills playing Jess Oakroyd, Judi Dench Miss Trant, Christopher Gable Inigo Jollifant and Marti Webb Susie Dean.

The production opened at the Palace Theatre in Manchester on 12th June, attended by JB and his wife. He returned full of enthusiasm. The London premiere was to be on 14th July, but first came some charity previews. Invited to one of these he decided to take his eldest granddaughter, Sadie, pointing out to her that they would be guests of the Variety Club, "a magnificent charity". As he had been asked to wear a black tie she could "dress up" as much as she pleased. He broke off here to explain to me how much women like to dress up and be admired.

Perhaps it was the thought of the cost of clothes that caused him to consider finances again, for he asked me to investigate the maintenance costs of the house over the last ten years so that he could send the figure to the Rating Officer with a request for a reduction in his rates. He felt that if he was keeping a fine old house in good order then he should not be sledge-hammered with enormous rate demands. In due course the Rating Officer visited, examined the house, in the process pouncing suspiciously on the book cupboard because its door had a Yale lock like a front door, and agreed that some reduction was due.

On the day after attending the preview Mr Priestley wrote to Braham Murray:

"The last thing I would want to do would be to appear before an unwilling or indifferent audience, but if there is any real warmth in the reception next Thursday I have worked out a little speech that would add to the warmth and might give a good line to any critics who are not unsympathetic. I shall be around of course, and after you and Previn and Mercer and Ronnie have taken your calls (as in my opinion you must) I could be brought on either by Ronnie or by Johnny Mills.

If the latter, unlike Ronnie, he would need a tiny script – roughly as follows:

'Now just a minute – there is a chap round here who started it all before most of you were born – good old JB!' – and then he brings me on.

I do not particularly enjoy curtain speeches and appearances but both with *An Inspector Calls* and *Eden End* they worked very well and I believe that this one could be particularly valuable."

While I kept my face impassive he went on to outline an improvement for the final scene. His idea for the impromptu speech reminded me of the meeting he had planned all those years ago between myself and Jean Young! John Mills would probably play his part better than I had though!

After the first night, although enthusiastic about it, he still had a few suggestions to make to Ronald Harwood, this time to improve the opening scene. With so much enthusiasm about it seemed astonishing that the musical came off after a run of only eight months. Afterwards Judi Dench told John Braine that she was sure the prevailing bomb scare had caused this, for her husband had seen it nine times and enjoyed it each time, while she herself loved doing it.

While this production was still in the initial stages, in 1972 Peter Hoar did an adaptation of the book as a serial for radio, running to twenty five episodes. It was in 1978 that Alan Plater adapted the story for Yorkshire Television. It went into production in May 1979, and was sent out in nine episodes.

But for me nothing could ever entirely match the spirit of the book and in time I had to see for myself the region that had inspired it.

BRADFORD

It was not until July 1986 that I saw Bradford, my husband and I driving there on a hot summer day. I surprised us both by taking the wheel as we neared the city, entering confidently as if I had known it for years. There were changes since JB's time there, a Sikh temple, a white goat tethered by the side of the road outside a garage, women in colourful saris, a long flow of traffic.

As we neared the centre I recognised the *Bradford Telegraph and Argus* offices in Hall Ings; we had dealt with them frequently. Then there was the Victoria Hotel where they had dedicated a lounge and bar to him, putting up photographs and old programmes of his plays. We parked on the fourth floor of a multi-storey car park from where the places he had described were spread before me. To the right was the City Hall, to the left the Central Library with the Alhambra Theatre behind it. There were some fine old buildings and distant vistas of green, but I could see the Bradford he had bewailed, the concrete and glass that had so offended him.

We emerged from the car park and I was seized with a sense of his presence, an old man in a dark coat and black fedora, a yellow tie, his stick tapping sharply as he walked alongside. The sense was companionable. I, who get lost anywhere, headed straight as a rocket to the Information Office. Here we encountered tremendous helpfulness. They had run out of street plans, but pointed out Mannheim Road and Saltburn Place on the office copy, eventually photocopying the maps and marking our route with arrows. The first was where JB was born, the second where he later lived and did his early writing in an attic room. They also marked the way to Green Lane School where his father had been headmaster. Before we left the Office we noticed the signs of that active Bradford life described so often, posters on the walls about plays and concerts, an advertisement for the Tridentine Latin Mass in the St John's Ambulance Hall on Sundays, evidence enough of independence.

Then I led the way straight to the Wool Exchange. JB had begun his working life as a junior clerk in the wool trade at the offices of Helm and Company in the regrettably demolished Swan Arcade. By now I was so much aware of him that I could almost hear his stick, once the property of Dickens, tapping the ground, his breath coming heavily, for he was old and the exercise tired him. If I looked sideways I would see him, surely, with tendrils of snowy hair brushing his collar, his pipe at his lips? He would remove it to smile his approval, for I had come to see his place.

The Wool Exchange was a fine building. There were richly patterned tiles at its entrances, and within, great arches, Gothic windows and fireplace, huge beams with handsomely carved figureheads, each with a shield. Polished pillars rose to the ceiling, ringed at the top with acanthus leaves or Prince of Wales feathers. Windows were outlined in delicate tracery. Above us a gallery was edged with wrought iron. In one entrance lobby a glass case held wool samples, brown and lumpish looking. I thought of him among his tops and noils, handling the raw wool samples and hating it. There was an antique flea market on in that enormous hall, the contents of the stalls forming a social history. Old pictures showed idealised country scenes, gardens with simpering girls, fluffy kittens; there were sketches of earlier Bradford, portraits of grandparents. Books were displayed on every subject imaginable. There were chamber pots, toys, cheap glass jewellery, gold, cameras, clocks and gramophone records. Tea sets and tablecloths edged with crocheted lace made me think of those high teas he recalled with such joy, the tarts and pies vying with cakes and scones that he described in *When We Are Married*. He said nothing could compare to a Yorkshire tea, told of the splendour of Baptist chapel tea parties. Dealing was busily under way; there were shrewd faces, satisfied faces. None was bored. I looked about for the characters he had described and saw them everywhere.

We continued to the site of the old Kirkgate Market, which had been replaced by one of those modern covered-in shopping centres you have to go upstairs to reach. We ascended to it by escalator, hastily descended again to escape the music, crowds and that distinctive smell of fabric and plastic that seems to cling to such places. It is totally different from the old covered markets which had pleasing scents of food and flowers, sawdust and fruit, with light that was filtered gently though high windows, not flooding you garishly. I did not need any derisive snort from him to know what he thought of this concrete and glass replacement of something that was old and interesting. His roots were firmly woven in what had gone; there was no inspiration here.

Our next stop was the Alhambra Theatre. Here he had come to

relish the glittering delights of music hall, to relish too the gilt and plush of the theatre, richly Edwardian. They have extended it now, but not in a style that would displease him. The interior is preserved, the ornate details of the stucco are intact and you can sense already as you pause in the auditorium that here is something to carry you beyond the feet-on-the-ground routine of every day. Bradford, he said, was well supplied with theatres, music halls, concerts. It had a life of its own, needing no help from the south to feed the soul. He had gone almost every week to the theatre, attended all the good concerts and, as he said, "read half the world's greatest books and a mountain of trash as well." Here he had come to the cheapest seats, dressed in what he described often enough as his "elaborately careless and bohemian style" with peg topped trousers and floppy tie.

He had talked so often about those days that I felt as if I knew him then, knew the very young man and the old man, but the man between was almost a stranger. Of that time he spoke very little, made only occasional references to it. He did not paint it with the clarity and depth which he used for his youth. I had a clear picture of the tough little boy with his football, of the careless dandy, of the young man who walked "hundreds and hundreds of miles over our blessed moors", who fell desperately in love with "mysterious beautiful beings" and followed them to their homes in remote suburbs, spending hours of hope and despair watching their lighted but curtained windows. He described how he had talked for hours and hours, in trams, pubs, teashops and front parlours. He said,

"Knowing nothing, I could talk about everything; and I do not regret a word of it," and smiled satisfaction. "Do you talk much to your friends?"

I nodded.

He said, "We used to walk for mile after mile at week-ends, talking all the time, and then we would spend whole evenings talking. We were full of ideas, I remember the scent of dust on the roads on dry summer days, and after summer rain the scent of damp dust, newly washed. You never get that now. We would walk across moors and through woods that were magical with bluebells, later returning along highroads on which the dust was settling. You could stop at a farmhouse then for the most magnificent sevenpenny tea. Can you imagine that, a good tea for sevenpence?"

I shook my head.

"For that the table was laden. There was white bread, brown bread, scones, pasties, teacakes, Eccles cakes, custard tarts, all kinds of cake, jam. Often there was some kind of salad, tomatoes, lettuce, watercress, beetroot, mustard and cress, celery and you might get raspberries and cream or stewed fruit as well!"

"All for sevenpence!" I said.

"And as we ate that wonderful tea we would be talking all the time. We had so much to say. I never wanted any other life then. My idea of success was to have a little cottage on the moors where I could write, and if I could make enough money to pay the rent and keep myself I would be satisfied."

I thought he still sounded quite wistful at this notion.

"Those friends were all lost in the war," he said. There was a pause while he reflected on it, and then, "I can still see those farmhouses now, the roses and sunflowers in front of them, the smell of cows, ham and whitewash, the smiling, comfortable women who used to provide the teas, the hollyhocks and honeysuckle peering in at the windows, the Dales rolling beyond."

I told him of my childhood walks with my Aunt Kate in the Northumberland countryside and of the splendid lunches we were given by Mrs Newton at the Feather Inn. She used to lay it all out for us in her front 'parlour', a feast of eggs and bacon and all that accompanied it, with newly baked bread and fresh butter. It was a fine restorative for weary hikers.

He rejoiced to hear of it, and then returned to talk again on Bradford and the youth that had been such a great trial to his father, looking at me confidingly and bending closer, as if this was to be something entirely between the two of us although I knew perfectly well that I was likely to find he had told the whole world in his writing.

"At eighteen I was my own most important work of art! No wonder my father sometimes thought I was a 'great fribble' of a fellow! My appearance proclaimed 'This young man may be compelled just now to work in a wool office, but he has dedicated his soul and much of his spare time to poetry, drama, music, Art, Friendship, Love!'" The memory of this soulful character was clearly highly amusing. "Once I got hold of some kind of dark green stock that made even my employer protest. I thought it looked fine! It wasn't to impress the girls that I dressed in this style, you know. It was to give me courage, as a soldier's uniform gives him courage, and to defy the wool business. I wanted to proclaim my difference. Youth generally does. And I did not shrink from travelling on trams dressed like that, which took some nerve in Bradford."

He did not talk much of the plays he had seen then, but would enthuse about music hall and the comedians. He was particularly keen on Jimmy Learmouth, a North Country comic he considered outstanding. The Sunbeams were part of the cast at the Alhambra and I wondered if they might have inspired the Dinky Doos who became *The Good Companions*, but I do not know.

Mr Priestley said, "I enjoyed, and I still enjoy, glittering nonsense and vaudeville. The lights and noise and the cheerful crowd stimulate my mind and give me ideas for my own work which are not connected at all with what I am seeing. I can relax and watch them in a dreamy kind of way and this seems to free my mind so that it can follow its own direction."

Standing in the foyer of the Alhambra now I imagined his pleasure in it all, the stirring scene, the noise and bustle. In his teens he had written a sketch called *At the Pantomime*, which seemed to me to show preliminary signs of the careful directions he was to give in later work. The characters were labelled Small Boy, Little Sister, Placid Parent, Humorous Youth, Giggling Sweetheart, First Young Blood, Second Y.B., Superior Youth and Man with eyeglasses who became Eyeglasses after the first mention of him. Nobody has an actual name. At the end was, "Curtain falls. Lights go up. Four bars of the National Anthem played as a two-step by the orchestra. Everybody goes out, and nothing remains but chewed programmes and the smell of oranges."

We had found the Promotions Officer at the Alhambra, John Martin, as helpful as everybody else we met in Yorkshire. Now we left him to return to our car and at the entrance to the car park I sensed Mr Priestley leaving us, felt that if I turned I would see the back of that broad, round figure, with his raincoat stirring in the breeze and his hat, bohemian as any in his youth, well down.

On we drove to his home area of Manningham. It was like Pakistan transported. In the bright sunlight of late afternoon we felt as if we had travelled to another country, but the houses were English enough, small, decent, terraced rows and streets where little Pakistani children kicked their balls as he had done himself. An old man wearing a round beaded hat nursed a fine brown baby in his porch. An attractive young woman in pantaloons and tunic was busy among her roses. We scarcely saw an English person on all the route to Green Lane School.

JB was always proud of his father, told me often that he had been a Headmaster, stressing the point so that I wondered why he made so much of it. When we arrived at Green Lane Junior School and talked to the Headmaster there, Mr A. C. Wheatley, I began to understand, however, that this was no ordinary school for, apart from anything else, it had been the first in the country to have a free meals service, and that was in the period when Jonathan Priestley was Headmaster there. It was no ordinary junior school size either, for there were 450 pupils. In Jonathan Priestley's time, of course, it was an elementary school.

His father, Mr Priestley said, was a dedicated educationalist, devoted to his teaching, ready to spend all his free time continuing to impart the information he had gathered, to be the schoolmaster out of hours. He would enthusiastically teach people wherever he went, on trams and trains and buses, in country pubs and seaside boarding houses. His was a generation that believed in education and he pursued knowledge eagerly, for to him it had come as a privilege to be prized and respected. A mill worker, his own father had not had the opportunity to learn, but managed somehow to help his son to go to a teacher training college in London. Such opportunity was not to be treated lightly and Jonathan Priestley made the most of it. Many of his friends were also teachers and the young JB spent hours listening to their heated debate, their voices assuming classroom pitch as the talk advanced. He thought there was too much about Education, but enjoyed the visitors as comic characters, absorbing them for use in future work, acquiring a huge store of material.

The school seemed to have changed little. My husband aimed his camera at it, but immediately the caretaker appeared announcing that photographs were not allowed. My husband argued. We were told then to approach the Headmaster and were afterwards glad that we had, for as he talked fluently and informatively I began to get a picture of his Priestley predecessor. We learnt that there had been only five headmasters since the school was formed so obviously they were a breed of stayers.

Jonathan Priestley was at White Abbey Mixed School which closed in 1902, when he transferred to Green Lane. JB had told me something of the period, of the poverty, children in rags and shoeless, their food inadequate, of his father's Socialism, but he had said nothing about the free meals service nor about the baths which were installed at Green Lane. It was Mr Wheatley who described these, producing a fat folder of photographs. There were the school kitchens with gigantic stew pots and ovens, Jonathan Priestley among a row of boys and girls with the description 'Before and After'. One, of the school dining room, showed rows of solemn children seated on benches at long tables covered with white cloths, their Headmaster watchful at the side of them. There was something in his posture which evoked his son. A chart illustrated how these children's weight went down in the holidays. We found the picture of the baths most fascinating of all for the boys looked like so many puddings boiling in tubs because these tubs were round as pudding basins.

The problems at the school now are of a different kind from food and cleanliness. It is a question of language these days since Mr Wheatley told us that 90% of his 450 pupils are from Pakistan, 5% from other countries, and only 5% are English. He is clearly not a man to be defeated by difficulty and spoke with enthusiasm of his plans for helping these pupils to learn English, many of them not speaking it at all when they come to him. Listening to him I was very much aware of Jonathan Priestley, could imagine him going about the business of baths and kitchens with the same eagerness, the same determination to educate. It was hardly surprising that his son should have retained such pride in him, and I had a sense of seeing him through JB's eyes, his faults included.

"He had the most fearful temper, but there was neither malice nor ill will in him. There would be a terrible outburst which cost us some crockery, but then the storm would pass. I never ever heard him swear though. In fact it would have been less trouble and expense for us if he had sworn instead of smashing things! Holidays were often enough to make him lose his temper and we would set out for ours with him in a storm. Once," he paused to dwell for a moment on the enormity of it, "he ripped the tablecloth off the breakfast table and broke everything on it."

I looked suitably impressed.

"I have made sure that I never developed a temper like that. It can terrify the women in the family, make them miserable. You've never seen me rage."

"Never," I said.

But you must not think that I did not love my father. I was very fond of him indeed." There was a smile then. "We used to have to carry our luggage to the station because of one of his economies. He was not a mean man, but there were some things that he would not waste his money on and a cab was one of them. He would struggle with a hundredweight of luggage rather than pay for a cab. And we used to have to take sandwiches on all our outings because he refused to eat in hotels, restaurants and teashops. It was the despair of his womenfolk!"

"It must have been," I said.

"Fundamentally he was a generous man. It was only in these small things that he was careful. He was a modest drinker, enjoyed his pipe and an occasional cigar, loved company and fun, relished good humorous fiction. But he thought, unlike the rest of my family, that it was a waste of time and money to go to shows, music halls and theatres. We had many scenes over this in which he shouted and I sulked. I think he was afraid that I might have inherited frivolous tendencies from my mother's family. She came from back o' t' mill people, happy-go-lucky and never a penny between them because they spent it on jugs of beer! I never knew her myself because she died when I was a baby. I had a very good stepmother then who was always kind to me so that I never missed my real mother." He obviously believed this.

There was not time enough for us to visit Belle Vue Grammar School where he was taught English by Richard Pendlebury to whom he felt a lasting sense of gratitude. We set out for his place of birth, parking near Toller Lane and crossing to Mannheim Road. He was again beside me and I sensed the old man's companionship, the boy, the youth. They were all there in those streets, kicking a football, sauntering, walking with a stick, all one. Three boys kicked a ball and a cat, seated fatly on one of the front paths, reminded me of that character he had described so often:

"We had a cat once, a huge tom – big as any dog. He would stroll along the street as if he owned it, casually. If any dog approached him he would carry on, ignoring it. But if the dog persisted he would turn and GLARE and the dog would make off in terror!" With eyes bulging furiously he would mime this, his arms the stalking legs of an all-conquering cat, his head turning to confront and subdue the dog.

My husband, having heard about this cat, produced his camera and aimed it.

Number 34 was a small house and there was nothing of much note about it. I remembered seeing a photograph some years previously in a birthday piece about JB, but they had used the wrong one then, the house next door which had diamond windows. His was good enough for me, though I felt no sense of the infant Priestley in it.

We went then to 5 Saltburn Place with its attic room from which you could look out across the streets of Bradford. I was still walking confidently and still aware of him, almost as if I had only to stretch out a hand to encounter the smooth silky feel of his raincoat. The house was terraced with bay windows, its roof broken by the big, square, projecting window of his room. There was a new front door which I regarded with indignation. Pakistani children watched us curiously, and presently two Pakistani women walked down the street and stopped at the door. My husband urged me to approach them but as I was momentarily shy went himself, explained that I had worked for Mr Priestley for the last sixteen years of his life and wished to see the places he had described to me. At first they were reluctant to show the room but relented suddenly and we were ushered inside.

The room was bare now. There was no longer any gas fire. And it seemed small to have contained all that he described in it.

"I had a combined bed-sitting room at the top of the house where I kept my books in shelves contrived out of orange boxes sawn in two and painted. On the walls I pinned up reproductions of pictures I admired. There was a gas fire there to which I would draw up close and write, never doubting that an eager world was waiting for my words."

"As it was," I said.

Although he had always done well at school, had won a scholarship and often come top of his form, he felt no desire to continue his education and go to university. His father had accepted this and, although he had never thought much of the wool men, agreed that the wool trade would provide a solid future for his son. JB then infuriated him by refusing to learn more about the business, finding it bored him even more than school had done. He declined to spend his evenings at the Technical College learning about the hair of sheep, goats and camels, and when he sneered at a neighbouring youth who was "working like a bee" at the theories of wool-combing and spinning, at commercial French, German and Spanish, his father's response was that this fellow would be a man when JB was a monkey.

Always sure that he wanted to write, for J. B. Helm and Company was simply a front, while the real work seeded in his mind and onto paper in that attic room. Here it was that he trained for his true role, changing his name to J. Boynton Priestley which he thought would sound more impressive to editors. There is no Boynton on his birth certificate but, as he told me, "At sixteen I felt I needed more weight, and I thought it sounded good, J. Boynton Priestley." He laughed at these notions happily. With this new name and a pipe filled with Cut Black Cavendish at 3½d an ounce, which he bought in the Swan Arcade, he produced ponderous articles about whatever aspect of the world occurred to him. As he said, he was at the age when he knew he could do anything, act in great dramas, conduct an orchestra or two, and produce Literature. He wrote *The Fallacy of 'Realism'*, beginning, "No School of Fiction has perhaps ever possessed such a hold upon the vacillating taste of the British Public, as the work of the so-called 'Realists'." He wrote *The Renaissance of the Cinema*. "One of the most striking features of the social life of our country during the last two years is the extraordinary growth of that species of entertainment known as the 'Cinema'. Picture Palaces have sprung up like mushrooms in the night, and the remarkable hold they have at present upon the public is well-nigh incredible." There were short stories and poetry and he had *The Chapman of Rhymes* printed privately, ever since trying to abolish the memory of it.

Helm and Company provided him with some material for his later writing, but his work there failed to interest him and he escaped whenever possible. Sent on an errand he would spend an hour on a task that should have taken five minutes, and sometimes he would take off to the moors for a day. Perhaps this was why in later days he was highly suspicious of his own staff, accused the sick of malingering, watched at the door for their return from errands, marking the time resentfully.

His father despaired of his son with his fanciful clothes and liking for music halls, told him he would be a Jack of all trades and master of none. Nevertheless he did take a pride in some of his son's "monkey tricks", especially when he managed to get into print and be paid for it, which he did young.

Mr Priestley said, "I think he usually saw me as a conceited young dilettante who would never make his mark at anything and might eventually be hard put to it to keep himself decently at all. He was a man with superb courage when any important principle was at stake, but in small matters he was timidly conventional and had a real bourgeois horror of offending his neighbours' prejudices and a passion for solid respectability. He was afraid of what the neighbours might think of me, and I could not see at all what they had to do with my habits and appearance. It caused us many differences at that time. He really worried about what people would think and say, even when he had no particular respect for those people. There was, too, a curious vein of rigid Sabbatarianism in him, curious because he had an ethical rather than a religious outlook, although he was a regular chapel goer. On Sundays we were allowed no newspapers in the house, no frivolous music or noisy nonsense. In spite of his liberal outlook there lingered in him something of the old Puritanism of industrial communities where repression is often mixed with a taste for bouts of debauchery. He had seen bad examples of this and I think they probably stiffened his own good resolutions of never breaking with the old Puritanism. He was afraid that I had inherited from my mother's side a tendency towards extravagant and idle amusement. To him my magnificently careless and picturesque appearance, my air of being a romantic genius of some kind, must have been painful. When all the other hard-working lads were about their studying, I would be lingering in my bed. When all decent people, especially our neighbours, had gone to bed, I would be up and quite likely out in the night. When he was having some Sunday morning gathering of 'respectable folk' I would arrive looking like a character out of a touring production of *La Boheme*. I can understand his worry."

His father, to JB's lasting sorrow, died of cancer before the real success came, but he did live long enough to see the beginning of his son's achievements and was proud of the book that was dedicated to him.

Mr Priestley described how he and his father, in those moments when they might have come to an affectionate understanding, were both held back by shyness, but in the war their differences vanished. After being wounded, when he was in hospital in Leicester, he woke to find his father beside him, his eyes full of tears. Later he discovered all his letters home from the army carefully tied up and preserved.

In his father's last days their shyness was gone, but with the irony of fate Jonathan Priestley's memory had failed so that no real talk was possible. There had been a space in the final year though when their relationship returned to what it had been when JB was a little boy, his father immediately glad to see him. Afterwards they would walk together almost in silence up Toller Lane, where he felt that every step they took was haunted, for it was the old familiar road climbing from the house. Looking from the window I could picture it now, could feel the reality of those streets that had fuelled the writer.

We said farewell to our hostess, who spoke little English, and shook her hand. She and her neighbour-friend consulted, decided, and we were invited to tea. Much touched we thanked her and were ushered into the front room where all those eager gatherings must have occurred, the loud discussions on education, the Christmas parties that abounded in games and songs and the piano, the Sunday visits from deacons with upholstered wives, and Baptist tea parties. It seemed right that the room should still be hospitable.

He did not come into the Dales with us. Perhaps he did not need to for I knew them immediately from his painting, saw the source of all his golden light as the sun poured down onto the hills. Their peaks really did have those dark spreading shadows; they were cast by the clouds, as if someone had thrown quilts over them. There were his dark stony summits, the stretches of varying green, streaks of gold where buttercups clustered, clumps of trees and their shadows. We went to his favourite Hubberholme where his ashes lie and there is a plaque to his memory. Afterwards we walked beyond along the Dales Way. The silence was broken only by the lark's song and the cry of the peewit, the bleating of sheep, the ripple of water, and there was the rich fragrance of an English country summer.

ECHOES OF WAR

"August," he said, "is a month I have never cared for and I'm glad we're coming to the end of it. It is a dull month. Nothing ever seems to happen in August; it is stale and flat."

"Perhaps it's because so many people go away for holidays."

He gave a doubtful grunt.

The scene outside was of that almost over-rich growth, with so much green that it becomes stifling, its ripeness having a quality of tiredness, the very air still and heavy with high summer as if it too was resting from all the earlier effort of awakening to new life. Soon gold would creep into the green and the early mornings have a crisp vitality.

Striving to cheer I said, "There are still some nice flowers."

Another humphing sound.

"It's good to be warm, too."

This did not impress him at all and he replied, with truth, that he was always warm, continued a shade resentfully that it was a sombre month. He seemed so determined to find no good in it that I remained silent.

"All those storms," he said. "I hope we're finished with them now."

There had been several of these, with great rumbles of thunder sounding like heavy artillery, streaks of lightning overhead that made me uncomfortably aware of my steel desk and its place in the bay of enormous windows. If I had been alone in the house I might have reclined under the billiard table, but as it was whenever there was time I busied myself in the stationery cupboard where there was neither glass nor chimney.

At our first storm he had come, at his most reassuring, into my room.

"Do you mind storms?"

"Not too much." I tried to make it clear that I was too brisk and efficient for storms to upset me.

"Good!" He took a puff at his pipe and remained reassuring. "If ever you should mind you could always come into my room and sit with me."

"It's all right."

I tried not to flinch at the particularly fiery fork of lightning that seemed to be coming straight for us. If he had not been here I could have closed the curtains and sorted out books at the further end of the room.

"Busy?"

"I'm always busy," I responded smartly, willing him to go away now.

"What are you busy with?"

"The letters."

"Are there many?"

"Mrs Priestley has given me quite a lot this morning and they are long ones."

"She says too much when she writes letters. Not like me. I keep them short and to the point. You'd agree with that, wouldn't you?"

It was true, but there hardly seemed a need for my agreement as he was clearly so pleased with his letter-writing.

Thunder clashed then; the sort that sounds like a giant in armour falling down a cliff. My heart jumped and settled.

"You're sure you don't mind?"

"No," I replied, my voice sharpened by alarm. "It's only a storm."

"I'll leave you to get on then." He gave another puff. "But if you should feel uneasy just come to my study." His tone was honey.

As soon as he had gone I leapt to my feet and closed the curtains, but the worst was over. Later it occurred to me that he might not like storms himself. Whenever we had one he appeared to sit reading through it. I never found him at his desk then, but always seated on the sofa, very still and calm looking. I was sure that even if he felt fear inside he would never show it. He would present a placid exterior for the world and carry on. He must have been like that in the terrible war. I wondered, sometimes, if the rumble of thunder reminded him of the rumble of guns, and could imagine the young J. B. Priestley marching stolidly on through the horror of it. He spent his 21st birthday in the front line trenches in 1915, when he was in the 10th Battalion, the Duke of Wellington's West Riding Regiment.[16] They were nearly all West Riding men and he soon made good friends among them, but the closest of these were all killed before the war was half way through. When he talked of the war it was briefly and he gave no details of it, even of being buried alive in the summer of 1916.

"They soon dug me out," he said cheerfully. "I was portioning out the rations when it happened and they needed those. A German Minenwerfer landed in the dugout where the rations and I were and that's about all I knew of it. If it hadn't been for the food they might have left me under the mud!"

He might treat it as a bit of a joke but I could picture only too clearly the noise and the sense of suffocation. He was taken then from Souchez to a military hospital in a suburb of Leicester, North Evington, and it must have been there that he awoke to find the tear-filled eyes of his father regarding him.

"There was nothing much wrong with me," he replied when I asked about damage. "I had a touch of deafness and a few minor injuries – no serious wounds."

The rest of his war experience was mentioned at different times, he never dwelt for long on it. After Leicester he had been sent to convalesce in a country house in Rutland, which was pleasant, and then in the autumn to a terrible convalescent camp at Ripon, finally moving on to another at Alnwick. Alnwick was brought up more often for he had liked it there and had good memories of walks in the surrounding countryside.

Passed fit, he went to the Third Battalion on Tyneside and from there to an Officer's Training Camp. His first posting on being newly commissioned was to the Devon Regiment at its headquarters and barracks at Devonport, returning to France in the late summer of 1918. Two particular friends he had made at Devonport were killed within days of his arrival and he himself was slightly gassed through a seepage through his gas mask, after which he was declared unfit for service. Having enlisted in his 20th year he was demobilised in his 25th, in March 1919.

His regret for the generation of men lost in that war was infinite. "Something ended then," he would say, as he said in his writing, and he wrote in *Margin Released* of the appalling conditions in France and the pointless fighting:

"Outside any plan of campaign, without any battle being fought, any honours being won, we went through the mincer. It was not long before our own B Company, with a nominal fighting strength of 270, had been reduced to a grim and weary seventy. Two hundred men had gone somehow and somewhere, with nothing to show for it."

All his days that war haunted him, filled him with a sense of its futility and horror. He emerged from it with a fatalism that he was never to lose, for death had been close.

The second war was entirely different for him, without the wholesale slaughter of his friends and with a new and particular role for him. As it began he was travelling to Broadcasting House to read the first instalment of his novel specially commissioned by the BBC, *Let the People Sing*. After this opening by him the serial would be handed over to professional readers. He set out from the Isle of Wight on Sunday, 2nd September, 1939, in bright sunshine, leaving early in order to collect several things from his house at The Grove in Highgate. The crossing from Cowes to Southampton was pleasanter than usual, the road out through Winchester quiet even for a Sunday morning. It was only when they were half way to London that they encountered busyness, with cars full of people coming away from the capital. He assumed they were going to the coast to make the most of the beautiful September weather. On they drove through Bagshot, Sunningdale and Virginia Water, all the time passing loaded cars. It was when they were in the middle of Staines that the loud, wavering wail of the siren started, a noise that he found more frightening than the thought of a rain of bombs. He was fearful too that there might be appalling scenes of panic, but there were none, only a lot of noise and bustle, the continuing cry of the siren reminding him of some trapped animal, the hooting of cars, and wardens in tin hats rushing about shouting instructions and gesticulating. The chauffeur halted the car and they asked if this was a practice alarm. The reply was that war had been declared an hour previously.

As the skies were calm, with no sign of enemy bombers, they continued to London. He had last seen it in July and found it now completely changed. There were sandbags, shelters and trenches everywhere, air raid wardens, auxiliary police and firemen at their posts, barrage balloons floating like inflated elephants above. They drove to 3 The Grove, which seemed to him uncannily silent, went through the house collecting things, including the children's winter clothes. Although he was not due to make his broadcast for several hours they went on to Broadcasting House to be sure of getting there, for at that point the entire population was braced for attack from the air and he might find himself trapped in some remote street.

He said, "Broadcasting House looked as if it had changed from peace to wartime months before. There were steel shutters, sandbags, uniforms and steel hats everywhere. I found I had returned to the deep dug-out life of the old French line for everything had moved below, down into the basements where the corridors were beginning to look like trench traverses. There were even nurses there, ready to deal with casualties."

What an expressive voice he had! It was not just the words he used but the tones that carried you into the scene and the sense of it. His voice could portray such depth and breadth and immensity, so much tenderness and compassion, humour and tolerance, such brevity if he was feeling put out. Now it took me into those basements and the very atmosphere that prevailed there.

"They told me the king was on the air when I arrived, and tucked me away in an empty subterranean corner where I was to wait. By that time I could no longer believe that anyone apart from my family would want to hear me reading."

Nevertheless the moment did arrive in that strange day and he duly delivered his chapter. Afterwards, having sent the car on to escape the still expected but never arriving bomb attack, he made his way through empty streets to Paddington, where there were crowds, and went home by train, stopping for the night at Basingstoke.

In that first week he helped, in the still hot September sun, to dig an air-raid shelter in the garden on the Isle of Wight, feeling that his womenfolk looked on him with new respect as he dug deep into the clay. It was roofed with timbers, corrugated iron and then deeply with more clay. I could not feel surprise, however, to learn that in the heavy rains of autumn the trench filled with water and the sides caved in. Finally the gardener took it all away.

Excavations completed he returned to London and began a tour of the country to visit camps, dockyards, aerodromes, munitions factories and write about them for the daily press. Soon he was making his famous wartime broadcasts after the nine o'clock news on Sundays. When he was in his eighties he was still receiving thanks for them from unknown writers, the most memorable broadcast of all appearing to involve a pie shop in Bradford. Even here, in my Warwickshire village, I have heard a man speak of it who had never himself been to Bradford but had heard that talk. His voice became so well known that on one occasion when he was groping his way through the thick dark of the black-out in the London streets, he bumped into a man and apologised. His voice was instantly recognised and he was told that he must not be late for his broadcast. It was he himself who presently requested a break from these talks, and when he later returned, responding to popular demand, he gave what he described as "a sharper edge" to them, with more of politics. This time it was outside sources who terminated the broadcasts and he was always convinced that Churchill was behind that decision.

Besides these Sunday evening *Postscripts* he broadcast several times a week to America and the Dominions, with recordings going out to the entire English speaking world. As they were made very late at night he used to stay at the Langham Hotel, close to Broadcasting House, so as to get some sleep. Fate seemed determined to preserve him, as he had a narrow escape from being blown up there. It was a particularly busy session of several broadcasts when, feeling completely exhausted, he planned an early night. An appeal came to him to do an extra talk for Canada. Responding rather reluctantly he gave up this much needed rest and went to Broadcasting House. It was that night that, during a heavy bombing raid on the area, the room in Langham in which he had planned to sleep was totally destroyed.

Many years later someone wrote and recalled seeing him in the early hours of misted mornings walking up Highgate Hill after making a broadcast, always deep in thought. They never spoke, for Mr Priestley did not appear to see him and the writer, sensing a need for solitude, did not break the silence.

Later, in the flying-bomb period, JB lived at Albany, where he spent much time fire-watching and sometimes had to make do with only two hours sleep. Despite being desperately tired, he said that he almost enjoyed being in such a deserted West End, that the English responded to danger and at that period he found people more companionable, more light-hearted in their approach, than at any less hazardous time.

It was while he was doing his Second World War tour of the country that he returned to the site of his early First World War activity, the barracks at Halifax which he had known as a raw recruit in 1914. The change in conditions was tremendous, so that it seemed to him now, in comparison, like a holiday camp. There were steel cupboards for kit, shower baths, drying rooms, central heating, suitcases, sitting rooms and, instead of the old cookhouse where he had spent days scraping tins that were encrusted with stale fat, there was now a kitchen worthy of a large hotel. Taken around by the Commanding Officer he was introduced to several mild, intelligent-looking, polite young men who turned out to be sergeant-majors. Gone were the purple faced, ferociously moustached types of his time with their hoarse and terrible blasphemies. Safe from their piercing glance he found that he missed them, that without their vast beery presences this was no longer the army. He spoke to a new recruit, found him calm and quiet, not objecting to anything but not welcoming anything. Asked if he found it a bit rough this young man replied that he didn't, but neither did he show any eagerness. In JBP's time they had found it very rough indeed, had had to sleep anywhere, eat anything, drill and work until they were ready to drop, and were much harried by their sergeant-majors. In spite of this, although they were cursed and protested, they were carried forward by great eagerness. In 1914 there had been a mad Bank Holiday air with flags, songs, cheers, drinks for the gallant boys, the women urging them on. He could see none of this in 1939. Then, men, because they were men, went blithely to the test of battle and their women, because they were not men, admired them for it. Now the war affected everyone, there was no blood sacrifice offered by the chosen few and the vicarious element had gone. Warfare on a scale that involves everybody's aunts and grandmothers strips it of glamour. He felt that the earlier war was the final occasion when a number of great powers, none of them dangerously threatened, produced a vast romanticised explosion of human belligerency. The later war was in the liberal tradition of Western Europe fighting for its life.

There is a piece written by Lce. Cpl. J. B. Priestley, Duke of Wellington's, in 1915 from Armentières, which was published in *The Phoenix*, 'The Magazine of a Command Depot', in January 1917, written, presumably, before he had become totally disenchanted with the scene, loathing the waste of life and its pointlessness.

A Little Nocturne

It was a gloomy, autumn evening, and we were on our way to the trenches, moving slowly and somewhat laboriously over the greasy cobblestones. We passed through the dirty, uninteresting streets of A....., passed the noisy crowds of children, the groups of English soldiers – nonchalantly attentive, the dismal looking houses with women standing about the doorsteps in strange subdued attitudes, the lighted windows of the cafes, passed on toward the firing line. And the shrill voices of the children, the deeper hum of conversation, the rattle of the carts, and all the other noises of the town pursued us as we slowly proceeded down the street; but it was a ghostly hour and the noises seemed like things heard in a dream, and the houses and the lights were only trembling on the verge of reality. The whole world was grey and ghostly, and the only reality was ourselves marching – marching –

We had come to the very edge of what we have called civilisation. In the distance we could see the bright flares from the firing line, as if the combatants were holding some fantastic carnival. There was open country on each side of the road, and such buildings that remained were partially ruined by shell fire, looking for all the world as if they had been gnawed by giant rats. There were no lights, no people, nothing but a strange unnatural silence, broken by the sound of our own footsteps and the distant roar of the guns. And then there loomed up on our left a row of houses, many of them with broken windows and roofs, all in darkness and apparently without inmates. But from out of one of them came to our ears, tuned to a greater sensitiveness by long night vigils in the trenches, the sound of a violin. A violin, played by an unknown hand in the darkness, and the tune that it played seemed a symbol of the spirit of our little company as we went down to the trenches, seemed a symbol of the spirit of all humanity as it strutted on its fantastic and fateful way under the calm and ageless stars! It was a tender, wistful little tune, full of cadences that began with a laugh and ended with a sob. Who the player could be was beyond speculation – who played in the darkness in those ruined houses? – who made such tender music on the fringe of hell?

I shall never know, and, indeed, what does it matter? It was enough to know that the Spirit of Romance walks abroad as of old, tinting the drab surfaces of our lives with the colours of sunsets and oceans, blowing a clarion-call that rings through the echoing spaces of our hearts. So we moved on through the darkness, strangely exalted by a little tune.

J. B. Priestley

Only a few pages further on a poem, *Death and The Soldier*, is initialled by JBP. It has a jaunty swing to it and an air of positive cheerfulness towards a soldier's end with Death declaring himself to be "ever a soldier's friend" and "always gentle with soldiers", the last of the seven verses ending with:

"I have marched with them into battle,
When they shared the last drop and crumb;
And I called them away so gently
From the tap of the little drum.
They marched away singing the glory of God
Who never made souls to lie under the sod."

If, as he sat through those August storms, he heard any echoes of gunfire in the rumble of thunder, it would surely be from behind the lines of that first Great War. The romance and eagerness of it gone, his whole direction was changed by it. Until war came he had never had the smallest ambition to live away from Bradford, the height of his hopes centred on that Dales cottage. The city offered him all he desired in the way of music, theatre, entertainment, interest and companionship, but the companions were all swept away. Bradford was no longer home for the survivor. If he waited now, sitting out the storm and recalling the roaring of the guns, he would see a lost world behind him.

"If you should mind the storm, you must come and sit with me." The world might be lost, but not him. There was never any sense of weakness in him, and if the thunder meant guns he did not shrink, but continued to sit, impassive, calm, the strength in him so deep that it could reach out to others. He offered it as protection if he felt a need.

I could imagine him, in that first war, holding the company together as he described in *Margin Released*, when, due to the absence of both the major and his senior lieutenant, he found himself in charge of a move to the Lille-Roubaix, Tourcoing area to do salvage work. It was after the Armistice, but conditions remained difficult. The company consisted of about eighty British troops, none of them fit for active service, and between six and seven hundred prisoners. He wrote:

"This was easily the most responsible job that had come my way in the Army, and it lasted for a couple of weeks or so and I enjoyed every moment of it, planning and working hard with several decent and conscientious senior non-coms. I cannot believe there was in me somewhere a master of logistics, a first-class staff officer; I make no claim to any peculiar merit; but I must set on record the fact that I did the job for once, in my four-and-a-half years of army knockabout, really enjoyed doing it. We had to march the company through Tourcoing, which had had years of German occupation, and its citizens lined the streets to curse and scream at our columns of prisoners, whom we had to guard not against possible escape but lynching."

In spite of the difficulties he got them all through successfully, but found on arrival that the site of their proposed camp was waterlogged and totally unsuitable. After an argument with the Army he succeeded in locating and setting up an alternative new camp in the ruins of a German hut encampment, the prisoners themselves setting to work to make it habitable. Clearly his success in this situation gave him some well-earned satisfaction, but it did not prevent him from ending his chapter on the war with:

"No awards for gallantry had come – or were to come – my way; but I was entitled to certain medals and ribbons. I never applied for them; I was never sent them; I have never had them. Feeling that the giant locusts that had eaten my four-and-a-half years could have them, glad to remember that never again would anybody tell me to carry on, I shrugged the shoulders of a civvy coat that was a bad fit, and carried on."

Storms pass, and he would settle again into his corner, bend over his typewriter, and work.

THE FREEMAN

Two widely separated places dominated 1973, for it was the year he discovered New Zealand and in which Bradford at last acknowledged his achievements by making him a Freeman of the city.

Recovery from his operation was neither as quick nor as complete as he would wish and he felt he needed some kind of challenge to liven him up or else, as he said, he would decline into "a fat-lazy-fireside old codger, demanding and unproductive". He sat there, hunched into his seat, growling to demonstrate this being. Visits were made to his surgeon in January and February and he was pronounced fit enough to take up this challenge if he was decided on it. New Zealand had already entered his mind in the previous December. He had visited New Zealand House then and was favourably impressed with his experience there, afterwards telling his publishers that he would like to write a book about that country, so the project grew. He had never been there before, although he had visited and not much cared for Australia a while prior to my joining him. New Zealand, however, was to enchant him and when he returned, safe in the establishment of age, he went so far as to announce that were he a younger man he might well consider going to live there. It not only enchanted him, it acted like a tonic on him, stimulating fresh enthusiasm and giving him something new to think about; quite an achievement for a man of his age who had travelled so widely. The outcome was *A Visit to New Zealand*, illustrated with paintings by himself and by various New Zealand artists. Both painting and writing had life in them, and although there were now and again melancholy references to this "final journey" there was also much humour.

Shortly before the Priestleys set out, A. D. Peters, his agent for fifty years, died. Receiving reports of his final illness, Mr Priestley came to tell me that Peters thought he was playing a game of bridge and was making calls for it. It seemed to JB a good way to go, having a game of something you enjoyed in life. The Memorial Service was on 1st March and on the 4th they set out for New Zealand. The result of his operation was that he had spells of feeling below par, but in between he was himself again, enjoying the whole thing keenly.

They flew via Boston where they spent two nights visiting friends, among them Susan Cooper. Another aircraft, with annoying piped music, took them to Los Angeles where they were met by the New Zealand vice consul for Southern California. By the time their Air New Zealand plane took off JB was feeling exhausted, was suffering from gripes and nausea and, unusual for him, had lost his appetite completely. The New Zealand staff began immediately to show the common sense and kindness that he encountered throughout his stay. As if they knew his ways already they produced pills. He did not know what they were but they made him feel better, which was just as well as on landing they were immediately confronted with a Television interview in the airport lounge.

The Ministry of Foreign Affairs in Wellington had assigned Derek Morris to take care of them. This man, who soon proved a friend, met them at the airport, drove them to their hotel, devised their itinerary, made all their arrangements and for some of the time accompanied and drove them himself, always keeping in touch when he was not present.

A night's sleep restored them sufficiently for him to attend to various business matters before going on to spend some fairly quiet days at Waitomo prior to starting on the full programme ahead of them. They broke off their journey to see the local museum at Hamilton, afterwards continuing another fifty miles to their destination.

Already he was taken with the quality of the New Zealand light, finding it a problem to paint because it was so different from the light he was accustomed to. The vegetation too delighted him. Everything seemed to grow to an enormous size. There were familiar flowers and trees, many imported, but they were bigger than he had ever seen before, and lush. Both town and country pleased him and among the earlier paintings that he did was a distant view of Wellington, its houses tumbling down the hills to converge beside the sea, all green, blue and dazzling white against a dark mountain. Although he himself was not totally satisfied with this painting, it was chosen to appear on the cover of his book and again inside it.

It was at Wellington that their itinerary gathered momentum and he gave a series of interviews to press, radio and television. He considered that they were conducted politely, without fuss, and with no trick questions thrown at him. It was here that they met the Prime Minister, Mr Norman Kirk, with whom they discussed the position of writers in New Zealand, conservation and the arts. Mr Kirk inscribed two books as gifts for them, a handsome art volume for JB and a rare out-of-print work on volcanoes for Mrs Priestley, which she afterwards had the misfortune to mislay in Auckland. In return JB later sent Mr Kirk a viewpoint he had sketched high above Waitomo. It was in Wellington too that, seeking suitable pictures for his book, he visited various galleries, did some painting himself, dined with academics, lunched with various notables, met members of the New Zealand Symphony Orchestra and gave a lecture on 'Duality in the Drama' at the University.

Their travel included a stay at a homestead in the mountainous sheep country, then Queenstown, Dunedin, Christchurch. It was at Dunedin airport that they discovered a strike on with no flights that day or the following. They had intended to fly to Christchurch where their old friend, Dame Ngaio Marsh, had arranged a dinner party for them that evening. The suggestion that he should charter a plane from the Aero Club astounded him, but he eventually agreed to it, watching with trepidation the tiny aircraft that approached. He said that it looked as if it was made from three deckchairs and was scarcely big enough to take them, let alone their luggage. Somehow all was got on board and, having braced himself for a bumpy ride he was relieved to discover that he was in for the best flight of his life, soaring smoothly above wonderful scenery "like a giant bee". They arrived in plenty of time for the "exceptionally good" dinner party where they met and made friends with Helen Holmes, already a friend of his eldest daughter.

After touring the North Island they went on to discover the delights of the South Island. He found Lake Taupo magical, enjoyed the thermal region where he was captivated by the effects of steam and fascinated by the pools of bubbling mud.

Whenever he travelled he was always eager to get home again, but for once there was a certain amount of reluctance in their departure from Auckland. New Zealand had so enchanted him that he would have liked to stay longer, see more of it, visit again the places he had got to know a little and see his new friends. They took off with a flurry of farewells and a telegram from Norman Kirk. If he had hoped to find a challenge to act as a restorative he had made the right choice. He returned revitalised, full of admiration for the New Zealanders and the way they had and were building their country, for the land itself. Derek Morris continued to send information required for the book, new friends sent news of themselves and details that he needed. Denis Glover, 'poet, publisher, typographer' whom he had met in Wellington sent amusing letters and compared the whitebait scale of his own mail to the whale dimensions that JB must receive. The visit was referred to always with pleasure and there was never a word of criticism for the country or its inhabitants. He was even heard to tell young people they should go there.

In his absence Bradford began to prepare a new event for him. "Go back to your roots," he would advise novice writers. "A writer needs roots from which to grow." His were in Bradford, strong roots in good ground that showed in his work. The people there were more real than any people would ever be again, his experiences were more vivid, for they had nurtured him. There was engraved in his mind a rich store of family scenes, aunts, uncles, characters comic and stern; there were all the fine buildings, occasions, ideas and the shop in Lumb Lane where he once found the window full of the heads of ventriloquists dolls and bought one. It was the place of youthful dreams that showed in his novel, *Bright Day*, with his early belief that somewhere people lived differently and more wonderfully in a better world. Bradford was deep in his heart but it had ignored him. He felt this keenly enough not to comment, shrugging as if he did not care. As late as 1967 out of a sub-committee of eight members considering candidates for the Freedom of the City only one had voted for Priestley. It was not until now, in 1973, that it was offered to him.

"They should have done it years ago," he remarked immediately, but there was pleasure there. Bradford commissioned David Hockney, another Bradfordian, to do a portrait of him. He sat for it in an armchair in his Albany drawing room and it hangs now in the Cartwright Museum.[17]

Congratulations poured in, including a wire from the unfailing Percy Monkman[18], two years older than JB, whose lifelong friendship with him began when they were still at school and used to play twenty a side soccer on the Belle Vue football pitch at Scotchman Road. Later, giving an interview to his local newspaper for his ninetieth birthday, Mr Monkman said of JB, "He was a very fair footballer, but afterwards he would bury his nose in the classics. He could recite great chunks by heart." He had spent his life as a bank manager, but was a talented artist and sent Mr Priestley cards every Christmas and birthday which were generally his own work. For many years he was president of the

Bradford Art Club. Replying to the wire JB told him, "oddly enough, just before receiving it I was looking with renewed admiration at the reproduction of your watercolour of Kirkland Lane that you sent me as a Christmas card." He made no reference to the honour but mentioned New Zealand and said what a country it was for painters. Mr Owen wrote from Hemel Hempstead and in return was told:

"Bradford had been messing about with the Freeman business for years and years and years and what should have been private committee proceedings has been constantly leaked to the Press, to my annoyance. Indeed, at one time I was so irritated that I said I would not accept the thing ever if it were offered to me, and if I recently changed my mind it was chiefly because I knew there were friends of mine in Bradford who had worked for a long time to obtain this honour for me."

As the date for the ceremony neared he grew more cheerful about it, pointing out to his daughter Sylvia that he understood he would be the last Freeman that Bradford could appoint due to the new regional distribution, so that the ceremony might be well worth seeing. He sent to Bradford the suggestion that they should provide a car for the journey from Kissing Tree to the Victoria Hotel, where he would pay for accommodation for himself, his wife, his two eldest daughters whose mother had come from West Riding, and his sister Winnie.

To me he said, "I first heard of this Freeman business soon after the war from Maurice Webb. He told me the local Tories had stopped it. I have always felt this must be unusual. After all, most men have political opinions of some kind or other, but the Establishment never did like me." He viewed the Establishment darkly as unfriendly shadows stalking him.

As the day grew close he showed mounting enthusiasm, sent requested photographs to Bradford, wrote a couple of articles and agreed to a number of interviews.

There were many activities besides, including meetings with Peter Hall of the National Theatre who wanted to do *Eden End*, with Ronald Harwood concerning *The Good Companions*, with Sir Bernard Miles about *An Inspector Calls*. There was Lord Clark's 70th birthday lunch at the Savoy, week-end visitors, including Laurens van der Post, his work on the New Zealand book, a Literary Luncheon at the

Dorchester. He opened the Walter de la Mare exhibition in Stratford, the poet having been a valued friend of his. There were plans for the annual event of Birthday and in time for this *The English* was to be published on September 10th, and also a new edition of *Delight*.

On 8th September "John Boynton Priestley, Esquire, MA (Cantab), LL. D. (St. Andrews), D.Litt. (Universities of Colorado, Birmingham, Bradford)" was "admitted to be an Honorary Freeman of the City" of Bradford and had a fine scroll to tell him so. After the civic lunch the Priestleys returned to Kissing Tree, but went up to London next day where he had a TV interview for the BBC. He was a guest on *Woman's Hour*, afterwards doing another recording with John Drummond again for the BBC.

He attended a dinner at the Savoy given by the publishers of his illustrated books, Rainbirds, and there was the birthday buffet too on the 13th. It was this birthday that Ralph Richardson mislaid somewhere, because he wrote on 8th November:

> "I have just come back from
> Australia – how are you?
> I saw a little Greek figure
> here today that I would like
> to offer you – in advance
> for your BIRTHDAY, it is a
> dancer but reminds me a
> bit of your TIME plays. Come
> to this shop if you can and
> see it but you can't take
> it away until the exhibition
> is over – BUT, if you DON'T
> like it they will change it
> for you for anything else."

The shop was Charles Ede Ltd., in Brook Street, and with the letter came a small cutting showing a picture of the Greek figure with the caption:

"Ritual dancer, her whole body enveloped in the himation which is drawn across to mask the lower part of her face and swirls out as she moves. Mid-4th century BC,

probably Boeotia. 6" (174mm)
For the type, see Louvre 1, pl. 45, C54-6"

Mr Priestley found the figure enchanting.

On September 17th the Priestleys again went up to Bradford for a Civic Gala performance at the theatre, and to recover from it all had a few days in Swaledale.

At about this time Henry Moore and his wife were commanded to come to lunch! JB had written to suggest it, but Henry Moore, living in Hertfordshire, had replied that due to work, shortage of time and energy he must regretfully decline for the present. Mr Priestley looked at me in astonishment.

"It isn't far!"

"It's not very close either."

"How long would it take him to drive here?"

"Around two hours I should think."

"That's nothing!"

I was ordered to get Mr Moore on the telephone, JB standing over me. He took the instrument and I heard the voice at the other end pleading fatigue, but this was put aside.

"It'll do you good – no distance at all!"

Protests were ignored.

"You can't be as busy as all that – and I *want* you to come."

Surprisingly the protests faded and the Moores drove up to lunch on 13th October. It was unusual for JB to urge invitations in this way, but Henry Moore was a Yorkshireman. Enlivened by the New Zealand air and the Freemanship, perhaps JB felt that Yorkshiremen could not be allowed fatigue.

There was further acclaim from Bradford when in 1975 the University there dedicated its fine new library to him.[20] The opening, on 18th October, was attended by the Chancellor, Harold Wilson, and to record the occasion there are some pleasing photographs of the two keen pipe smokers deep in conversation. There are also some photographs of him taken outside the building in which he is wearing his outdoor coat and his hat, exactly as I had pictured him walking beside me through Bradford.

FOUR SCORE

Reaching eighty calls for some special acknowledgement, and as the year of his eightieth birthday arrived, with him grumbling still about the world overlooking him, it appeared to me to bring many tributes and festivities. In that year the musical of *The Good Companions* opened at last, the National Theatre produced *Eden End* with Laurence Olivier directing it, and there was a revival of *Time and the Conways*. This had opened in Manchester the previous December with casting difficulties apparently overcome. Marion Lines played Kay. The production had gone ahead rapidly as it was only in October that Braham Murray wrote to JB about the cast, telling him, "I have found a marvellous girl called Marion Lines." Later that year *Dangerous Corner* opened at the Yvonne Arnaud Theatre in Guildford. This meant that in 1974 four of his plays were staged in mainline theatres.

JB had felt for some time that *Eden End* should be put on by either the National or the Royal Shakespeare Theatre, so that when Laurence Olivier expressed a wish to do the play as a birthday tribute he was well pleased. The cast included Leslie Sands as Dr Kirby and Joan Plowright as Stella Kirby. The production involved meetings, telephone calls and letters so numerous that when he wrote on 28th January Lord Olivier began, "You will think I have ambitions to be a pen pal."

It was fitting that the end of winter visit was to his well-loved Arizona. Before the war it had prompted his book *Midnight on the Desert* and he had referred to it ever since in terms of praise. He was now to do a piece on it for *The New York Times* and another, longer one, for *Travel and Leisure*. Having arrived there he should have been revitalised, but unfortunately he suffered some kind of flu or chest infection and became quite ill. The Priestleys returned on 27th February and after a week he had a chest x-ray. Much to our relief it showed no damage and the following evening he was able to attend the dinner of the Society of Yorkshiremen at the London Zoo.

On 21st March he presented the prizes at the Bradford School of Nursing, paused briefly at Kissing Tree House and went on to London where he lunched with his publisher, gave an interview to *The New York Times* and saw a preview of *Eden End*. Back at Kissing Tree he wrote about Alistair Cooke's *America* for *Travel and Leisure*, and on

4th April he was again in London for the opening of *Eden End*.

All this Theatre relieved his mind for a time of the problem of money. It was not that there was any real problem, but he always foresaw that there might be, quoted well-known people who had gone bankrupt because they had suddenly received enormous demands for income tax which they could not meet. At any moment, he felt, his royalties might drop and there be no demand for him. The cost of postage, too, roused his ire, and although they generally got a reply from him, he was justifiably annoyed by people sending him letters with queries in them and not sending the postage.

"Have they sent stamps?" he would ask.

"I'm afraid not."

"So I'm expected to pay for the answer! What do *you* think I should do?"

I would shift mutely.

"You think I'd better write back all the same I suppose. It would make them happy. I must have spent a *fortune* on people who don't bother about sending stamps. What it's like for an author who has only a book or two and gets £10 a week if he's lucky I don't like to imagine."

"Perhaps they don't get much mail."

"Authors are appallingly badly paid. Do you realise that?"

I assured him that I did, although I did not think that he was one of them. I was aware, however, that even secretaries were better paid than the average author.

"Do I have a private aeroplane?"

"No."

"Do I have a yacht?"

"No."

"So you can't describe me as living in luxury, can you?"

Their house was enormous and there was Albany, but I understood what he meant. The house needed a staff to run it, a gardener, and he needed me. With so much space, heating costs were high. I could quite see that his income was accounted for without indulging in aeroplanes, so I shook my head.

"I'm not a rich man. I do not travel in a Rolls-Royce even."

For years he had made me feel that at any moment he might have to sell all he had to make ends meet. He himself was convinced that he only managed to scrape along, and his talent for drama convinced me too, so that I listened with the utmost alarm to his tales of the simple life ahead and impending poverty. Eventually though I began to think that his fears were groundless.

"Income tax and postage," he would say. "The Government take it away by any means they can think of. If I went abroad to live I might be a rich man, but not here."

"Have you ever thought of living abroad?" I saw before me sunlit shores and the faithful secretary.

"No, I have not. I will not be driven out of my country by the tax man. I have always lived in England and I intend to go on living in England, even if they drain my blood!"

As there seemed no suitable reply I simply nodded. Whenever any kind of tax was mentioned there was an outcry. He took tax demands as a personal insult and behaved as if nobody else, myself included, paid tax. If they did, he was positive that it was not as much as he paid, and if it was not as much he did not seem to connect it with the fact that they must earn less proportionately. There was one occasion, however, when on reading of some wealthy pop star who had gone into tax exile, he surprised me by saying that if you earned your money in a country then you should pay your taxes in it and not run away. This was a sentiment he never again repeated.

He had the curious idea that money coming in to him was infinitesimal, but if it was going out from him then the sums were vast. Therefore, he considered his royalties modest, and when I told him at the end of each year how much he had earned in it he was sure I had got it wrong somewhere. On the other hand, the low pay of his staff was, he thought, more than adequate, although as he signed the pay cheques he remarked more than once, amused by it but I did not find it madly hilarious, "I'm a mean sod!" Apart from this, everything else for which he had to pay was, he considered, charged for at enormous rates and must be making huge profits for the sellers. He would say, resentfully, "This is far more than anyone ever pays me!"

Happily, with the money coming in from so much Theatre, his alarms were lulled and he was able to enjoy the prospect of eighty in peace.

A local tribute was a *J. B. Priestley* exhibition at the Shakespeare Centre, which involved much rummaging around and going through things. It was during this that he came upon a first edition of a book by J. M. Barrie which, hoping it was still of value, he sent to his stepdaughter, Angela de Hartog. The exhibition was opened on 6th July by his friend J. W. Lambert, Literary Editor of *The Sunday Times*. Included was a display of his novels, plays, essays, travel books and social histories, examples of his wartime radio broadcasts, a notebook containing some of his ideas, the original manuscript of his latest book, many photographs spanning his lifetime and the chair in which he sat to write *The Good Companions*. There was also the musical cigarette box from which he got the idea for his play *Dangerous Corner*. At the end of the year the exhibits were included in an Exhibition of J. B. Priestley and the Bradford of his Day which was held in that city at the Wool Exchange. Percy Monkman was among the first visitors. JB himself went up to see it in the following January when he was given lunch by the Lord Mayor. He was also taken to see the Central Library.

Another birthday activity was to be guest speaker at the Shakespeare Lunch in April, then in July he flew out to Canada to lecture at McMaster University's Shakespeare Seminar. Aptly he and his wife stayed at the Windsor Hotel in Stratford, Ontario. He had warned them in advance:

"I absolutely refuse to sit through *King John*, having left the one here at the interval. I know yours is different, but I do not like this play and no longer enjoy sitting in theatres as a way of passing the evening."

He returned from Canada on 1st August in time to entertain week-end visitors two days later, among them Ngaio Marsh, who was over from New Zealand, and the Ronald Harwoods. Dame Ngaio was a favourite of his and after her visit he wrote to ask Diana Collins[20] to include her in the music party she was giving to honour his birthday.

Since early spring there had been recordings taken of interviews with him and on 13th August he went to Leeds to record a version of *The World of J. B. Priestley* for Yorkshire Television for a programme that lasted an hour-and-a-half. As well as himself and Leslie Sands the cast included Robert Stephens, Michael Cashman, Noel Dyson, Paddy Glynn, Frank Middlemass, Michael Newell, Philip Stone and Marcia Warren. Reviewing it in *The Times* of September 5th, Stanley Reynolds began:

"The highbrows have always seen Priestley as a lowbrow and the lowbrows have thought of him as a highbrow. He has also been cursed as a middlebrow, that most pernicious and asinine of labels. Can J. B. Priestley possibly be in fashion now?"

He ended with:

"...the bits and pieces of the novels and plays took up most of the time from 8.30 to 10 o'clock and they were brilliantly done, done as well, if not better, than the BBC's previous adaptations of Priestley. We were also spared any showbiz gush about the grand old man celebrating his eightieth birthday. Priestley is obviously too much of a hard-nosed Yorkshireman to stand for any of that."

Above the review the page was dominated by Himself smiling like a contented toad (I like toads) beneath the sweep of his broad black hat. Those hats were very much a part of him and were seized upon by photographers, written about by journalists. Even when hanging tidily on their pegs in the cloakroom they evoked him.

Leeds was followed by two days at home and then it was London again for a reception for his book at New Zealand House, the Collins coming to dine at Albany afterwards. On the day after that he recorded an interview for television with Robert Robinson. There were then a few quietish days and we were into September, the telephone ringing with queries, congratulations and requests for interviews. A photographer came from *The Sunday Times*. On the 8th a production of *The Linden Tree* was the Sunday evening 'Play of the Month' on BBC television. Andrew Cruickshank played Professor Linden, Margaret Tyzack his wife. JB wrote to thank them the following morning, telling Andrew Cruickshank that he had been "very strong and sincere", Margaret Tyzack that her "beautifully controlled performance was just right for TV." He also wrote to the director, Moira Armstrong, saying that in spite of some necessary cuts he thought most of it came through very well. Praising the two stars he went on to remark that the casting throughout was good and ended:

"...altogether a good TV reproduction of a play that cannot have been easy to do. Please accept my congratulations."

In the first stage version long ago Professor and Mrs Linden had been played by Sir Lewis Casson and his wife, Sybil Thorndike. Having seen the TV version Dame Sybil wrote to tell JB how much she had enjoyed it. He replied that he liked to think of her watching it and remembering how "wonderfully good Lewis was in the part".

The *Radio Times* took up his birthday with enthusiasm. It carried a full page cover picture of him seated against a background of daffodils that matched his tie. He popped up here and there inside and ended with a three page interview with David Pryce-Jones. There was enough Priestley work on that week to make a festival. As well as Sunday's *Linden Tree* there was a Radio 4 broadcast of *Eden End* on Saturday, *Priestley at 80* on Radio 3 on Thursday, a programme on his life and work presented by Paul Bailey with Phyllis Bentley, Sir Arthur Bliss, Peter Hall, David Hughes, Pamela Hansford Johnson, Henry Moore, Benedict Nightingale, Sir Ralph Richardson and Dame Sybil Thorndike contributing. The Robert Robinson interview went out on BBC 2 Television on the birthday itself, Friday 13th. This presented no threat to him as he considered the 13th to be his lucky date.

No birthday was complete without the publication of a book and this time it was *Outcries and Asides*, a collection of short, informal pieces. They included a few memories of his youth and that much dwelt-on topic, the gigantic high tea. There was also a grouse about Nature which he had already tried on me, and probably everyone else.

"When you are old Nature no longer has any use for you and so she plays you up."

I thought that she did that at any time and perhaps my thought showed as he then stabbed with a forefinger.

"You wait and see. There's no escape! Nature comes and sniffs you out, decides that you're no longer any use to her, and she ATTACKS. A pain here, a twinge there, a good dose of stiffness to make you want to sit and do nothing. Nature likes you to be young, doing your job, having children, doing the thing she intends you to do for her benefit. She has no time for old age, for idleness."

"You're not idle!"

"Perhaps she resents me carrying on after my time. She'll finish me off soon I expect. That's what she's waiting for."

"You don't look like a man who might be finished off!"

"Well I feel like it sometimes."

The house was by now fairly bursting with a sense of occasion. It was a sense that had been there all through the year as an undertone, inevitable with the advance interviewing and preparation there had been, but when the actual week arrived it had grown to a crescendo, post pouring in, gifts being left, food being prepared for the family luncheon party. Eighty was something to celebrate, especially if you were born at a time when the expectation of life was fairly modest. JB smiled from the cover of *The Listener*, from the pages of newspapers. There were occasional idiots who asked in surprise, "Is he still alive?" With so much evidence of him about I wondered how they managed not to notice it.

On Wednesday, the 11th, the household departed for London and JB went to the first of three sittings he had agreed to with Paul Vincze the medallion maker. That evening the Collins gave their musical party for him. The 12th began with an interview at Broadcasting House, went on with a visit from Heinemann's publicity man, and in the evening there was a dinner for 120 guests given for him at the Savoy by Heinemann's. Speeches were made by Paul Johnson, Ralph Richardson and Evelyn Ames, JB's longstanding American friend, over for the occasion. He himself followed his custom of keeping his own speech short, ending with:

"I've had a long run and done what I could. If I'd been better it would have been better; if I'd been worse it would have been worse. I've done what I could."

The birthday itself was a family affair, although he managed to be at his appointment with Paul Vincze at half past ten; this after a fairly late night and the stir of the dinner. About twenty members of his family gathered for the buffet lunch at Albany.

He enjoyed the role of family man, perhaps enjoying it more when it was all over. He could grumble then, and enjoy not having to look happy, for he complained that having to look as if he was having a splendid time immediately put him off having it. He had had a splendid time on this occasion though and had enjoyed it hugely. Back at Kissing Tree he sat comfortably against his sheepskin rug and began to answer all the correspondence, grumbling that there was too much of it. Percy Monkman had painted and sent him a small picture, 'Back Lane, Buckden', with a cottage, tree, hills behind and two lively looking lambs in the foreground. He was thanked for "a delightful little watercolour". The size of the mail became too much for him in the end and he was obliged to dictate a standard letter for all general telegrams and another for people other than friends.

He had arranged the purchase of a picture for Ralph Richardson which was to be called for. He wrote to this friend:

"I hope by this time you will have collected 'The Dry Point' by Segonzac and hung it beside its companion. It represents a gesture of thanks for what you said on the radio programme and at the dinner afterwards.

You may be interested to know that at this very moment I am writing something about you, the point being that I am writing a book, rather against time, called *Particular Pleasures*, which is divided into four sections – Painting, Music, Acting, Clowning. For the Acting section I am doing about 20 brief accounts, running to about 700 words or so, of actors and actresses whose work I have enjoyed, and of course you are high among them. This explains why there has been no chance of our meeting in London just now, simply because I must stay down here and get on with this book before old age overtakes me and I lose all will, energy and memory..."

He turned then to work again. Stan Barstow had written with a suggestion that he should adapt *Bright Day* for Television, considering that it would make a fine serial. Mr Priestley replied that he gave his permission, only stipulating that it should be done for either the BBC or ITV network and not just for one or two channels. There was work ahead of him yet, more interviews, too many in his opinion, more Radio and Television, more plays revived, first nights to attend, applause to respond to, more to be written; old age had not yet overtaken him. He had written in *Outcries and Asides* in connection with Nature:

"Life at my age is like staying in a certain Scottish castle, with Lady Macbeth smiling her goodnight and adding sweetly she hopes I have everything I want."

This may have been a cry against hubris, for will and energy were there. There was a decade yet ahead of him, and now he went to his desk, stuffed his ears, contemplated a fresh sheet of paper and began to type furiously.

A FEW ASIDES

He complained about dull days and about afternoons, which did not appeal to him. In endless rain he grew impatient, finding it put him off work and he could not settle, causing him to pace about, peer through windows, watching the steaming glass and the trees dripping, frustrated by it. Afternoons also frustrated him and he would come into my room, hoping for solace.

"The afternoon is a dull time."

"Why don't you read?"

"I don't want to."

"Go for a walk?"

"I have done."

It was like dealing with a petulant child on these occasions and I had no answer for him.

"I have never liked the afternoons. They seem to hang about with no purpose. Don't you find that?"

I replied with some regret that afternoons did not bother me, did not stretch out as they did for him, made further useless suggestions and accepted that whatever I said would make no difference. In the mornings he was occupied with work, in the evenings there was the routine of early work, a drink, dinner and then television or some other form of entertainment. Sometimes in the afternoons he played his gramophone, he would read a little, walk the long length of the hall in search of post, very occasionally play the piano, and for a brief period he took to painting old cigar boxes, giving them away as Christmas or birthday presents. Always in the afternoons he came to speak to me, sometimes at length and sometimes briefly. He said that he enjoyed my company.

Another area in which I failed to find an answer for him was in the matter of quenching his thirst. He might come and stand over me, dismal, or raise his head from the book he was reading on his seat on the sofa.

"I've got an awful thirst – a dry mouth. What I need is a drink of something sharp – not water, not alcohol, not squash. What do you suggest I ought to have?"

"How about a squeeze of lemon in soda water?"

"No."

"Lime cordial in soda?"

"That might help, but it isn't really what I want."

"Tonic water?"

"No."

Fresh orange juice would mean more oranges than were available, and it was not right in any case. Apple juice was not the answer. The drink he sought seemed to be another of the elusive treasures in his life and he would turn despondently to one of my suggested stop-gaps, making do with it. I wish I had then discovered Perrier water because it might just have been the right solution.

Another blight on his life was my hair, or at least the cutting of it. Fine and straight, but at the same time with a nasty tendency to fuzziness, it has filled me with lifelong resentment. The easy way out was to grow it long, set it on rollers to dry, and tie it back in a tail that formed two ringlets, using chiffon bows to soften it and of course covering it with scarves at any sign of damp or wind. He liked the result of my efforts, constantly admired the bows and said they suited me. Perhaps they carried him back to the days before 1914. After many years with him though I decided on a new image. A friend had just returned from Manchester where she had had her own straight hair cut most becomingly. I was so impressed that I decided I would go all the way there myself. It would be worth it to look like she did.

He said, "You can't have your hair cut!"

Lips pursed, I assured him I was going to.

"But I like it like that."

It wasn't his hair, I thought indignantly.

For days he moaned about it, said I should leave it as it was, wondered how he would get through life without my two ringlets, seemed to think my hair was his business and that I was staging a mutiny.

At last the day arrived. My husband, eager to see this new, more youthful, freer modern image, drove me to Manchester. Isobel did not have to do anything with her hair. It just fell into place as mine would do in the future. I sat and let them get on with it.

The result was so terrible that I had indeed found freedom. There was nothing that could possibly make it, or me, look worse. I strode through the wind and rain that prevailed that day, liberated. But the sight of myself in shop windows made me feel sick with horror, and I could not refrain from peering at them, hoping it was not as bad as I thought it was. My husband said nothing at all, but what would JB say?

In readiness for disaster I had bought heated curling tongs, and once home struggled in vain with them. The short, straight fuzz slithered away from them and, gulping, I had to make the best of the disaster, going to work the next morning in a state of real dread.

He looked at it impassively, said eventually, "You look like an intellectual horse," but not unkindly, and never referred to it again, for which I was grateful.

In time the disaster grew again, but I continued to leave it loose and found a perm that would give it some curl. He, who had constantly admired the bows and ringlets, never again mentioned my hair so I suppose he still felt I should tie it back for his benefit.

It is surprising how often other writers quote him or refer to him. Even this week, in speaking of the death of Henry Moore [1986], *The Daily Telegraph* said he had "the look of a four-square creation by J. B. Priestley" and a biography being currently read by a friend, as well as a book about Yorkshire being read by my husband, both bring him in. He is so much a part of the English scene and has even brought new words into the language, for it was he who coined Admass to describe a system which turns people into nothing more than consumers. His descriptive phrases turn up not only in writing but in talk, on radio and television. Once when I remarked on it to him he smiled modestly, but on another occasion when something I was reading quoted him and I again referred to the way he so often appeared he replied, "And quite right too!" He seems to have covered every subject and left a legacy of lifelong reading, of compassion, concern, humour, irony, wonder at the beauty of the world and good sound sense.

AWARD FOR MERIT

"I have never accepted any honours."

It was on a lukewarm summer afternoon a year or two after I arrived that he first said it. He was signing letters on the billiard table when he broke off and turned to me.

"I was offered a knighthood and I turned it down. Later they offered me a peerage and I turned that one down too."

Mentally I tried 'Lord Priestley', but it did not jell.

"I have written against honours, and I never write one thing and do another. It wouldn't have been possible for me to accept them and I would not want to. What do they mean? They're often awarded for the wrong reasons and I want none of them."

But there was one honour that he did respect, would accept with pride, and that was the Order of Merit. Created by Edward VII as the highest honour he could bestow it was limited to twenty four holders. Writing of this in his book *The Edwardians* JB said of the king that he,

"...created an Order of Merit that really was – and still is – an order of merit, not just another title and ribbon to reward contributors to party funds or to compensate politicians kicked out of the Cabinet."

The award remains the personal gift of the Sovereign and no recommendation is required for it from any Minister. It is given for exceptionally meritorious service in the Armed Services or towards the advancement of Art, Literature, Science and Learning.

The years passed and he became older. Readers often wrote, not knowing what he had turned down, saying that it was a shame he had not been given some official recognition for his work. Often he was told that he deserved a knighthood. That one so highly respected honour seemed to be passing him by. Sometimes now he was a little hunched, a little slow, his footsteps shuffling down the hall. It had always been his habit to go down to peer into the letterbox, searching for mail, complaining that the afternoon post was always irregular or that there had not been any, convinced sometimes that his mail had been taken elsewhere and that someone was sitting on it. There were occasions when he seemed to be dejected, complained again that the world had forgotten him. And then it came.

Surely that letter that arrived on 19th October 1977 from Buckingham Palace must, if only for a short while, have made him feel that the treasure he awaited so long had arrived? At last the one award he would accept, the one that meant so much to him, was offered. Even then it had taken its time about coming to him, having gone first to Albany and being a week in its forwarding. It reached him in the early morning, before I arrived. He announced the news as I entered the room and then walked to the window to peer at the view outside as if he had never seen it before and was wholly taken with it. Until an official announcement the matter was still confidential and only his household were told. We hugged it close and rejoiced for him. When his long scrutiny of the scene from the window had satisfied him, he turned to the room and said, very casually:

"As this year is the 75th anniversary of the institution of the Order the Queen is inviting all the Members and their wives to attend a Service in the Chapel Royal on 17th November and lunch at the Palace afterwards. Make sure you put it in the diary."

I assured him I would not forget!

The announcement was made the following week. His new fellow members of the elite twenty four were to be Lord Franks, Lord Todd and Sir Frederick Ashton. The newspapers all carried pictures of him, mostly in various hats. It was his big beret that he wore when he painted that was used in our local Stratford Herald. When they telephoned to ask what he thought about it he replied, "I am very proud. It makes me very happy. I suppose it is because I am very old and have done a lot of work. Anyway, I deserve it."

The editorial in the *Bradford Telegraph and Argus* said:

"The reluctance of Mr J. B. Priestley to accept 'establishment honours' was for long years matched by the reluctance of his native Bradford to bestow on him the one honour he ranked above all – the Freeman of his city.

It was that typical Bradford cussedness which was responsible for the years rolling by without Mr Priestley becoming a Freeman. It is not surprising. It was a clash of Bradfordians and J.B.P. could be as cussed as the councillors.

Happily, four years ago, the cussedness melted. He was named a

Freeman and was as proud of the honour as Bradford was proud of him.

Now at the age of 83, he becomes a member of the Order of Merit – a rare and special distinction for eminent people and the most prestigious of all honours which do not carry the addition of a title.

He is a most worthy recipient of the Order, and on behalf of all our readers we send him our warm and sincere congratulations.

Of all of Bradford's notable men of past and present, one other name can be weighted against that of John Boynton Priestley. We refer to composer Frederick Delius who became a Companion of Honour. That is a title which, with *The Good Companions* in mind, would have aptly clothed Mr Priestley.

But, eminent as that distinction is, the Order of Merit outranks it, and we can now fairly claim that J. B. Priestley is Bradford's most famous son.

The massive output of his pen continues to delight a world-wide readership and to captivate playgoers in every corner of the globe. That is merit enough."

Obviously the editor of the *Telegraph and Argus* did not know that JB had also turned down Companion of Honour.[21]

In *The Author*, the journal of the Society of Authors, was:

"The appointment in October of J. B. Priestley to the Order of Merit must have given pleasure to all British writers ... There is also the pleasure of observing, at a time when many people understandably feel that the honours system has been devalued, one state award that really *is* an honour going to a leading member of a profession that is, officially, oddly undervalued..."

That week something else pleasant happened for him when his play *Laburnum Grove* opened at the Duke of York's in London, with Arthur Lowe in the leading role.

When he returned from seeing the play he began the task of thanking everyone who had written to him, telling Dr Edwards at Bradford University, "Bradford University is close to my heart and if it welcomes anything that has happened to me then I am delighted." Percy Monkman, as usual one of the first to send congratulations, was told, "I think that 'the great debt' that Bradfordians owe to me, as you suggest, is far smaller than my debt to Bradford and Bradfordians." Ralph Richardson was thanked with, "Thank you very much for your toastmaster piece of October 25th – the most original and perhaps the most welcome of all congratulatory message I have had. How I wish we were working on a play again!"

As the day of the ceremony neared he began to make his customary careful arrangements, asking me to order International to meet them at Euston and take them to the Palace, where the car was to wait for them. It was to collect them again from Albany four days later to take them to the Chapel Royal, wait, and then drive them on to the Palace for the lunch. These instructions were exact as to time and sequence, for there was no vague writer air about JB. When he thought of a thing he never left loose ends. When the London car had been attended to I was to find the time of trains from Coventry to Euston, which were every half hour, and ask Carters to drive them to the station. He was again careful about the time, allowing extra in case there were any traffic delays, discussing it at length with me who tended to err on the side of caution. Between us we were sure to have enough time in hand for him to smoke a pipe and read a paper! He did not object to this; it was last minute hustles that he found upsetting.

The big day was Monday, 14th November. They returned to Kissing Tree on Thursday when he proudly laid out the insignia for us all to see. He had found the Queen "very likeable indeed", which put her in his top bracket of popularity.

He was anxious then that we should appreciate that the O. M. was not like other honours but went with his name. He was now J. B. Priestley, O. M., and it should be put on his headed paper. I was able to assure him that it had already been ordered, but sometimes he used to come to look at it, as if he feared it might somehow get rubbed off. That most valued award was a source of pleasure to him for the rest of his days. Celebrations for it went on into the following spring when his club, the Savile, gave a dinner for him. It proved the best attended they had ever given. Jack Longland took the chair and David Hardman, John Hadfield and Ralph Richardson spoke on their various collaborations with him in their own fields.

He remarked occasionally that they had only given him the award because he was too old to hold it for long and they would be able to give it to someone else, but I think he would have been put out if the response had not been a smile of disagreement.

AT KISSING TREE

Under his dressing table his slippers are laid in a row as if they still expected him. They are small, neat slippers.

Once, as we sat and talked, we somehow got onto the subject of skin. Then it was that he rolled up his sleeves and told me to feel his arm. It was smooth as silk. Next he gleefully rolled up his trouser leg.

"Feel that! Nothing rough there!" He was obviously proud of it. "Soft as a woman's – not that I'm lacking masculinity!"

I ran a cautious hand between knee and ankle and agreed that it felt like satin. We sat and admired this really remarkable skin and then he rolled down the trouser and put back his foot into the small slipper.

Besides his slippers there are still the books. His bedroom is full of murder and mystery. On his bedside table when he died was John Le Carré's *Smiley's People* and Arnold Bennett's *Imperial Palace*. The shelves by the window are packed with his favourites, Rex Stout, Ngaio Marsh, Agatha Christie, Ross Macdonald, Georges Simenon, Margery Allingham, Elizabeth Ferrars, Hillary Waugh. He said they entertained him at night when he could not sleep.

"A good detective story, and here I am talking about the worth-while stuff, not the rubbish, is in its own way a picture of life spiced with an element of puzzle. Unlike many modern novels it has a tale to tell. When I am in bed, wide awake as I often am, I don't want to read a book that is full of somebody's deep psychological insight. I want to escape and be entertained, but at the same time I want something that will give me some suggestion of real life. A good detective story does this. It gets away from the muddle of the world into its own tidy little problem and its own neat solution. It is an excellent form of fiction in its own right and tends to be underrated."

Eric Ambler's *Mask of Dimitrios* and C. M. Bowra's *The Romantic Imagination* lie on the chest of drawers. There are a few books on the shelves that are not detective stories; *Brideshead Revisited* is one of them.

On the back of the wardrobe doors his ties still hang; they are mainly yellow. Inside, the plum velvet jacket hangs, as if awaiting a dinner party, alongside the work-a-day tweeds, and there is his dark blazer. For rare heatwaves there is a light linen suit which made him look like a tea planter, or a character from Somerset Maugham.

On the shelf facing the bed is his wife's silver framed photograph. Anxious for me to appreciate it he used to say that he had a very good marriage. Beside her is his daughter Mary, posed with her violin. Most of the pictures which line the walls are his own work.

The dressing table top and first drawer of it contain a feast of pills, powders, potions and some old passports.

"When I was young you didn't need passports or visas. The world was more civilised then and a man with a liking for liberty could breathe in it. In my late teens I visited five foreign countries and the only preparations I made were to pack a rucksack and put a few sovereigns into my purse. There was no need for traveller's cheques. You could change a sovereign anywhere."

He had already told me about his early trip in a butter boat to Copenhagen when he also explored a part of northern Denmark and southern Sweden, saying that none of the vast travel he had done since could touch it.

"I used to breakfast in a shaded courtyard watching the pretty girls who worked behind the windows opposite. They occasionally smiled at me! There were more pretty girls in the Tivoli Gardens where I spent my evenings. It was all just looking though! I never got any closer, never even exchanged a word with any of them!"

That was in the June of 1913. The following June he went to Amsterdam where he saw the Rembrandts and Vermeers, afterwards travelling on by train to Cologne.

"I spent a week walking in the Rhine valley, staying at little inns where I sometimes played the piano. I lived richly then on a few shillings a day. I returned via Brussels and Antwerp and sailed to Goole." The forefinger came into action. "All that, remember, without any of this passport nonsense. It has always amazed me that when the passport system was retained after the war nobody protested. If you cannot leave your country without a passport, then your government has you completely at its mercy."

Brought up with passports I could not imagine a world without them and murmured about illegal immigrants and crooks and spies. These, he replied, were always able to get false papers, but my doubts remained.

In his bathroom the tube of shaving cream, always "the lather kind, not the brushless", half squeezed, lingers. There are his throw-away plastic razors and the odd remedy for ills. He was ready to share these.

"Try one of my throat tablets. They're very strong and effective."

Ever polite I would gaze gloomily into the proffered box, wondering about age and the state of the contents, take a pill and bravely put it into my mouth.

In early days, when my back troubled me, he suggested that I should try his sun lamp in the lunch hour. It took a good deal of setting up in Gertrude's bedroom and I was not at all sure that I was getting it right; nor was Gertrude. Eventually the lamp disappeared into the attic. In those days he also had one of those steam machines in which you sat with your head poking out and a towel round it. It was already there when I arrived so that, not being involved in the purchase of it, I was not aware of the reason for having it. Only very occasionally did he use this, Gertrude clucking exasperation about towels and damp. It was a great performance, not that I actually saw it but the preliminaries were noticeable and he was long absent. That too did not appear to endure and vanished into a distant corner of the house.

His study is different now because the piano is no longer there. It has gone to his granddaughter, Beth. It was seldom used, but very occasionally in the afternoons he would play it, complaining that he was out of practice and could only bungle things. The peace of the house was, at these times, sometimes shaken with a sudden explosion of ragtime.

It is in his desk, the big one by the window in which he keeps things, that I find small signs of his vulnerability. Underneath that self-assured exterior is perhaps a note of shyness, a need for praise. There is a drawer in which he has kept letters that have meant something. They have come from people he cared about or whose opinion he valued and they are spread over a long period. His son-in-law tells him that the best thing that ever happened in his life was marrying his daughter Barbara, and the second best "was coming to know you a little". Susan Cooper's parents write to say, "We are always delighted when she makes time to come and see you both. She seems to charge her batteries again. You will never know quite how much you have helped and continue to enrich her life…" He has kept Susan Cooper's own letters clipped together in his working desk; for her he had a deep affection. A letter from William S. Trout to Mrs Priestley begins with, "And bless JBP for <u>being</u>. Across some black years of grief and loneliness, he has been the shadow of a great rock." Most of the letters are from friends thanking him for a recently published book, or for a play of his just seen, or just for his friendship. T. S. Skillman, whose book *Good Old Age* JB had, at the author's request, read and commented on, writes:

"Let me tell you again what an influence you have had on my life. That wind that blew across the countryside in *The Good Companions* must have refreshed every Englishman who read it. Your *English Journey* must have had great political impact. Your plays, of course, are unique. I remember a textbook on play writing, written by a most successful playwright (whom I know well, but can't at the moment name) who came back always to your techniques as those of "the old master" – so perfect as to be invisible to all but the expert. But it was the idealism in things like *They Came to a City*, and some of your poignant short stories involving time, that always moved me."

Most of his letters he gave me to file or destroy when replied to; a few were to be divided into two boxes, one for family and one for well-known people. The latter were to go eventually to Texas University. Because he knew how I admired them, he gave me some of those he received from Ralph Richardson to keep for myself. Now it is my job to go through the desk and sort things – discover what it was he chose to keep there. No sign here of any hard-headed Yorkshireman. He could be hurt, offended, could withdraw into a wounded silence. He could be moved by a word of praise from someone he cared about, whose opinion he valued. He could be pleased, pretending not to be, when a friend published an appreciative article about him, praised his work sincerely and sensitively, or simply thanked him.

There is a letter here from Noel Coward dated 30th September 1941:

"Dear JB,

I read 'Out of the People' the other day and thought it so clear and accurate and above all so full of warm, human common sense that I felt I must write and tell you so. It seems to give the impetus to individual thought which is so badly needed in this country.

You really are doing a magnificent job and I am sure many thousands of ordinary English people are deeply grateful to you.

Yours ever,"

There was another letter, written in 1969, that I recall him reading. It is long, four pages of foolscap typed in double space. The sender is another Yorkshire writer, Malachi Whitaker.

"That's a good letter," he said, passing it over. "Read it and give it back to me. It's a great pity she stopped writing."

A year younger than himself she had gone to the same Belle Vue School and had stood on the steps to peer into the boys' playground. She reminded him of the night-soil men's huge carts whose creaking wooden wheels woke everyone, said that her family were among the first to install a bathroom and people came from miles around asking if they could pull the chain. Once, she told him, she had met him for tea in Bradford, at his invitation, but, "I was an ass. Not interesting a bit, though I can be even yet." Miserably worried because she was late, Hopkinson's car having broken down, "an impossible thing in the thirties, we thought we were so last minute in Bradford, didn't we?" she had arrived in a state. Her husband was talking with JB, but she was so disintegrated that she could hardly remember it. She ended by saying she wrote simply because she liked him and was not angling for an answer. This did not prevent her receiving one and they corresponded occasionally afterwards. He prized her letters.

The drawer is full of appreciation, gratitude, people telling him how much he means to them whether they are friend or stranger, famous or unheard of. They speak of the pleasure or the depth of insight he has given them, thank him for speaking for them, for his good sound sense. Sometimes he would take a letter from this drawer and read it and I wonder now if he found consolation here in low moments. Some of them thank him for support when it was badly needed.

I remember now how he was when my mother died, how when I rang to tell him there was so much care in his voice, such kindness and sympathy.

He might call himself "a mean old sod", but where he met need he responded generously. When a young girl in the village needed a kidney machine he gave £500 towards it – a considerable sum then.

There was a time with me, too, when he gave support. It was in 1977. I had an experience then that soured my world, and I know it changed me. Although I did not speak of it to him he was keenly aware of it and used to come and stand close to me, watching anxiously, giving me openings to talk of it, tell me how fortunate he was to have my company.

"Is everything all right with you?"

"Yes, thank you."

"You deserve to be happy."

"Thank you."

He said one day, "You have been with me eight years now and never for one moment of that time have I tired of your company. You have always been interesting and you have a lovely personality. I really do not know what I'd do without you."

The wound in me was so deep that words could not touch me, but I remembered them.

It was clear that he was troubled for me. He used to come and walk round the billiard table, pat my shoulder. So strong was his sense of concern that even I was aware of it, as if he wrung his hands. At one of these times he came to a halt by the bookshelves opposite my desk, stared at them and then turned to speak.

"Negative emotions are a bad thing. They do harm to the person who harbours them. You must not allow negative emotions in. Anger is negative, and bitterness. Bitterness is wholly corrosive – it achieves nothing. Try never to be bitter about anything."

Replying through a well of bitterness I agreed politely.

He came in another day, walked round the billiard table, stopped in front of me and spoke very gently.

"If you had a hundred pounds to spend on yourself, what would you do with it? It would not have to be used for anybody else, just you."

I thought for a while and my reply surprised me. "I would go to Crete."

"I am going to give you a cheque for one hundred pounds, and so long as it is spent on you, you may do what you like with it. Go to Crete if that is what you want to do."

Somewhere through the darkness in me there stirred a thin thread of wonder.

"Ssh!" he said. "It is a secret between us."

Little more than a week later I went, entirely alone, and found it wonderful. Put on the train by my husband I was transferred at the London end by my student daughter to the Gatwick train. Expecting a degree of loneliness I had taken books and painting things, but found time for neither. Mr Priestley now was doomed to a constant topic. It was no longer safe to mention Greece or anything Greek or I was off, eulogising. Soon, as family responsibilities eased, I could pay my own way and went once, even twice, a year to Greece. He must have sighed at times over the door he had opened for me, particularly when I began to learn the language.

"Never trust a Greek."

Snort from me.

"Beware Greeks bearing gifts!"

"Pff!"

"Going to Greece again!"

I would breathe ecstatically.

"You should stay at home."

"Greece is the home of my spirit!"

He would fall into a silence that let me know what he thought of that.

The wound of that year was so deep that I ceased to write my unpublished, probably unpublishable books. He did not know about those as I never mentioned them, but sometimes I felt quite humphy when he spoke of the problems of writing, for he at least had all day to do his. Mine was scrabbled in at the end of working for him and looking after the family, a house and a garden. I clattered my way through six in those early days with him, so that I could follow with sympathy when he spoke of writing and I wondered that he was not surprised at my understanding. Greece helped to fill the gap and inspired in me an enduring gratitude. He had made the big gesture in a barren landscape, and it was never so bleak again.

As well as responding to need, he was loyal to his friends, sprang to remedy injustice if he heard of it. This did not prevent his speaking so bluntly on occasion to people that it sounded rude. He was generally forgiven, and being totally unaware of his culpability, never knew either of the forgiveness or the fact that there was anything to pardon. Perhaps it balanced his tremendous courtesy. It is that I remember. I know that sometimes he would make me catch my breath and quiver with indignation or laugh inside, incredulous, but I cannot recall the occasions, only that gentle, smiling consideration.

Affection was important to him, for had he not quoted those words of Wordsworth repeatedly, "We live by admiration, hope and love." He endeavoured to live by them, hoping to receive in return.

"You don't care," he would say to me sometimes. "You don't give a damn!"

He was wrong there, for I cared very much and as he grew older I often wanted to put my arms round him and comfort him, mother him, but he could be a flighty fellow and I did not want to give him any false ideas. A kiss was allowed at Christmas and another at birthdays, although once after driving him to the station I reached up and kissed him goodbye because it seemed so fitting. His face lit up and at the entrance he turned to look back with an expression that was heart-warming.

On one occasion, when everyone else was away, we ate our lunch in the staff dining room. I was busy that day and it seemed a waste of time to take our things through to the proper dining room and do it formally. Miss Pudduck had left some good stock and meat and, watched and encouraged, I put them together with my own additions to make a casserole. Thanks to the stock the result was delicious and he was always convinced I was a marvellous cook. He fell in agreeably with the staff room suggestion, obviously intrigued by it, and as we ate he peered about the room as if he could not quite believe it, peeping at me too with eyes full of suppressed laughter. I suspect he enjoyed the lack of fuss, because usually he was made much of. Afterwards he helped me to clear up, telling me how fortunate his wife was in her domesticated husband.

"You don't care at all," he would say reproachfully.

I wished my words to the contrary did not sound insincere. I mumbled awkwardly that I did care, the awkwardness making it sound quite false.

"I'm very fond of you," he would say.

"I'm fond of you too," I would mutter stiffly.

"I do not know what I should do if you were ever to leave me."

Anxious to reassure I would reply in that stilted voice that I had no intention of leaving him.

Later, when he was very old, I would hold his hand, just for an instant or two. He would reach out to mine as I passed him and I would take it, pausing at his side as I did so. There is no need for words in such gestures; they are words in themselves and comforting.

Recently I heard three notes on the piano. They came loud and clear from his study, but the piano is with his granddaughter Beth now. I went to see, saw nothing, but felt.

A FINAL VOLUME

The years might advance and he protest at what they brought to him, but there was still more activity for him than many younger men could expect in a lifetime. In 1976 The Whittington Press produced a beautiful limited edition of his essay *The Happy Dream*. Ludovic Kennedy came to Kissing Tree to interview him for BBC TV's *Newsday*. There was a successful TV film later in the year, *An Englishman's Journey*, which was based on his return to some of the places he had visited for his thirties book, *English Journey*. This took him into home territory when the Priestleys stayed at the Devonshire Arms near Bolton Abbey. He attended and spoke at the Crime Writers' Association annual conference dinner, held this year at a local hotel. He donated one of his own paintings to be auctioned in aid of the British Epilepsy Association, took the opportunity while in London to visit the Constable Exhibition at the Tate, saw Ibsen's *John Gabriel Borkman* at the Lyttelton. In October both he and Mrs Priestley attended the official opening of the National Theatre by the Queen in the presence of Prince Philip and Princess Margaret. The play was Tom Stoppard's *Jumpers*.

His own play, *Time and the Conways,* was being taken on tour that year by Triumph Theatre Productions, Michael Denison directing it and his wife, Dulcie Gray, playing Mrs Conway. JB was taken to see it at Wolverhampton by Duncan Weldon, a director of Triumph. He expressed much doubt to me about the journey being too far and I consoled him by saying airily that it was not as far as all that and as he didn't have to drive he would hardly notice it. He afterwards presented me with tickets so that my husband had to drive us all the way to Wolverhampton!

The book he was working on that year was to be a final volume of biography, to be called *Instead of the Trees*. Publication was to be in the spring of 1977, but on Saturday, October 16th 1976, *The Times Sunday Review* gave him a whole page to complain about old age. It was taken from the book entitled *Crabbed Old Age*:

"Why not a piece, as honest as I can make it, on Old Age? A lot of people have told us how they are enjoying their old age. I am not one of these complacent ancients. I detest being old. I can't settle down to make the most of it – whatever that may be – but resent almost every aspect of it. There is still in me a younger man, trapped, struggling to get out. It is rather as if I were press-ganged at a stage door, dragged in to submit to old-man make-up, and then pushed on the stage to play an objectionable character part. For instance, I am increasingly fussy about engagements and arrangements and time-tables. Meanwhile, there is a self that is aware of all this fussiness and deplores it..."

At the receiving end, on reading this I wondered why, if he was aware of his fussiness, he did not check it. Going away had become increasingly wearing to him. He wanted to stay at home where all his comforts were, to sit and be himself, read what he chose to, enjoy the food that appealed to him. He did not want to be disturbed. If there was a journey to be made he would indeed fuss over the timetable, come to my room repeatedly to check the details. Engagements had to be gone over again and he grumbled about having undertaken them. Sometimes all this was trying, but he occasionally caught my eye, smiled and said, "I'm an old fuss-pot!" Patience restored I shook my head, told him he had every right to want the details right, and we would begin again.

When the time came to leave he did not want to go and would try to avoid it, refusing to pack or unpacking the things already in his case, losing the items that were vital. He would be discovered mournfully in front of the chest of drawers in his bedroom.

"Why am I going away?"

"You wanted to go."

"Well I don't want to go now."

"The arrangements are made."

"They can be unmade, can't they?" There would be a note of desperation here.

"Not really."

This would cause a look of resentment, as though the whole thing were my doing. I would make equally desperate replies, doing my best to kindle enthusiasm.

"You're going on holiday. You'll like it there."

"I don't need a holiday."

"You always like it when you arrive."

"How do you know?"

"You tell me so afterwards."

This would produce a sound of scorn.

If it was not a holiday that awaited him it might be a talk or an interview. I would point out that people expected him.

"Can't they find someone else to give their talk for them?"

"They want you."

"That's their story."

"They do. That's why they invited you, and you did accept."

"Why do they want *me*? There are plenty of other people about who could do it as well."

"No there are not. You do it better than anybody and we all want *you*."

"Are my cigars packed?"

"They are."

"Show me."

We would peer into his case for proof.

Then it was newspapers, and I would have to go down to the study to fetch them. He would begin to wonder if he should take matches as well, for when his lighter "let him down." Unless Mrs Priestley was driving them in their Mercedes the car would arrive and he turn himself into a pathetic, shaky old man, shuffling and shambling, as if there was no certainty that his legs would take him as far as the front door. Once in the car he would resign himself, make much to-do over the safety strap, and then he would turn and wave, as was expected of him.

In his piece on age he summarised a typical day, taking it through to bedtime, complaining:

"...Because I am old, almost everything mentioned above demands both effort and patience. Nothing runs itself. What – even getting dressed or going to bed? Certainly. They are both workouts ... To get by from nine in the morning until midnight I use enough willpower to command an army corps."

He used to grumble to me about the effort of it, starting with an outburst on shaving.

"Have I shaved?"

"Yes."

"You're sure?"

"I think so."

A face would be held out for me to check.

"Is it smooth?"

"Perfectly."

"Can't be perfect. I probably cut myself."

"There is one little mark."

"When you get old you don't want to struggle with all the performance of everyday things. Putting on a pair of trousers for instance. Have you any idea what an effort that is? You may think you have, but you haven't really. You have to be as old as I am to find out. Then there's shaving and teeth, getting a tie on. You know you'll only have to do the whole thing in reverse again at night. We should live in our dressing gowns."

I listened gravely.

"Do you think I should just keep my dressing gown on?"

"No."

"Why not?"

"It would look sloppy."

"You find my dressing gown sloppy do you?"

"It's a very nice dressing gown, but not to be worn all day."

Old age might be trying to him, but he would put it off casually if the need arose. If there was something to be enjoyed age was forgotten. He would spring to life for the TV camera, possibly keeping them in suspense first though. He could be a shade vague at one moment, but at the next offer lively talk for the Press or telephone. Time continued to cost him valued friends and at this period both Agatha Christie and Neville Cardus died. Although he said he wished it had come earlier when he would have been better able to cope with the ceremonies, his O. M. was opportune in bringing new light to a more wintry portion of his life.

Instead of the Trees came out in March 1977, bringing a new surge of correspondence. Reviewing it in *The Observer* Anthony Burgess[22] began:

"A final Chapter of Autobiography is a sad subtitle, and the content of the book leaves us in no doubt that Mr Priestley will not be writing about himself any more. He also says, more than once, that he has written far too much in his long lifetime. I disagree, and I hope that the writing habit will still prevail in what seems to be a hale enough old age."

It was a long review and must have given JB much pleasure, particularly when it mentioned *The Image Men*:

"He talks of his books and thinks that *The Image Men* (due out shortly in a single big volume) is his best novel. I agree. I have read it at least five times. More than I can say of the work of any other living British author with the exception of Amis (K)."

The review ended:

"The best overall tribute I can think of is to suggest that he has hardly written a line too many, and that the entire oeuvre coheres into a unity marked by a strong and inimitable personality. The critics have not taken him seriously enough. Let them make this book a pretext for a revaluation which avoids the condescension they would never dream of according to Samuel Beckett and attempt however hard it may be, a little of the humility and gratitude due to a writer who has written hard, long, much and mostly well."

It was heart-warming praise from a respected fellow writer, the warmth of it filtering through the house like a small gleam of sunlight as these things did. *Instead of the Trees* proved to be not just a last chapter of autobiography, but a last volume of any kind. He wrote no further book and after that it was merely the occasional introduction or article, JB remarking that he had done enough.

There were still plenty of radio and television doings and he contributed to *The Intrusive State* for the BBC's World Service, recorded an introduction to a new series of *My Delight*, in which one of the essays to be read was his own *Fountains* from his book *Delight*. The Cambridge Theatre Company presented a new production of *An Inspector Calls* directed by Patrick Lowe. In May the Priestleys went to the Isle of Wight for a holiday and he wrote about it for *The Observer Colour Magazine*. The piece was accompanied by a photograph of JB standing on a grassy slope against the sea, looking old, but not too old, and certainly not defeated. He also did a painting to accompany this piece. Later, in December, he presented the award of the year at a special Society of London Theatre dinner at the Café

Royal when he shared a table with Duncan Weldon, Claire Bloom, Glenda Jackson and Ingrid Bergman. He admired Ingrid Bergman particularly, considered her very beautiful indeed, and, having sat next to her, returned in excellent humour to brood over catalogues of food hampers which were to be his family Christmas gifts.

It was strange to hear the silence of his typewriter. There, in its corner it remained ready, a pile of paper beside it and a few notes. He said he might get around to writing a new book one day, but he did not really believe it. It should not be supposed, however, that the future lacked interest.

THE END OF A DECADE

Important activity was to open 1978, for he had a new suit.

"What's wrong with the old ones?"

A good deal if you studied them, but one could hardly tell him this.

"You need a new suit for public appearances and things."

"Don't make any."

"You're always having visitors and being interviewed."

Mrs Priestley must have prevailed on him eventually because Mr Hall was sent for. He had been introduced by me, a fact that gave me satisfaction. As well as a tailor, he was also chairman of the *Leamington Literary Society*, and his sister, I learnt, had been at school with Mrs Priestley, and he had a fine top coat of his own making. I explained that he was a first rate tailor, quoting his price for a suit which was about half the sum JB had been given by another firm, grumbling about it ever since. Doubt was expressed, and no hope. However, Mr Hall was sent for and appeared wearing, to my delight, his fine top coat. Promptly he produced a suit for Mr Priestley that could not be faulted. After that he became the Priestley tailor, making several jackets and several pairs of trousers. The jackets provided happy feeling of cloth and study of colour, JB reminiscing about the Bradford wool trade, telling me how to judge the quality of cloth by the feel of it. This led to talk of how he used to take days off from work to walk on the moors, and then he nudged me jovially.

"Do you take days off when we're away?"

My reply was affronted. "No, I don't."

"Never?"

"Never."

If I could have my legal day off each month I would have plenty of time to myself, I thought rather crossly.

The year began well enough with talk about Vera Brittain and plans for a February holiday for some winter sun. Vera Brittain arose because somebody asked for his opinion of her and I, having recently read glowing references to her work, was also interested. He explained that he was prejudiced against women who did not seem to him to have much feminine charm and at the same time were sharply opinionated. Vera Brittain, he said, did not appeal to him, but he did not know much about her and the only time he had spent alone with her that he could think of was when they met by accident at breakfast on a train. I said that her autobiographical works seemed to be well thought of, but he stuck out his lower lip and remarked:

"If I ever read them then they can't have made much of an impression on me because I can't remember them."

To his correspondent he wrote:

"You are probably right when you say she suffered from being so closely associated with Winifred Holtby, who was a splendid woman. At a venture I would say that during the period you mention Vera created the more stir, but Winifred claims the more affection."

He was more enthusiastic about the forthcoming visit to Amalfi. It was unusual for the Priestleys to holiday with friends, but they were to spend this one with the Collins. JB had arrived at an age when he would like some company if it was congenial company, and Canon Collins, who was also growing older, was the ideal man. He was also very fond of Mrs Collins. He was still meticulous in his arrangements, working it out that the car I was to order should call for the Collins at 6.45 and then for the Priestleys at 7 am. They would be staying at the Hotel Cappuccini Convento and I must have its telephone number in case they were needed. I was sent for necessities which included his latest favourite lighters, the throw-away kind. It did not much matter if they went wrong and he thought this happened less than with the more expensive kind. Although it was short, the holiday went well and was the first of many they shared with the Collins.

He returned to write a Foreword to David Frith's book, *The Golden Age of Cricket*, and also an Introduction to a new volume of six of his plays. Such limited writing left him dissatisfied and he wrote to Susan Cooper complaining that he felt bored with everything, including headlines in newspapers. He said, "We often read that we should be living to over 100, but I think it would only work in a better world than this one, neither nasty nor boring." Telling her that he was writing short bits and pieces these days he added, "Publishers fire off instructions to write introductions as if one could do them in one's sleep, but in point of fact I find them rather tricky and awkward to do." This, he pointed out, might be because he was getting old and stupid, but although he did feel old he did not really feel stupid, and

"I have just asked Mrs Batten if she feels I am stupid and she says I am not." He ended with a grouse about the weather, that although it was May it was really February and he was beginning to suspect the whole movement of the solar system.

That month he heard that he had been elected an honorary Fellow of his old Cambridge College, Trinity Hall. Although he appreciated this, he had never felt himself to be a Cambridge man, explaining that for him the place held no cherished memories.

He opened an exhibition of Henry Moore's work in Bradford, took part in a BBC recording on Proust, and attended the Malvern Festival for the last time. In July, 1978, he and his wife celebrated their Silver Wedding anniversary with a modest party and afterwards a holiday in Monmouthshire. Thanking his daughter Rachel for her letter of good wishes, he told her that marriages were not always worth celebrating, but a very happy one like his certainly called for congratulations.

He was finding it strange still not to be writing anything of length and complained again to Susan Cooper that he did not find himself happily situated these days, being essentially a creative man and feeling that he ought to be busy creating something. "I suppose the truth is the really creative period is over, but I find this hard to accept and rather sad." On the subject of health he told her that apart from occasional touches of familiar complaints like gout and hay fever he was pretty well and could not complain, "though of course I do."

In November he heard that he had been elected Pipeman of the Year and in response told the organisers that he should have been elected years ago. They agreed with this, but were glad that he would be able to attend their Pipeman of the Year lunch at the Savoy in January. When the occasion came he was presented with a silver model pipe on a stand with an inscription on it. This took up a permanent position by his desk.

There was never a year without some kind of TV and radio interviewing, and 1979 brought a Yorkshire TV film about him that was produced in February. In the same week he was interviewed for Kaleidoscope.

In May there was a remarkable exhibition of painting at the Annexe Gallery in Wimbledon entitled *J. B. Priestley and Family*. This was part of a series designed to demonstrate inherited talent and included work by all five of his children, as well as gouache and oil paintings by himself. Carrying it into the third generation was his granddaughter Vicki (Victoria Goaman) a botanical artist awarded the RHS Gold Medal in 1978.

It was at this time that Alan Plater was adapting *The Good Companions* for Television. He came to lunch with the producer, Leonard Lewis and later JB visited several locations for the film of himself which was to precede the first episode.

In September he opened his publisher's new offices in Grosvenor Street and on the 13th attended his birthday party there. It was on this occasion that I was seized with a stab of nervousness and he, watching, beckoned me to sit by him and put himself out to amuse me.

In November he entered the King Edward VII hospital for Officers in London for an operation. In spite of this he was able to attend the National production of *When We Are Married* on 11th December and to have supper afterwards with Lord Rayne in the Theatre restaurant, other guests including Lord Goodman and Henry Moore. In spite of this brave show of spirit the operation inevitably affected him, and although he did make a remarkable recovery his pace was beginning to slow and his memory to trouble him. The 1970s took their leave on a quieter note, as if the stage was being prepared for the last act, but there was event ahead yet, for they were to name a train for him.

INTO THE EIGHTIES

He had been born in 1894 and now we were arrived at 1980. Sometimes he came down the hall as if he was acting the part he had demonstrated ten years previously of an old man, but then he would suddenly stir and smile, move more lightly, and you would realise it was only the shadows playing tricks, his slippers being loose, his leg being stiff with gout or rheumatism. He was old, but not as old as all that. He would still pause in the doorway waving his stick in readiness for being Harry Lauder, still demonstrate what age might have in store for him so that you could see there was plenty of vigour yet. It was the year they named a locomotive for him. It was done with due ceremony at Euston and they photographed him sitting beside it in his hat. It was a terrible picture, making him look a bit dotty, probably due to the angle he was taken at with his head slightly turned and his eyes to the side because that was where the train was. To our horror the photograph was then taken up all round the world and often sent to be autographed; presumably other people did not see it in the way we did, but it seemed curious that with so many pleasing pictures of him they should choose that one.

British Rail made a day of it, Sir Peter Parker sending his Rolls-Royce to collect the Priestleys from Albany so that they entered Euston Station in style. The locomotive, duly christened, bore a big brass plate on its side announcing that it was the J. B. Priestley. There was a special lunch to celebrate with a menu that stated it was "In honour of J. B. Priestley O. M., on the occasion of his naming Electric locomotive 86234 on 11th December 1980."

That year he was photographed by Lord Snowdon twice, once for *Vogue* and once for a German magazine.

In March an extract from the Victor Saville film version of *The Good Companions* with Jessie Matthews and John Gielgud was included in a film on British musicals at the Royal Film Performance.

August brought a letter from Ralph Richardson:

> "Just a line to you,
> I have nothing to
> say but to tell
> you that I am

often thinking of you.
I think it is about
a year since I saw
you and Jacquetta
and I can remember
the TEA you gave me
easily for a year.
I have no NEWS
really, banging
along filming just
now; quite good for
one, getting up early
in the morning I
mean, unless paid
have never liked heat
therapy.
Have had a little
holiday at Biarritz
never been there
before, very bracing,
never got up early.
Haven't painted
lately but teaching
myself FRENCH POLISHING
– very interesting,
same smell as
painting – very bracing!
Well you have all my
NEWS –
You and Jacquetta
have all my love.
Send me a word
one day
EVER
Ralph"

Sometimes now he put off replying to things and I brought this letter up several times because, having developed concern for Sir Ralph's welfare, I wanted him to have the pleasure of a reply. It was always put aside "for later", but in the end I believe that they spoke on the telephone.

At the end of the year his play *Dangerous Corner* opened in London. On 2nd December it was heralded in *Londoner's Diary* in *The New Standard*:

"The Priestley boom continues. After Yorkshire TV's successful adaptation of *The Good Companions*, and two London revivals of his plays earlier this year, J.B.'s first, *Dangerous Corner*, opens at the Ambassador's Theatre in a fortnight."

In the new year of 1981 he went to see the play for himself on 14th January when, in a curtain speech, he said, "I want to give the audience a clap and the cast, who were marvellous, a clap, then I'll give myself a clap and after that I'll go home." He was photographed on stage with some of the cast afterwards, and went on to give several press interviews next day, including one to Stephen Pile for the *Atticus* column in *The Sunday Times*. In this, having been described as our last link with Shaw, Bennett and H. G. Wells, his appearance was described as resembling a North Country mole gasser or farmer "dressed in a large, checked jacket to cover his pear-shaped frame."

Granada re-issued several of his novels in paperback in February and Sarah Crompton, in the *Coventry Evening Telegraph* described them as illustrating Priestley's dazzling range of topics "and show that after a lifetime in the business, he is as popular as ever."

At the end of May they spent another holiday with John and Diana Collins, this time in England at Castle Combe, Wiltshire. In order to attend the unveiling of a statue of Elgar by Prince Charles, they returned via Worcester on 2nd June. There was a concert first, after which the Priestleys were presented to the Prince in the Giffard Hotel, from where they afterwards watched the unveiling ceremony from an upper window. This was followed by a reception and supper in Worcester's Guildhall.

On 29th June the *Yorkshire Evening Press* published an interview with him under the title *86-Year-Old-Priestley Discovers Patience Comes With Age*. Asked if he took a lot of interest in the production of his plays he replied that he interfered all the time. "I'm a great interferer", but later remarked that being old he was not as impatient as he had been. This was true, for he no longer paced the hall waiting for my return from a shopping trip, and if a visitor was five minutes late for an appointment he no longer expostulated against their wasting his time. The interview ended with the often asked question of whether he had not wanted to write a book about the First World War. He replied:

"I was in that war. When it was ended, I wanted to get on with something else. A good many things happened to me in the war. I'm a kind of survivor, you know. I made the best of my survival. And I hoped people would be more tolerant and not so quarrelsome and try to free themselves from the desire of power. I think the desire for power is bad."

A big change was made in September when he gave up his remaining set of chambers in Albany, B3, retaining only the housekeeper's room on the top floor for his wife's use. In earlier days, oppressed by his sense of financial doom, I had worried at the expense of keeping Albany even though, as he liked to point out, it came off tax because he needed somewhere in London to entertain and stay when he was there on business. We discussed it spasmodically.

"Can we afford it?"

"It is an expense."

"But it comes off tax."

"All the same..."

"Mrs Priestley likes to have Albany. I keep it for her."

"You could stay in hotels."

"Me? Stay in hotels? In London? They cost the earth!"

I thought to myself that he could buy a flat, a capital investment, security against the day financial disaster finally caught up with him.

"We can pay the rent? The money *is* in the Bank?"

"Yes, it is there, but you have to remember to keep some for tax."

"You will let me know if we get too low?"

"I always do tell you when your balance goes low."

It had taken him long enough to give up B4 so that it was not surprising that years of brooding went into the wisdom of maintaining B3. When the quarterly demands for its rent arrived it gave us a regular topic to chew over. We might have been a pair of destitutes discussing the next meal. Now he so seldom went to London that there was no longer any good reason for keeping a flat there, and so he surrendered Albany. It gave him something new to grumble about, where to stay in London, hotels and their cost and his dislike of them.

Anna Ford, who was writing her book about men, came to have a talk with him, but I do not know if she quoted him. Then there was another holiday in Dorset where his daughter Sylvia had a cottage. This brought a happy round of family outings, picnics and lunch parties. On his return his sister Winnie came to stay with him for a few days, alert as ever and eager for talk.

It was at this time that John Atkins' book, *J. B. Priestley, The Last of the Sages*, was published by Calder. Writing about it in *The Literary Review* Colin Wilson hailed it as by far the best book that had ever been written on Priestley and "could be the beginning of a real revival". It was a long review, taking up the better part of three pages, covering not only the book but also Mr Wilson's own view of Priestley, which was that he rather agreed that JB was one of the dozen or so great writers of the twentieth century. At the end he said:

"If my enthusiasm carries me too far, it is only because Mr Atkins has written a book that captures some of the sheer exhilaration of Priestley at his best."

In November Pru Sandiford came to do a TV programme about JB. She proved to be the daughter of his old friends the Sandifords on the Isle of Wight. The fact pleased him, but did not stop him remarking that he had had enough of this kind of thing, said all he had to say and had no desire to make any more appearances on television.

On Christmas Day *When We Are Married* was broadcast on radio, so that we could point out afterwards this further proof that he was not forgotten. He smiled and lit his pipe, making a muffled sound over it that could be taken as we liked. To us it seemed a pleasant close to 1981.

On 1st April, 1982, the Queen gave a lunch for her O. M. s at Windsor Castle. We were a little concerned about this because his memory tended to play tricks with him, but our fears for him were groundless and all went happily. He enjoyed showing us all again his gleaming insignia, reminding us what a singular honour the O. M. was.

Another holiday was taken with the Collins in Wales, though JB's actions to prevent leaving the house were growing more strenuous. The hours and minutes would pass while he remained resolutely unadvanced with dressing himself, standing in his bedroom. In turn we would look in on him.

"The car'll be here soon," or if Mrs Priestley was to drive that she was waiting.

"What for?"

"You're going away."

"Why?"

"It's time you had a holiday."

"I don't want one."

I would regard him anxiously, convinced that new scenes gave him fresh vigour.

"You need a change."

"But I'm happy here."

"That's what you always say, but you come back better for a holiday."

"There's nothing wrong with me."

In the end he was always somehow got into the car and driven off, turning to wave quite cheerfully once someone had succeeded in getting him strapped in. The holiday in Wales, at Llanwrtyd Wells, proved pleasant, he admitted afterwards, although he pointed out as he always did when the food was good that it was good at home, where he didn't have to be surrounded by strangers.

In September his son Tom came to make a film about him for Central Television. Called *Time and the Priestleys* it was to cover his life, using scenes from old home movies, various photographs and newsreel of old Bradford and other archive material researched by his granddaughter, Sadie. This was interwoven into talk with Tom, the pair of them walking round and round the garden or seated inside the house, Tom probing gently, JB rumbling on comfortably, for the camera never made him ill at ease.

His 87th birthday was quietly celebrated with a small dinner party of four friends and was followed by a visit to Yorkshire where he stayed first at the Wilson Arms Hotel at Grassington and then the Feversham Arms at Helmsley. Alas, there was no painting done this time as he felt his interest and energy for this had faded. On his return he wrote a Postscript for his piece *Seeing Stratford*. Originally appearing in his book *Apes and Angels* in 1928, this was being published in a limited edition by the Celandine Press.

One of Stratford's oldest hotels, the White Swan, renamed a bar for him that year, calling it *The Good Companions* bar.

By then plans were already afoot for his ninetieth birthday, nearly two years ahead. There were to be special tributes, a new illustrated edition of a book, Tom's television film, and that was only a beginning, for, as we pointed out to him, ninety called for something notable to mark it.

PREPARING FOR NINETY

Age caught up with him at last, having a push-pull struggle with him. He would forget what day it was, would come twenty times in a few hours to ask about his royalty statement, would sit over a letter to repeat and repeat again a single statement. Then he would smile, sweetly and patiently.

"Have I said that before?"

"You have actually."

"Read it to me."

Sometimes I would have to read the sentence a dozen times, but he would persevere until the letter was finished at last and the next one might be got through quite quickly, or we might spend a whole morning struggling together. I would suggest a fresh point, trying to take his mind forward, but he would prefer, for the most part, to go at his own pace, no matter if it took an hour or two, remarking at the end so that my heart ached for him,

"I'm sorry if I've kept you," his voice dove gentle.

"That's all right."

"I hope I haven't bored you."

"Of course not."

He had tired me though. It was a wearing thing to sit there, still, trying not to distract him, or to lead him back to the matter in hand, not sure if he had wandered off into his inner world or forgotten what he was about, or whether he had simply fallen asleep. The hours would pass slowly, while I recalled the patience he had always shown to me and endeavoured to repay it. Occasionally, desperate, I would ask,

"Have you finished with me yet? Shall I come back later when you have thought about it?"

He might reply with a sharp, "No!" or he might agree that I should return presently. I did not know if time had encapsulated and compressed itself, making the hours minutes for him, or whether he was aware of the time spent on the correspondence, knew how we lingered. People seemed to have no idea for they would make demands that seemed to me unreasonable. I wanted to cry out in protest, "Don't you know how old he is? Do you never think?" He would push their letters aside, strangers wanting his opinion of their work, wanting him to write introductions, solve some problem, but as I went to pick up this discarded mail he might change his mind, seize it, study it and begin to reply. I wondered whether he would feel neglected if they did not write, but then wondered again why they could not imagine what it is like to be old and write to amuse him or thank him, not to make demands on him, for he was tired now and his body was often a trial to him. He did not like to ask me outright to deal with things, but would say, "You'd better look after this," and hand me a letter to which I would reply for him to sign. If it was somebody he knew who wanted his help I would try to discover what it was that he would mainly wish to reply, but often he could not be bothered and I would remove it and deal with it. He always supported me, always approved whatever I did or suggested, so that it was easy to help him and do things for him.

For his ninetieth birthday they were going to publish a splendid new illustrated version of *English Journey*[23] with only a few minor alterations to the text, taking out small sections so that the book should not be too large when the pictures were added to it. *English Journey* was much in demand. There was a series based on it on radio, Granada Television wanted to do it, travelling his road fifty years on, but it was already contracted to the BBC who were making a film with Beryl Bainbridge. There was an article in *The Sunday Times Colour Magazine*, 'Jack's Journeys', based on it. It was written by Ian Jack with photographs by David Montgomery and covered the Cotswolds plus a visit to Priestley when:

"The interview was not a great success. The author is 88 and lives in a fine house, built over several centuries, with a door opened by his secretary. But neither old age nor an autocratic lack of hospitality can be blamed, for Mr Priestley was sharp and welcoming. The problem, probably, is that the author is tired of remembering things for the benefit of other people. 'Interviews,' he said at one point, 'are a dead loss. They take time. You don't get paid for them. All you get is misrepresented'."

John Hadfield came to lunch to consult about the new edition and the pictures for it. He had found himself travelling on the J. B. Priestley, a fact that excited him, and us too. It is not every 86 year old who has a train namesake.

In May the Priestleys went down to Chichester for the opening of *Time and the Conways* at the theatre there. Although his memory troubled him much of the time, he retained the ability to rise to an occasion and, arriving in Chichester after several hours travel, he was interviewed soon afterwards by Southern TV. Again, that evening, he addressed the audience at the end of the performance and delighted them.

In June there was another Dorset holiday with its happy round of children, grandchildren and now great-grandchildren. On his return there was a short visit by Susan Cooper and her daughter Kate, and in August his sister came to stay. These visits were increasingly important, so many of his friends had died now. Canon Collins went early in that year and then Lord Clark. There had been a final, shaky letter from Ralph Richardson:

> "Dear Jack,
> This is just to
> say Hullow –
> because I've been thinking
> about you
> I've become DON
> reading about the QUIXOTE
> that you gave me.
> Hope to take up
> your invitation
> to call on you,
> must SEE you
> EVER
> Love to
>   Jacquetta
> R"

We were concerned about his health which was variable, but for no particular reason. He would be all right one day, feel out-of-sorts the next. His back was often painful and his leg hurt. Physiotherapy sessions were tried with Stratford based Mrs McFarlane who dealt with his protests firmly and cheerfully, making him come to her sometimes to "get him out a bit". Although he said he did not need treatment, these sessions seemed to ease him and he was generally brighter for them.

The ninetieth birthday year arrived and began with a stay at the Lords of the Manor Hotel in Upper Slaughter, less than an hour away. In February he was interviewed again about *English Journey* for *The Sunday Telegraph Colour Magazine* and the *Radio Times*. The jubilee edition was launched on March 26th and well received, praised for its text, relevance to the present time, and the splendid photographs of the period which had been selected so carefully by John Hadfield. Simultaneously the TV series opened, his voice heard in each episode reading from the book, a shade tired but still effective. Friends rushed to tell him of the pleasure it gave them, how for them it had all its old enchantment. Strangers wrote that they had been so impressed by it that they had bought the book. This cheered him, as they so often wrote that they had borrowed his work from libraries.

In March he suddenly became quite ill and within days was in the London Clinic for an operation to remove an internal blockage. It was the most awful leave-taking, for he had lost some weight, and though he had much to lose this made him look frail to our eyes. We were all alarmed at the thought of an operation at his age, and he himself was not optimistic, replied to our forced cheer about how we looked forward to having him back, "If I do come back!"

I wondered then about the letter, but knew it would hardly be cheering to write as if I was saying goodbye to him. Clearly the moment had not come yet. Instead, I sent a card with a message I hoped would convey some note of feeling to him. "We are all missing you, thinking of you, and looking forward to your return." Sadly, I do not know if he ever received it. On his return they brought an envelope of cards sent to the hospital, and mine was not among them.

Soon he was about again and ninety was looming. Heinemann were giving him a birthday lunch, there were plans for a future ITV production of his book, *Lost Empires*, *The Illustrated London News* wanted an interview for a birthday tribute, Tom's film was to go out in September. He was needed, wanted and loved, his work was in demand, and if he should have a stab of anxiety, ask, "How is the money?" I could smile reassuringly, "It's coming in. You've nothing to worry about."

"You're sure?"

"Quite sure."

"What about tax?"

"That's set aside. You are all right."

He could smile then, a little at himself. He could wander into the garden to sit in the sun and I could run for his hat, fretting for him. There were times when he needed company now and Mrs Priestley even asked me to sit with him. I would do so, chattering on, he listening patiently, turning now and again to speak.

"Are you happy?"

"Reasonably happy."

"I hope that you are. You deserve to be."

How could one old man so fill a room with companionship?

THE END AND ONWARDS

He was planning and looking forward to things, even if only for some of the time. Often he sat lost in thought, remembering old friends, resenting his age but enduring it, being as cheerful as he could about it when he stirred himself. "It's a tiresome business," he would say, but he would still imitate an older, doddering self, quavering about with his stick, his acting so good that even his hair appeared whiter. Friends came to dine, he gave interviews, listened to people's notions for his birthday festivities, though with fainter enthusiasm than in earlier days. Mr Hall was making him new coats. These were not his idea, but he was persuaded. His family visited him in turn and if Mrs Priestley had to be away she arranged for someone to stay with him, Barbara perhaps, or Mrs Collins. In case he should need us, the household staggered their visits to Stratford so that he was never alone in the house. Occasionally I stayed to make his afternoon tea if his wife was detained and his housekeeper, exceptionally absent.

"Why aren't you going home? It's past time."

"I'm making your tea for you."

"I'll make my own."

Terrified at the thought of accidents with a boiling kettle, though he was always careful I would demur.

"I like making your tea."

"Miss Pudduck can make it."

"She isn't here today and I don't want to leave you alone."

"Why not?"

"I just don't want to."

"You think I'm too old and have to be looked after, do you?"

He did not like to keep me later and never had, but seeing my determination he would either put on the old man act or quietly settle for his tea.

Roger Berthoud came to do his *Illustrated London News* interview together with Charles Pick his publisher, and lunched with him. In July, John St John, who was writing the history of Heinemann, visited in search of JB's recollections. Several photographers came to take pictures of him, some of them students who wanted the 'grand old man' for their portfolios. An experienced hand at these things, he went through the motions, obeyed instructions to sit or lean, to look out of the window or into the fire, and he would watch them, "Youngsters barely out of the egg," his eyes amused or resigned according to what he thought of them.

John Pickford had arranged to record an interview with him for a BBC World Service feature to celebrate his birthday. JB had been out of sorts that week and had even rested on his bed, but on Tuesday August 7th, in the afternoon, he agreed that he could make the necessary recording. At first it was planned for the study, but by the time Mr Pickford arrived JB had decided he was better in bed, propped up with pillows to support his back. In this position, reclining somewhat awkwardly, his voice was recorded for the last time. Faint it came, and tired, but still it had its old appeal and that rich Yorkshire roundness, its message as firm as it had ever been. Asked about his writing he replied,

"I've enjoyed it; certainly I've enjoyed it. I think if they hadn't been paying me for it, I would still have gone on and done it, you know. And a great many people enjoy what I've written and I'm all for that. I enjoyed writing it and if they enjoy what I've written we are all going to be happy together."

Asked if he had written mainly for a sense of enjoyment he answered, chuckling,

"That and money."

In this interview he, who had written more than a hundred books, described himself, as he often did, as "a lazy sod". About half way through there was a record of one of his wartime broadcasts which ended,

"Soon I hope the all clear will come. Soon I hope London, which has worked hard all this week, can go quietly to bed, can go to sleep. I hope it will dream of a better world. Dream that dream and not sleep too long but make that dream of a better world come true."

Finally, asked if he had a birthday message, the answer came, a shade breathless but yet with the vigour of someone with something to say,

"I would simply say this. Try to enjoy as much as you can. Try to enjoy as much as you can."

He was up again on Wednesday, moving slowly, seated in his blue velvet chair by the fire in the study, rousing himself to give an interview for a newspaper to Peter Lewis. He was not too good on

Thursday, but neither too bad and when I left on Friday there seemed to be a real improvement. He was looking forward then to a visit from Sylvia and Barbara who were to stay overnight on Sunday.

Everything had changed by Monday. He was extremely ill. The atmosphere in the house was tense; voices were lowered; his daughters hurried about performing small tasks, trying to help against a wave of helplessness. The household went about its business, but quietly. Nurses came and went. Sylvia and I went into Stratford to fetch oxygen. We tried to sustain ourselves with false hope so that I said, foolishly,

"It's the thirteenth today. His lucky number! He said it always brought good things to him. Perhaps he will change for the better tonight."

Barbara, knowing better, said, "Yes," kindly.

Throughout the day the door of his bedroom softly opened and closed as nurses or family crept in and out of it. I could see his reflection then in the mirror of his dressing table. His hands stirred restively against the counterpane and his face might have been moulded from wax, whiter than white candles, sharply edged with none of the comfortable roundness of him. I knew then how false it was to hope.

He had asked me to write a letter to him at the end, but then he must have envisaged himself sitting up cheerfully, able to read and still to enjoy what remained of life. Outside the bedroom door I knew that there was no letter to be written and read now. He was beyond that.

On Tuesday he was worse and nobody pretended. In the afternoon a doctor came to X-ray him; gestures still had to be made. I carried the X-ray plates into the room and held them. Himself lay on the bed, his expression watchful, but not watching us. The doctor asked me something and as I replied I saw the eyes of Himself attentive. Mrs Priestley said the room was too crowded and asked me to leave. I went and stood outside, as if standing and waiting might be of some comfort to him.

The door continued to open and close and I saw his hands plucking at the sheets and longed to hold them for an instant, to pour my strength into him. He died at midnight.

He was an old man and his time had come, but what a void he left among us.

They are putting up a statue of him in Bradford[24], outside the National Media Museum[25]. The lad who kicked footballs around its back streets, the teenage dandy slipping out of the office to select some tobacco and dream, the soldier whose world shattered and darkened. What would he think of that? He would be pleased, he would chuckle and remember and prepare himself for yet another game, playing the part of the man of consequence who did not give a damn, but woe betide you if you did not give him his due! Bradford was a part of him. He would probably remark, as if it was some amusing thing they did to please themselves, that they were putting up a statue to him there, but he would rejoice in it.

The business attendant on death had to be dealt with. I went in on Saturday and Sunday to open the letters that poured in. The Post Office sent a special delivery on Sunday. The house seemed empty at first, as if its vital force had gone, but presently it was not empty any more. There was a comfortable feel of him there, and then came the day when I heard that sharp rap of his pipe. It was only once, but the sound was unmistakeable. The house felt safe again, warm with him. One old man. How could he make so much difference to a house? How could he make so much difference to a world? He could though. He could change a world by sharing with it hopes and dreams and humour, he could pass on to it his wisdom. Over the years so many people wrote to tell him so, to say what a comfort he had been to them at difficult times, how they had laughed with him, agreed with him, how he had said what they had always felt. My own world is wider for having been so close to him.

Stan Barstow wrote a long tribute to him in *The Author* and said:

"I cannot remember ever coming away from his work feeling worse than when I went to it. Always it yields something that gives a little lift to the spirit. If I must offer a concrete image, it is an abiding impression that somewhere round the corner, and not too far away, the fire is lit, the table is laid, and love and warmth, faith and reason are waiting in the lamplight."

John Pickford's interview was turned into a touching memorial on the World Service. *Time and the Priestleys*, intended for his birthday celebration, was shown as an obituary. In Bradford the flags flew at half-mast for him until after the funeral and the City bell tolled sombrely, once every minute for an hour. There were, of course, long tributes to him in the newspapers, his friend J. W. Lambert in *The Sunday Times* beginning:

"So he has gone, after 89 busy years, this amazing, exhilarating, exasperating, lovable man, this unstoppable, stimulating, disappointing, provocative writer..."

After a long and appreciative piece about him he ended with:

"Capable of startlingly disagreeable ungraciousness when required to go through his formal paces, especially on special occasions, he was in relaxation the embodiment of a delicious spirit of mischief, his little eyes glinting, his pipe-laden lower lip as expressive as his wrinkled brow, his cavernous mumble as gleefully derisive as his well of absurd similes ... Take him for all in all, a man not to be underrated, or a writer to be forgotten."

No blind admiration here, for you could not know him without admitting that he had his faults, but then you could not know him and not forgive him for them.

The funeral service was in Stratford's old Guild Chapel with local schoolboy Julian Cawdrey playing the flute for him, and local organist Howard Bould. They ended with *Nimrod*, from Elgar's *Enigma Variations*. In October there was a Service of Thanksgiving in Westminster Abbey. Julian Cawdrey played the flute there too, and the Address was delivered by Diana Collins. He would have been proud of the way she did it. There were readings from his works with Charles Pick giving *The Swan Arcadian* from *Margin Released*, Dame Peggy Ashcroft *What Happened to Falstaff* from *The Moments and Other Pieces*. Finally, before we rose to sing *Jerusalem*, Richard Pasco delivered the lines from *Johnson Over Jordan*:

"I have been a foolish, greedy and ignorant man;
Yet I have had my time beneath the sun and stars;
I have known the returning strength and sweetness of the seasons,
Blossom on the branch and the ripening of fruit,
The deep rest of the grass, the salt of the sea,
The frozen ecstasy of mountains.

The earth is nobler than the world we have built upon it;
The earth is long-suffering, solid and fruitful;
The world still shifting, dark, half-evil.
But what have I done that I should have a better world,
Even though there is in me something that will not rest
Until it sees Paradise…?"

In November there was Bradford's own Memorial at the morning service in the cathedral there, and in the afternoon a tribute was given to *John Boynton Priestley, 1894–1984*, at the Bradford Playhouse. It included, for how could it not, an excerpt from *The Good Companions*.

In the final years, as I looked at him looking at me, I would think fiercely, rebelliously, "I *won't* write a book about you. I can't write a book about you." If he read my thoughts he kept them to himself, looking back solemnly. "You should write a book about me one day." No reply. Now I remembered him. And I had not had a chance to say goodbye to him, had not taken his hand for a final moment, had not written the special letter he desired, though whatever made him suppose that I could write it! They lit a fire in his study on one of those dull, chill November afternoons, filling the room with dancing flickers of light, bringing it to life again. The flames leaped, the logs crackled and hissed and sent a thousand brilliant sparks racing into the black of the chimney like stars into the vault of heaven. I stood at the side of his seat watching it, as I had done so many times with him. He seemed so near that if I reached out my hand it might touch his shoulder, but I could not see him. It was then that I began to write about him. I can only hope that it is not causing him to pout and brood and growl a little somewhere. It is done with the best intentions, to thank him for admiring my lipstick, the style of my difficult hair, my knees and my smile, for making me feel wanted, admired and loved. Small things, but only a giant of a man could think of them. I have done my best and can only add the message that I put on my funeral flowers, that it comes with admiration, hope and love.

Notes

[1]J. B. Priestley and Jacquetta Hawkes purchased Kissing Tree House in 1959. Their former home was Brook Hill House on the Isle of Wight. Formerly known as Avonmore Alveston, Kissing Tree House was built in the early nineteenth century. The village of Alveston lies just over two miles from Stratford-upon-Avon and the Priestleys saw this as an advantage. There was also a cottage by the entrance for the Hayleses to live in (see note 2 below) and enough garden to grow vegetables. It is now a grade II listed building and remains unchanged (at least externally) from when the Priestleys lived there. In 2014, a planning application was made to erect 18 new houses in the garden but this was rejected by the local council.

[2]The term 'parlour maid' is one that was used in the Priestley household at the time. In fact Gertrude Jones was one of the two permanent live-in staff who helped to look after the house. The other, Miss (Ann) Pudduck, always known as Miss Pudduck, was the senior member of household staff and acted as cook and housekeeper. There was also, until about 1970/71 (Mr) Hayles, the gardener and his wife, who also helped out on an ad hoc basis. The Hayleses were from the Isle of Wight (they had previously worked for Priestley when he lived there), and thought long and hard before deciding to join the move to Warwickshire.

[3]The actor involved in this accident in 1934 was Frank Pettingell. As no replacement could be found, Priestley stepped in to take the part at St Martin's Theatre and had only about 24 hours to learn the lines and rehearse the part. To his relief the press and the audience reacted favourably to his performance.

[4]A. D. Peters (1892–1973) was Priestley's literary agent from the 1920s until his retirement in 1972.

[5]The play mentioned here was *Linda at Pulteney's* screened on 8 January 1969. One in the series *A Touch of Venus*, of which there were 13, each a 20 minute monologue. Authors such as J. B. Priestley, Terence Rattigan and John Mortimer were invited to contribute and write something for the actor of their choice. The scenario for this little known Priestley piece, is that Linda Carfield was on a night plane from

New York which crashed at London Airport and she lost all consciousness in the terror of the disaster. She had planned to stay at Pulteney's Hotel, and when she recovers some kind of consciousness apparently there she is, in a bedroom of the hotel.

[6]Albany, is an apartment complex in Piccadilly, London, set between Piccadilly to the south and Vigo Street to the north. Built in 1771–76, it was originally the home of the 1st Viscount Melbourne and named Melbourne House. In 1791 it became the main residence of Prince Frederick, Duke of York and Albany. He gave up his residency in 1802 and it was then converted into 69 bachelor apartments (known as "sets") by Henry Holland. Priestley rented two flats (B3 and B4) in the building from late 1943 onwards. He needed two flats to accommodate the whole family. B3 contained a bedroom, living room, kitchen and space to eat; B4 had two bedrooms and what was Priestley's study. Albany has been, and remains, a home for many famous personalities.

[7]John Hadfield (1907–1999) was a British author, editor and publisher, best known today for his 1959 comic novel *Love on a Branch Line*. He worked with Priestley on several books and became a good friend. In 1984 he edited the Jubilee Edition of Priestley's *English Journey*. Priestley was a regular contributor to *The Saturday Book*, an annual miscellany that Hadfield edited from 1952 until its demise in 1975.

[8]Priestley was a very keen amateur landscape painter. He painted using gouache and regularly took his paints with him when he travelled. In 2014 the J. B. Priestley Society curated an exhibition of his paintings at the Bradford Industrial Museum.

[9]Charles Pick (1917–2000) was Heinemann's (Priestley's main publisher for over 50 years) one-time managing director and a lifelong friend of Priestley.

[10]Iris Murdoch (1919–1999) and her husband John Bayley (1925–2015) became close friends of the Priestleys and were regular visitors to Kissing Tree House. When interviewed by John Braine for his biography of Priestley, Murdoch described him as "not only a vastly talented and *exceptionally* versatile and wise writer, he is also such a remarkable human being. And such an *Englishman*! I love him very much" (John Braine, *J. B. Priestley*, 1978, p.143). With Murdoch, Priestley dramatised her 1961 novel, *A Severed Head*. The play was

Priestley's last serious and successful venture into the theatre, running in the West End for two years from July 1963 after a successful preview at The Theatre Royal, Bristol. It also appeared on Broadway.

[11]Bradford born and bred, Roger Suddards CBE (1930–1995), was a solicitor, a writer of books about the law, architecture and Saltaire, and also an English Heritage Commissioner. As well as being active in the management of The Bradford Playhouse, he was also Chairman of the Council of Bradford Grammar School from 1987–1992. He was a long-time friend of Priestley and the two men would regularly meet when Priestley travelled back to his home county and city.

[12]Sir Ralph David Richardson (1902–1983) was a great friend of Priestley and starred in several of his most successful West End plays. *Cornelius* (1935) and *Johnson Over Jordan* (1939) were written for him and the latter presented him with one of his most challenging theatre roles. He also appeared in *Eden End* (1934), *Bees on the Boat Deck* (1936) and in 1946 he was the very first British actor to play Inspector Goole in what is arguably Priestley's most well-known and successful play, *An Inspector Calls*. In 1965, Richardson reprised his role in *Johnson Over Jordan* for a BBC television adaptation of the play.

[13]Susan Cooper was indeed the S.M.C. who had written the entry on Priestley for *The Sunday Times Magazine's 1000 Makers of the Twentieth Century*.

[14]Stephen Mitchell was a film and theatre producer, best remembered now for his work on the films *Mr. Denning Drives North* (1951), *The Lord's Taverners Ball* (1957) and also *Last Holiday* (1950), which was written by Priestley.

[15]*The Bradford Pioneer* was a weekly newspaper run by the local Labour Party. When he was just eighteen years old, Priestley managed to secure a regular feature called *'Round the Hearth'*. Here he would write reviews of concerts, plays and exhibitions and do his best to appear to the world as a grand, cultural correspondent. Up until the First World War, his dream was to become a local journalist and live in a cottage on the edge of the moors. The conflict changed all that for the Bradford he returned to was a very different place and just about all his friends had been killed in action.

[16]Priestley's decision to enlist in September 1914, was something he never managed to explain fully. In his 1962 memoir, *Margin Released* he described the decision as being "a signal from the unknown". What is interesting is his decision to go to Halifax and join the Duke of Wellington's West Riding Regiment rather than join the Bradford Pals Regiment as all his friends did. It almost certainly was a major factor in Priestley surviving the conflict, for at the Battle of the Somme in July 2016, the 1st and 2nd Bradford Pals, totalling approximately 2,000 men, suffered 1,770 casualties in the first hour of the offensive as they attacked the heavily fortified village of Serre. For the remainder of his life, Priestley was haunted and angered by the war that resulted in the loss of virtually all his childhood friends. *In Margin Released*, he wrote, "I still feel today and must go on feeling until I die, the open wound, never to be healed, of my generation's fate, the best sorted out and slaughtered ... Sliced up like sausage meat held above a swill bucket".

[17]David Hockney's drawing of Priestley is not currently on display in The Cartwright Hall Art Gallery in Bradford, but it is part of the collection. Postcards of the drawing are available from The 1853 Gallery in Salts Mill.

[18]As well as being a boyhood friend of Priestley, Percy Monkman (1892–1986), was also a locally celebrated town and landscape painter. He studied at the Bradford School of Art and painted predominantly in oils, watercolour and gouache. After retiring as chief cashier at The Westminster Bank in Bradford he took up painting full time. He was also an active member of the Bradford Civic Theatre.

[19]The library is also home to *The J. B. Priestley Archive* which includes scripts of plays, films and TV broadcasts, journal articles, books, lectures, press cuttings, theatre programmes and other publicity material, business and personal correspondence and a huge collection of photographs. Most of the material has been kindly donated by the Priestley Estate. Since 2003, the library has also held *The Jacquetta Hawkes Archive,* which provides a record of her life, including diaries, letters, photographs, notebooks and drafts of books, poems, plays and articles, from her school reports and nature diaries to her last writings and obituaries. Both archives can be viewed upon request.

[20]Canon John Collins (1905–1982) and his wife Dame Diana Collins

(1917–2003) had a lasting friendship with the Priestleys after they had met during the beginning of the Campaign for Nuclear Disarmament (CND) in 1957. Diana wrote a memoir of their friendship published by Alan Sutton Publishing in 1994 as *Time and the Priestleys: The Story of a Friendship.*

[21]Priestley said no to a Knighthood in 1965 and a Companion of Honour invitation in 1969 as well as the peerage mentioned in the text. He was firmly against honours awarded by political patronage.

[22]Priestley was one of Anthony Burgess' favourite writers. When Priestley died in 1984, he wrote a glowing piece in the Observer (19th August) and concluded it with the lines: "I've read nearly everything he ever wrote, and not for one moment did I ever feel I was wasting my time."

[23]See note [7] above.

[24]The bronze statue, created by the sculptor Ian Judd and commissioned by the City of Bradford Metropolitan District Council was unveiled on Friday 31 October, 1986 by Jacquetta Hawkes. It provides a striking image of Priestley with his coat flapping behind him, in a typical Bradford breeze. The inscription on the plaque on the granite plinth contains the following lines from one of his best novels, *Bright Day* (1946):

"Lost in its smoky valley among the Pennine hills, bristling with tall mill chimneys, with its face of blackened stone, Bruddersford [Bradford] is generally held to be an ugly city; and so I suppose it is, but it always seemed to me to have the kind of ugliness that could not only be tolerated but often enjoyed; it was grim but not mean. And the moors were always there and the horizon never without its promise. No Bruddersford man could be exiled from the upland and blue air, he always had one foot on the heather; he had only to pay his tuppence on the tram and then climb for half an hour to hear the larks and curlews, to feel the old rocks warming in the sun, to see the harebells trembling in the shade…"

[25]The museum changed its name to the National Science and Media Museum in 2017.

'He who must be obeyed' – Recollections of Priestley
by Sophie Fyson, Rosalie's Daughter

It was a good few years before we actually met 'he who must be obeyed'. At least that was how he appeared to my brother and I after listening to our mother. J. B. Priestley and the workings of his household were spoken of in tones of awe and we were left in no doubt that his words and his wishes were law. His appearance in our lives had a dramatic effect. Not only did we now have no mother at home when we got back after school but even Christmas was now a severely limited holiday.

Clearly Priestley was a powerful being. Never before had we seen our strong, determined and very knowledgeable mother allowing anyone to dictate to her how she should live her life.

In the event the meeting was brief and greatly lacking the expected terror. He was sitting by the window while everyone else (at his birthday party) was standing chatting. To me he resembled a benevolent toad (I am fond of toads). The jowls descended in gentle folds over an extended and rather large body below. He looked up at me with a beady twinkle in his eye and acknowledged my presence. He seemed to be someone at ease with himself and even rather pleased with himself. It was surprisingly comfortable to be next to him. I could understand why my mother enjoyed his presence as she worked.

There was another event that endeared Priestley to the family. It was the wonderfully exciting gift of theatre tickets to see *When We Are Married*. Not only were we given tickets but also permission to stay in his flat in Albany. This was tremendously exciting. We were to stay right in the middle of London, where all the posh people lived! The need for good behaviour was impressed upon my brother and I and we duly dressed carefully and behaved correctly. It was interesting to note that while we tiptoed around, convinced that speaking or being seen at all would mark us out as interlopers, the door keeper seemed totally comfortable with our presence and showed no signs of the expected scrutiny.

The play itself was a delight. The story held my attention, the characters were real and entertaining while the ending was most satisfactory. I was curious that Priestley, who from my mother's evidence was so very strict, serious and demanding, had proved himself capable of writing such an enjoyable play.

My final memory about Priestley is of visiting Kissing Tree House many years later after leaving home. I didn't meet him this time but his presence and that of his wife and the household was palpable as it was impressed upon me that they must NOT be disturbed. I crept into this large house through the French windows at the back and was walked past the billiard table topped by seemingly endless neat piles of papers. Each pile was explained to me along with various provisions of what had to be done or didn't need to be done. It was a formidable setup and I wondered what would happen if anything got muddled up.

We glimpsed through the door into the wide corridors and hallway where everything was clean and undisturbed. I was shown the door to the kitchen and where my mother ate with the staff. It was very quiet and should one dare to walk along the corridor I felt that the noise would echo everywhere and disturb the rest of the house. It was a relief to go outside again into the spacious, well ordered garden. Here there was a sense of peace. I suspected that this may be the part of his home that Priestley too enjoyed the most. It was easy to imagine him strolling over the lawn with his pipe or settling down to do some painting.

Also available from Great Northern Books:

Angel Pavement
by J B Priestley

Tucked away in the City of London, lies a dingy, almost forgotten side street known as Angel Pavement. Here can be found the headquarters of Twigg & Dersingham, suppliers of veneers and inlays to the cabinet-making trade. Business is bad and getting worse. The firm is fighting for its life and its staff are gripped by the fear of insolvency and redundancy. Into their midst descends the mysterious and charming Mr. Golspie and his beautiful daughter, Lena. Together they set in train a sequence of events that will transform the lives of everyone who works there.

Shot through with Priestley's trademark social conscience, Angel Pavement is one of the great London novels; a vivid evocation of the 1930s metropolis in an age of recession. It is also a brilliant and startlingly relevant examination of what happens to a group of workers when the destructive force of a rapacious financial predator is unleashed among them.

"There's a part of London no-one can take from me, because I invented it." **J. B. Priestley**

"The whole fabric of the few lives, are opened up to us with a warm and generous assiduity that is entirely convincing... Magnificent." **The Times**

"A novel by a man who thoroughly enjoys the whole spectacle of life and can communicate his enjoyment." **The Daily Telegraph**

"A marvellous writer" **David Hockney**

"A lost classic from the teeming world of Depression-era London." **DJ Taylor**

www.greatnorthernbooks.co.uk

Also available from Great Northern Books:

Bright Day
by J B Priestley

Disillusioned writer Gregory Dawson is holed up in a Cornish hotel writing a script he must finish. A chance encounter in the bar triggers memories of the doomed world of his youth before the slaughter of The First World War and forces him to remember his time within a close-knit Yorkshire community, his days spent with the Alington family and his first, tentative steps towards becoming an author. Caught up in this lost world, he realises that to have any chance of a bright future he must first exorcise the ghosts of his past and come to terms with a tragedy that has haunted him for decades.

Jungian, semi-autobiographical and Priestley's own personal favourite, *Bright Day* is a story and a journey laced with warmth, colour and Priestley's trademark compassion and tenderness.

"Bright Day is as bright as its title, so full of youth's golden hours that one could call it a Golden Retrospective, or the Golden Book of J. B. Priestley."
Manchester Evening News

"I do not think Priestley has ever written anything better than this book."
News Chronicle

"J. B. Priestley is one of our literary icons of the 20th Century and it is time that we all became re-acquainted with his genius." **Dame Judi Dench**

"A grand writer... a great writer." **Beryl Bainbridge**

"Bright Day is good Priestley... its republication is an event to be celebrated." **Melvyn Bragg**

"A gripping and readable novel, with a powerful page-turning plot."
Margaret Drabble

www.greatnorthernbooks.co.uk

Also available from Great Northern Books:

Lost Empires
by J B Priestley

Lost Empires is J. B. Priestley's late masterpiece. The First World War is looming and the music halls are thriving. Into the backstage world of dingy lodging houses, outrageous characters and decaying variety stages comes Richard Herncastle, an aspiring painter who has agreed to travel the country with his Uncle Nick, the half lovable, half-monster, master illusionist. Once inside this comic and tragic world Richard becomes caught in a triangle of love, jealousy, temptation and sexual adventure.

Vividly imagined, authentic and richly-coloured, *Lost Empires* is a humorous and occasionally disturbing coming-of-age story as well as a haunting portrait of a way of life and a society soon to change forever.

"His best for many books... Conveys a marvellous sense of period." **Sunday Telegraph**

"A Major novel. Nostalgic but often disturbing" **Sunday Express**

"If you've read this before, embark on a return journey. If you haven't, I envy you." **Barry Cryer**

"My favourite of all his work... a storyteller supreme, a master of his craft." **Roy Hudd**

"Priestley looks not only inwards at his characters, but outwards, towards the great events that shape their lives, outwards at history." **John Braine**

www.greatnorthernbooks.co.uk

Also available from Great Northern Books:

The Good Companions
by J B Priestley

In the great depression between the wars, ordinary Yorkshireman, Jess Oakroyd, disreputable schoolteacher, Inigo Jollifant and Colonel's daughter, Miss Trant are all unhappy and unsure about what to do with their lives. Each seizes the opportunity to flee their current situation to seek adventure on the open road. Fate then brings them together and into the presence of a down-at-heel and fractious theatrical touring company. With Miss Trant's money, their modest talents and buckets of enthusiasm they form a travelling troupe who proceed to sing, dance, drink and argue their way through the pavilions, provincial theatres, towns, seaside lodging houses and market fairs of Twenties' England.

The winner of the James Tait Black Memorial Prize for Fiction in 1929, *The Good Companions* is a captivating, hilarious, riotous and unforgettable carnival of English life.

"Priestley is a writer whom I admire. I remember reading The Good Companions *in one fell juvenile swoop."* **Melvyn Bragg**

"A truly great novel." **The Sunday Times**

"Wonderful vitality... describes with unfailing truth and humour the rich fabric of English provincial life." **The Daily Telegraph**

"One of the great novels of the 20th Century." **Paul Johnson, The Spectator**

"A wonderful story." **Dame Judi Dench**

"Picaresque, picturesque... If you have not read it I envy you, it lies ahead..." **Barry Cryer**

www.greatnorthernbooks.co.uk